SECURITY RISK SENATORS

SENATORS

Part 2: Michigan to Wisconsin

TREVOR LOUDON

Security Risk Senators — Part 2 by Trevor Loudon

Cover Design: W. Rainier
Typesetting: W. Rainier

ISBN: 9798359862035
Independently published

www.TrevorLoudon.com
www.keywiki.org

To the memory of the late US Representative
Larry McDonald (D-GA).

Born April 1, 1935, in Georgia, USA. Killed September 1,
1983, by Soviet fire, with 268 others, on board Korean Air
Lines Flight 007, over the Sea of Japan, September 1, 1983.

The last and the greatest of the anti-communist Democrats.

CONTENTS

WASHINGTON

WISCONSIN

SENATORS FROM THE STATE OF
MICHIGAN

DEBBIE STABENOW

BACKGROUND

DEBBIE STABENOW STARTED her political career at the Ingham County Board of Commissioners in 1974.[1] Stabenow served in the Michigan House of Representatives from 1979-1990 and served in the state Senate from 1991-1994. Stabenow served as a member of congress before she was elected to the United States Senate on the Democratic Party ticket, where she has served since 2000.

Debbie Stabenow received her bachelor's and master's degrees from Michigan State University.[2]

INFLUENCE

Debbie Stabenow chairs the Committee on Agriculture, Nutrition, and Forestry. She also chairs the Subcommittee on Health Care on the Committee on Finance. Stabenow also sits on the Committee on Environment and Public Works, Committee on the Budget, and the Joint Committee on Taxation.[3]

DIRECT SOCIALIST CONNECTIONS

Like many of her comrades in the Senate, Debbie Stabenow has numerous connections to radical left individuals and organizations. These associations have been critical in helping the senator get elected and maintain her power.

Mildred "Millie" McWilliams Jeffrey

For example, Mildred "Millie" McWilliams Jeffrey was close to many democrats but had a special bond with Debbie Stabenow. Jeffrey served as a "leader in the Stabenow for Governor Committee".[4] In 2000, Jeffrey was "pushing hard to get her friend Debbie Stabenow elected to the US Senate," according to the Toledo Blade. She even wore a "tiny gold 'Team Stabenow' megaphone on her lapel…"[5]

A lifelong socialist, Millie Jeffrey co-founded the Democratic Socialists Organizing Committee (DSOC) in the 1970s and America's largest Marxist organization, the Democratic Socialists of America (DSA) in 1982.[6] Jeffrey began her activism as a "fiery young socialist, organiz[ing] clothing workers in the South," and from there, "became the first director of the UAW's [United Auto Workers] Women's Bureau."[7]

NORMAN THOMAS CENTENNIAL

The Centennial of the birth of Norman Thomas, "America's conscience," will be marked by conferences and forums in the east and midwest. A symposium at Norman Thomas High School on November 17 will focus on "The Continuing Influence of Norman Thomas" and will feature as speakers three leaders of organizations with roots in the Socialist party that Thomas led for many years. They are Michael Harrington, co-chair of DSA, Bayard Rustin, chair of Social Democrats–U.S.A. and Frank Zeidler, chair of the Socialist Party–U.S.A. Other speakers include James Farmer, H.L. Mitchell, Fay Bennett, Gus Tyler, Aaron Levenstein and Millie Jeffrey. Harry Fleischman, a close friend, campaign manager

and biographer of Thomas who was also national secretary of the American Socialist Party, will be moderator for the symposium. Fleischman will be honored at the event for his half-century of activism and dedication to the ideals of socialism in the spirit of Norman Thomas.

Earlier in the month Thomas will be remembered at a conference on "Socialism in America" to be held at Princeton November 9-10.

On October 31 the life and influence of Thomas will be assessed at a symposium at Roosevelt University in Chicago. Speakers will look at Thomas's religion, his pacifism, his labor policy, his humanism, and end by asking, "What's Left of Thomas' Agenda?"

DEMOCRATIC LEFT   24   SEPT.-OCT. 1984

Screenshot, Democratic Left

In 1984, the DSA publication "Democratic Left" reported that Millie Jeffrey was among prominent socialist speakers at two events honoring Norman Thomas, a socialist Presbyterian minister, co-founder of the American Civil Liberties Union (ACLU) and repeat presidential candidate for the Socialist Party of America: the "Socialism in America" conference held at Thomas' alma mater Princeton University and the "Norman Thomas Centennial" held at the Norman Thomas High School in New York, which ultimately closed in 2014 after "years of poor performance reviews".[8, 9, 10]

The March – April 1990 edition of Democratic Left reported that "DSA Vice Chair" Millie Jeffrey "was on a twenty-woman team of elected public officials and education leaders who visited the Soviet Union last fall under the sponsorship of the Women's Peace Initiative and Women for Meaningful Summits [sic]."[11] Debbie Stabenow was in the delegation.[12]

Notably, disarmament activist Cora Weiss was co-founder[13] and on the board of Women for a Meaningful Summit.[14] Weiss was the daughter of Communist Party USA-affiliated businessman Samuel Rubin, founder of the Faberge cosmetics empire. Both Cora and Samuel were heavily involved in the founding of the far-left Institute for Policy Studies. Women for a Meaningful Summit brought US and Soviet female academics, politicians, activists, and journalists together to push for US nuclear disarmament - a long time Soviet policy goal.

Mildred Jeffrey

Both Mildred Jeffrey and Cora Weiss served on the Women for a Meaningful Summit's board alongside Cheryl Craig, National President[15] of the Communist Party USA front[16] Women for Racial and Economic Equality, Edith Villastrigo of the Soviet front World Peace Council,[17] Democratic Socialists of America supporters Eleanor LeCain[18, 19] and Diane Balser,[20, 21] Institute for Policy Studies activist Anne Zill[22] and far left Democratic Congressmembers Maxine Waters, Barbara Boxer and Bella Abzug.

Republican member of congress Claudine Schneider co-chaired the organization with Barbara Boxer. Schneider was one of the very few Republicans ever to have been endorsed by the disarmament organization Council for a Livable World.[23]

Paradoxically, the "peace" movement is and always has been about disarming America to the advantage of her enemies. Therefore, it is not surprising that Stabenow would be involved with disarmament activists, as she has been endorsed by the Council for a Livable World throughout her career. The Council was founded in 1962 by long-time socialist activist and alleged Soviet agent, Leo Szilard. Senator Stabenow earned a 100% rating on the Council's voting record for the 111th Congress.[24]

In 1995, Debbie Stabenow accompanied Millie Jeffrey to Communist China. Stabenow, along with former Democratic Senator Carl Levin, honored Millie Jeffrey in the Congressional Record upon her death, marveling at her influence. "As one who traveled with her to the Fourth World Conference on Women in Beijing," Stabenow said, "it was amazing to see people from all over the world, hearing we were from Michigan, asking if we knew Millie Jeffrey and if we could tell them where she was; or that their grandmother, their aunt, suggested they meet Millie Jeffrey."[25]

Millie Jeffrey died in 2004 at the age of 93. At the time, Adam Bernstein of the Washington Post wrote that Jeffrey "was a Democratic Party power broker for a series of women now in public office, including Gov. Jennifer M. Granholm, US Senator Debbie Stabenow and US Representative Carolyn Cheeks Kilpatrick."[26] Millie Jeffrey is also credited with securing the VP spot for leftist New York Democratic Congresswoman Geraldine Ferraro when Walter Mondale ran for President in 1984.[27]

As an aside, Jennifer Granholm is currently serving as the United States Secretary of Energy under President Joe Biden.

On August 28, 2010, Debbie Stabenow spoke at an event sponsored by the "Justice Caucus", the Michigan Democratic Party's most socialist-friendly subgroup. The Justice Caucus honored Jennifer Granholm with the "Spirit of Millie Award" honoring Granholm's contribution to Michigan's judiciary via judicial appointments.[28]

Elizabeth Bunn

Another socialist and high-ranking executive of the UAW, Elizabeth Bunn played a key role in electing both Debbie Stabenow and Jennifer Granholm though her creation of the "Woman to Woman Campaign".[29]

According to the Democratic Left,[30] Elizabeth Bunn was named as a co-chair in a 1999 dinner honoring Saul Wellman who "worked to promote Communism within Detroit auto plants"[31] and UAW Vice President and DSA member[32] Nate Gooden. During the dinner, the publication quoted Saul Wellman, then 87:

> I have always had a feeling I was never alone no matter where I was, because I was part of a great movement that would move us closer to a world where the exploitation of man by man would be eliminated – the movement for socialism.

Nate Gooden and Elizabeth Bunn were named in both a 2000[33] and a 2001[34] tribute to the DSA publication Democratic Left. Gooden, who died in 2006, was described by the New York Times as an "activist for the Democratic Party".[35] Also active in the Democratic Party despite being a member of the Democratic Socialists of America,[36] Elizabeth Bunn was a "Super Delegate" in Michigan in 2008.[37]

CUBA

In addition to her travels to the Soviet Union and China, Debbie Stabenow was also involved in advocacy for and travel to Cuba. In 2009, Stabenow approved a trip to Havana for her then-chief of staff and legislative advisor Amanda A. Renteria, sponsored by the Center for Democracy in Americas, which is connected to the Institute for Policy Studies (see more in the section "Radical Left Events"). The trip was described as a "fact-finding mission to learn more about Cuba's leadership transition and ongoing program of reforms in Cuban government."[38]

After from her tenure with Stabenow (as well as a stint working for Senator Dianne Feinstein), Amanda Renteria went on to serve as chief of operations for former California Attorney General Xavier Becerra, and then as National Political Director for Hillary Clinton's presidential campaign. Renteria is now the CEO for "Code for America," whose vague "goal" is to create "a resilient government that effectively and equitably serves everyone."

It was reported in April, 2022 that Code for America received commitments of $100 million over seven years to "transform America's social safety net," using the massive influx of funds to "work with state governments to reimagine and rebuild delivery of equitable and accessible benefits".[39] Code for America has received funds from the Bill & Melinda Gates Foundation, the Chan Zuckerberg Initiative, the Ford Foundation, the Rockefeller Foundation, and many others.[40]

In line with international communist policy, Senator Stabenow has been a long-time proponent of relaxing US trade and travel restrictions on Cuba. She has travelled to Cuba with congressional delegations in 2013[41] and again in 2015.

Cuba's official state news agency Cuba Prensa Latina reported[42] on the 2015 meeting of "senators and representatives of the Democratic Party of the United States", stating in part that the delegations of America and Cuba "will hold talks on migration…at the Palace of Accords in Havana," and further revealed that the conference was the "first meeting in the process of restoring diplomatic ties."

RADICAL LEFT EVENTS

Debbie Stabenow has been involved in many events directly or indirectly associated with radical activists. Here is a sample:

Call to Action

In 2010, Stabenow sent aides to a rally dubbed "Call to Action" co-sponsored by the Greater Detroit chapter of the Democratic Socialists of America.[43]

The purpose of the event was to "press members of the Michigan Congressional delegation, particularly in the Senate, to pass key components of the progressive agenda including health care reform, cap and trade energy legislation, immigration reform, and the Employee Free Choice Act."

Notably, then-members of Congress Sander Levin and John Conyers, Jr. both addressed the audience of 300, along with DSA member Al Fishman[44] and DSA Executive Board member Dave Ivers.[45]

Take Back America Conference

In 2004, Debbie Stabenow was on the speakers list along with leftist activist George Soros, AFL-CIO President and DSA comrade John Sweeney, former Planned Parenthood President Cecile Richards and IPS activist Robert Borosage among others at the "Take Back America" conference, which was organized by the blandly named, but radical-left Institute for Policy Studies and the Campaign for America's Future, which are both closely allied with DSA.[46]

Next Agenda: Blueprint for a New Progressive Movement

Debbie Stabenow was an invited "special guest" at the "Next Agenda: Blueprint for a New Progressive Movement" conference held at the National Press Club on February 28, 2001.[47]

The press release explained that the conference would discuss the "economic and demographic dynamics that make for a growing progressive electorate". It further read in part:

> ...the Conference on the Next Progressive Agenda has been endorsed by a who's who of prominent leaders from the labor

unions, women's organizations, civil rights groups, environmental-
ists and individual members of the House and Senate. Their goal:
to forge a progressive movement to fight for the 'working family'
agenda they insist was endorsed by a majority of the voters in the
2000 election.

The conference was organized by the "Campaign for America's Future", an organization deeply connected to the Democratic Socialists of America or one of its two predecessors Democratic Socialist Organizing Committee or the New American Movement through founding members John Atlas, Paul Berman, Norman Birnbaum, Julian Bond, Mitchell Cohen, Richard Cloward, William Domhoff, Peter Dreier, Barbara Ehrenreich, Richard Flacks, Adam Hochschild, Michael Kazin, Charles Knight, Peter Laarman, Nelson Lichtenstein, Steve Max, Jay Mazur, Harold Meyerson, Lawrence Mishel, Frances Fox-Piven, Frank Riessman, Richard Rorty, Sumner Rosen, Richard Rothstein, Theda Skocpol, Stanley Sheinbaum, Jack Sheinkman, John Sweeney, Michael Walzer, Roger Wilkins and William Julius Wilson.

In addition to Debbie Stabenow, then-Democratic senators Mark Dayton and Paul Wellstone (Minnesota), Jean Carnahan (Missouri), Jon Corzine (New Jersey) and Maria Cantwell (Washington) were also invited.[48] Speakers included Senator Richard Durbin and then-members of congress Jesse Jackson, Jan Schakowsky, Hilda Solis, John Conyers, Dennis Kucinich, George Miller, Rosa DeLauro, Barney Frank, and Luis Gutierrez.

The conference released a book of the same title[49] compiled of progressive strategy essays edited by co-directors of the Campaign for America's Future Roger Hickey and Robert Borasage.

PRICE CONTROLS FOR PHARMACEUTICALS

Socialists have long fought for government price controls in industry. This, despite the repeated catastrophic results of such policies. In 2007, Debbie Stabenow took part in a conference call with the afore-mentioned Roger Hickey in relation to mandating price controls for pharmaceuticals, which are notoriously expensive due in large part to exhaustive and stifling government regulations.

In 1979, Roger Hickey penned an OpEd for the Marxist publication "Democratic Left" titled "Fighting Inflation: Strategy for a New Majority"[50] arguing that greedy industry was jacking up costs, and the government should step in to control prices and provide for "life's necessities." Hickey was writing in his capacity as Executive Director of a leftist coalition closely associated with the Institute for Policy Studies and the Democratic Socialist Organizing Committee called "Consumers Opposed to Inflation in the Necessities" (COIN).

Fighting Inflation:
Strategy for a New Majority

by ROGER HICKEY

President Carter and the Democrats running for office in this 1978 election year have been struggling desperately to convince a worried electorate that they have a solution to the raging inflation that is rapidly eating away at the American dream. Many Democrats succeeded by stealing the bandwagon of tax-cutting, balanced budgets, tight money and corporate giveaways and riding it harder and faster than the Republicans. The new conservative bandwagon may have bought some politicians some time, but it will probably run smack into the brick wall of recession. *And* it won't make inflation go away.

The politics of the 1980s must focus on an equitable and demo-

ganize citizen activism to hold down price increases in four "basic necessity" sectors: food; energy; housing and health care.

At COIN's Washington press conference Alperovitz read telegrams of support from Doug Fraser of the UAW and George Meany of the AFL-CIO, both of whom are backing the effort.

Citing research by the Exploratory Project for Economic Alternatives, which Alperovitz co-directs with Jeff Faux, campaign leaders explained that most families spend 70 percent or more of their incomes on the four non-postponable necessities of life. A new "necessities price index" released jointly by EPEA and the COIN campaign for the first nine months of 1978 shows

"As old solutions fail to control inflation caused by these powerful interests, the COIN Campaign will be working with progressive politicians, community organizations, consumer, labor and senior citizen groups to propose ways to allow citizens to start voting on food costs, interest rates, hospital charges and energy prices," Hickey wrote in part.

On December 19, 1978, Hickey joined his COIN colleagues at the White House for a meeting with President Jimmy Carter.[51] The following day, Carter released a statement about the meeting:

> *Following our very constructive meeting with COIN, I have asked Alfred E. Kahn, my adviser on inflation, to have the working groups he has assembled cooperate with COIN and other consumer groups to plan additional specific steps to hold down inflation in the sectors of the economy that provide the basic necessities of life. I expect their recommendations soon.*

Consumers always seem to be the last to be consulted about the policies that determine what they pay for products and services in the marketplace. COIN has spoken up for consumers throughout this Nation effectively, and I want to hear their views before decisions are made. I want COIN to be a partner in our common effort to control inflation.[52]

Fast forward to April, 2007. In his capacity at Campaign for America's Future, Roger Hickey co-authored a report titled "Waste and Inefficiency in the Bush Medicare Prescription Drug Plan: Allowing Medicare to Negotiate Lower Prices Could Save $30 Billion a Year".[53] The report promoted government intervention in drug pricing. "If the Senate follows the House in passing legislation that will allow Medicare to negotiate for cheaper prescription drugs, the result will be savings for seniors, for the Medicare Part D program, and for the health care system as a whole," Hickey argued. Debbie Stabenow was enthusiastic about the idea.[54]

"When so many Americans struggle to pay for the prescription drugs they need, it doesn't make sense to prohibit the federal government from negotiating the lowest possible drug prices on behalf of the 44 million seniors and people with disabilities who rely on Medicare," she was quoted as saying.

Notably, Roger Hickey's 2007 report was later cited by then-candidate Barack Obama and Joe Biden in a campaign fact sheet titled: "Barack Obama and Joe Biden's Plan to Lower Health Care Costs and Ensure Affordable, Accessible Health Coverage for All."[55]

'REPARATIONS' FOR BLACK FARMERS

Oftentimes politicians attempt to sneak in legislation as a part of a large spending bill, as it would not pass on its own. Stabenow's proposal to spend in the arena of four billion dollars to forgive outstanding USDA loans to farmers *based solely on skin color* falls into that category. Like price controls, "reparations" – are a long-time communist priority.

Stabenow's proposal, which she referred to as an "important piece of reparations," is now Section 1005 of the American Rescue Plan Act of 2021.[56]

The effort was part of the "Emergency Relief for Farmers of Color Act" submitted by Senator Reverend Raphael Warnock (D-GA), Senator Cory Booker (D-NJ), Senator Ben Ray Luján (D- NM), and Senate Agriculture Chairwoman Debbie Stabenow (D-MI).

A March 4, 2021, press release[57] from Raphael Warnock revealed that "600 leaders and organizations" supported the "Emergency Relief for Farmers of Color Act." The supportive organizations include hard-left groups "National Farmers Union," and "Federation of Southern Cooperatives," both of which are well-known for their pro-reparations agenda.

As chair of the Senate Agriculture Committee, Debbie Stabenow has long-standing ties to the National Farmers Union (NFU).[58] The NFU, in most states, serves as a far-left pressure group. Founded in 1902, the NFU from the 1930s until the present day has been penetrated to varying degrees by the Communist Party USA.[59, 60]

From a 2001 report[62] to the Communist Party USA national committee by Washington dairy farmer and long-time communist Tim Wheeler:

> ... Our goal is to build up our ties and connections with the coalition of farmer organizations including the Institute for Agriculture and Trade Policy, the National Farmers Union, Coalition of

> *Family Farmers, and so on. Obviously, the goal is to recruit farmers*
> *and farm workers, Black, Latino and white to our Party.*[63]

Wheeler explained that during the 1999 "Battle of Seattle" protests,[64] thousands of farmers joined "organized labor, environmentalists, youth and other progressive groups to shut down the World Trade Organization". "A few months later," Wheeler continued, "[t]hese same forces brought about 3,000 farmers and their allies for a 'Rally for Rural America' in Washington DC. It was co-sponsored by the NFU, the AFL-CIO, the National Coalition of Family Farmers, the Corn Growers Association, the Federation of Southern Cooperatives and a dozen other rural organizations and movements."

The purpose of the Rally for Rural America was to demand higher taxpayer-funded subsidies for farmers.

Farmers rally in Washington for increased crop supports

Associated Press

WASHINGTON — Roger Winter lost $28,000 on his wheat and dairy farm in California, Minn. last year, and is in Washington this week trying to make sure that doesn't happen again.

"I'm here to be a voice for the rest of the United States," he said.

Winter is one of more than 1,000 farmers participating in the Rally for Rural America this week, aimed at increasing crop supports for struggling family farmers.

The main villain for the mostly Democratic gathering, dubbed "Rally for Rural America," was the 1996 Freedom to Farm law, which reduced crop subsidies.

"Family farmers have been the victim of bad public policy in this country, and it's time to straighten it out," said Sen. Byron Dorgan, D-N.D.

Agriculture Secretary Dan Glickman agreed.

"It is time to rewrite that 1996 Freedom to Farm bill," he said.

The legislation called for price supports to be gradually scaled back over seven years. The law, pushed by Republicans, was intended to wean farmers from federal support, but since its passage Congress has passed several multibillion-dollar bailouts. Last year, the package totaled $27 billion, with the bulk going to Midwestern Corn Belt farmers.

"It's made farmers more dependent on Congress," said Rep. Earl Pomeroy, D-N.D. "It's wrong — it's just dead wrong."

Sen. Richard Lugar, R-Ind., chairman of the Agriculture Committee, has resisted holding hearings on overhauling the law, which expires in 2002.

"We'll rewrite the farm policy in 2002 — we have a seven-year contract with American farmers, and it was something they wanted," Lugar spokesman Andy Fisher said.

Farm income dropped from $55 billion in 1996 to $48 billion last year, but Fisher said that was due to cyclical changes, not federal farm policies.

The farmers, many wearing baseball caps and a few sporting cowboy hats, were organized by the National Farmers Union and a coalition of other organizations. They were bused in from all over the country, with the largest contingents from Minnesota and North Dakota.

Farmers also complained about agribusiness mergers. The resulting mega-companies dominate the marketplace, making it harder for family farmers to get a good price for their crops, they said.

Sen. Paul Wellstone, D-Minn., promised to reintroduce legislation calling for a moratorium on agriculture mergers, after polling the crowd in a tent on the Capitol Mall.

"We'll bring it back!" he yelled. "We'll do it!"

Sen. Kent Conrad, D-N.D., used the rally to pitch legislation calling for the U.S. government to match what European nations pay their farmers in subsidies.

"I say don't blame them, let's match them," Conrad said.

65

From a Federation of Southern Cooperatives press release dated March 4, 2021:

> *The Federation is urging strategic partners, supporters, and mem-*
> *bers to rally behind the bill that will repeal major injuries to*
> *farmers of color. The American Rescue plan, which includes up to*
> *$16.1 billion in agriculture and food provisions, landed a success*
> *in the house on Feb. 27, raising hope for systemic restoration and*
> *repealing of USDA discrimination and injustices done to Black*
> *farmers. As the Emergency Relief for Farmers of Color Act now*
> *lies in the Senate, awaiting the passage of the Emergency Relief*
> *Bill, The Federation sees this as an opportunity to amplify the chal-*
> *lenges faced by Black farmers and to support champions of repar-*
> *ative action. The Federation has asked for its extensive network*

and cooperative partners to support the mission of Ag committee
members to recalibrate past discrepancies amongst socially disad-
vantaged farmers. 'The Emergency Relief for Farmers of Color Act
is an important step toward equity, justice, and inclusion as well as
putting our nation on a track toward resiliency and sustainability,'
says Cornelius Blanding, Executive Director.[66]

A white paper accompanying Raphael Warnock's press release
explains that $4 billion would be provided "in direct relief payments
to help farmers of color pay-off outstanding USDA farm loan debts
and related taxes," while an *additional* $1 billion would "support activ-
ities at USDA that will root out systemic racism, provide technical
and legal assistance to agricultural communities of color, and fund
under resourced programs that will shape the future for farmers and
communities of color."

"I am a supporter of reparations," Debbie Stabenow declared in July
1994 during a campaign event hosted by the Detroit chapter of the
NAACP. "And I will as governor be a supporter of reparations," she
continued.[67] It appears that the senator is consistent.

At the time of this writing, Section 1005 has been "stalled" in the
courts due to the blatant race-based discrimination of the measure.[68]

GARY PETERS

GARY PETERS IS THE JUNIOR US SENATOR FROM MICHIGAN

BACKGROUND

GARY PETERS HAS served as the junior senator from Michigan since 2015 on the Democratic Party ticket. In 1991, Peters began his career in politics as Rochester Hills City Councilman. In 1994, he was elected to the Michigan State Senate, where he served two terms. He served in the US Navy Reserve, where he became Lieutenant Commander. He also had high level jobs in the financial services industry, where he worked for twenty years. Peters was first elected to the US House of Representatives in 2008.

Gary Peters has several degrees, including a B.A. from Alma College, an M.B.A. in Finance from the University of Detroit Mercy, an M.A. in political science from Wayne State University, an M.A. in Philosophy from Michigan State University, and a law degree (J.D.) from Wayne State University Law School.[1]

INFLUENCE

Gary Peters chairs the Committee on Homeland Security and Governmental Affairs. He also chairs the Subcommittee on Surface

Transportation, Maritime, Freight, and Ports on the Committee on Commerce, Science, and Transportation. Peters also sits on the Committee on Armed Services.[2]

SOCIALIST CONNECTIONS

In January 2009, the newsletter for the Detroit branch of America's largest Marxist organization Democratic Socialists of America (DSA) carried a strange report:

> *Having been rebuffed in our offers of assistance to progressive Congressional candidates Gary Peters (9th district) and Mark Schauer (7th district)—both of whom were afraid of being red-baited--Detroit DSA focused instead on local and state races.*
>
> *Our strategy was simple: Given our limited resources and man-power, we concentrated on competitive races in which a progressive Democrat was running for an open seat. In such a setting, the efforts of a small, but disciplined, group such as ours might provide the margin of victory for the progressive Democrat. Furthermore, by helping to turn out the progressive vote in these state representative districts, we also helped to turn out the vote for Obama, and to a certain extent, for Gary Peters.[3]*

Indeed, the Peters and Schauer campaigns had turned down the very effective DSA help - not out of ideological incompatibility, but purely to avoid potential bad publicity.

Detroit DSA had been heavily involved several state legislative races with some success.

In an interview with socialist website In These Times, Detroit DSA chairman David Green explained his organization's tactics - open and covert:

> 'As a small organization, how can we make a difference? We leverage our forces. We put our efforts towards a progressive Democrat challenging a Republican, or a progressive Democrat challenging a centrist Democrat [in a primary].'
>
> 'We don't pick symbolic victories,' Green says, 'We pick things we can win.'
>
> After deciding whom to support, Detroit DSA carefully chooses

tactics that will have the greatest impact, all of which are based on the leftist tradition of on-the-ground, grassroots action.

Green holds initial fundraisers for progressive Democratic candidates in his own home, where he invites friends and allies to come meet the candidates and contribute to their campaigns. These fundraisers bring in several thousand dollars, which, according to Green, is more than enough to get a fledgling statehouse race off the ground, providing crucial support to underfunded progressive candidates entering politics for the first time.

To build on the initial fundraising push, a core of Detroit DSA goes door-to-door to distribute literature and answer questions about their candidates. These activists also participate in phone banking and email campaigns. As part of this effort, Green instructs his members not to identify themselves as DSA members, to avoid the knee-jerk reaction many still have toward people who self-identify as 'socialists.'[4]

However, the pro-free-market Mackinac Center for Public Policy and some Republican Party candidates began calling out DSA's infiltration of the Democratic Party leading to bad press for some Democratic candidates.[5]

From In These Times:

Such red baiting…has prevented Detroit DSA from getting involved in higher profile races. The group offered to support progressive Democratic candidates in two congressional races in 2008: Gary Peters (9th district) and Mark Schauer (7th district), both of whom went on to victory.

Green says that the candidates themselves were happy to have Detroit DSA's involvement, but that 'handlers' from the Democratic National Committee (DNC) refused the support, for fear that the candidates would be red-baited or branded as socialists.[6]

Congressman Peters must have overcome his initial reluctance to mingle with the Marxists because the May 2009 Detroit DSA newsletter carries a report "on Meeting with Gary Peters' Staff".[7]

Democratic Socialists of America Greater Detroit Local   May 2009

Agenda for May 2nd DSA General Membership Meeting

1. Treasury Report
2. Report on Jobs with Justice—Support for Rally on Immigration Reform
3. Report on MichUHCAN—Support for "Health Care Heroes" Dinner
4. Report on Michigan Alliance to Strengthen Social Security and Medicare
5. Report on Detroit Area Peace with Justice Network
6. MSU YDS Update—Proposal for Taking a Summer Intern from YDS
7. Report on Education Committee—next DSA Forum
8. Old Business—Pontiac Living Wage, Renegotiate NAFTA, new DSA Banner
9. Op-Ed Piece—What Socialists Really Think
10. Report on Meeting with Gary Peters' Staff
11. Michigan Policy Summit on Saturday, May 16th 0A
12. Speaker: Sister Mary Ellen Howard on "The Impact of the Recession on the Uninsured in Michigan"

Gary Peters' colleague Mark Schauer certainly wasn't shy about seeking DSA's help.

In March 2014, DSA's newsletter carries a report on a DSA fundraiser for Democratic candidate for Governor of Michigan Mark Schauer:

Detroit DSA chair David Green left, Mark Schauer second from left

Detroit DSA held its first in a series of proposed fundraising house parties for Democratic gubernatorial candidate Mark Schauer on November 13, 2013, at the home of Chris and Gillian Talwar. We raised over $5000 from 48 donors.

Mark Schauer shares DSA's values. He believes in universal health care. In fact, his courageous vote in favor of the Affordable

Care Act in 2010 was probably responsible for his losing his Congressional seat in 2012.

Detroit DSA proposes to organize a series of fundraising house parties for Schauer in 2013-2014 in Oakland, Wayne, Macomb, and Washtenaw Counties. The purpose of these house parties is two-fold:

1. *to raise money for Schauer who faces a huge fundraising disparity compared to Governor Snyder*
2. *to improve Schauer's name recognition and visibility in southeastern Michigan where he is not as well-known as on the west side of the state.*[8]

David Hecker

January 27, 2014 – the American Federation of Teachers (AFT) Michigan endorsed Mark Schauer for Michigan Governor and Gary Peters for the US Senate.

From the AFT press release:

> 'Michigan needs a Governor who understands that we need to invest in public education to compete for good jobs and build a strong economy,' said David Hecker, President of AFT Michigan. As the son of a teacher, Mark Schauer knows that education is the key to opportunity, and as Governor, he will make education a top priority to help our students compete for good 21st Century jobs. Our members are energized and ready to help make Mark our next Governor.
>
> 'We are very pleased to endorse Congressman Gary Peters for the US Senate. Gary Peters has always been a friend of education and is in tune with our members on issues like the accessibility of higher education, investments in strong pre-school programs, full support of public schools and collective bargaining rights for Michigan workers,' David Hecker, explained. 'Although no one can replace, Sen. Carl Levin, we believe Gary Peters will bring the same kind of work ethic and integrity to the job.'[9]

David Hecker even went out to personally canvass for Schauer and Peters.

David Hecker is an officer-at-large in the Michigan Democratic Party.[10] According to the May 2012 Detroit DSA newsletter, David Hecker is also a "lifetime DSA member."[11]

In May 2020, Senator Peters listed supporters for his COVID-19 "Heroes Fund" proposal and called on the Senate to work in a bipartisan manner and include it as part of a next Coronavirus package. The COVID-19 Heroes Fund would provide pandemic premium pay to reward and retain essential frontline workers.

According to Senator Peters' press release, David Hecker was one of those supporting the Senator's proposal:

> 'Essential workers all across Michigan have been working day in and day out during this pandemic to ensure families are safe and protected,' said Dave Hecker, President, American Federation of Teachers Michigan. 'Senator Peters' Heroes Fund is a sure way to show our teachers and school support staff they are appreciated.

*We are proud to support this proposal, and grateful we have a
leader like Senator Peters fighting for Michigan educators.'*[12]

Keynote Speaker at Radical Left Event

The Spirit of Millie Jeffrey Award Dinner is the far-left Michigan
Democratic Party's Justice Caucus annual award and fundraising
event in honor of the life of DSA Leader and Democratic Party
activist, Millie Jeffrey.[13]

Congressman Peters was the keynote speaker at the June 7, 2009,
dinner.[14]

Call to Action Rally

In February 2010, Detroit DSA helped organize an event that
demonstrated just how much DSA and the Michigan Democratic
Party actually overlap.

John Conyers with supporters at the Detroit DSA fundraiser.

For example, the late
Representative John Conyers
who spoke at the rally was a
decades-long DSA member.[15]

Most Michigan Demo-
cratic Congressmembers have
DSA ties.

From the Detroit DSA
newsletter:

*Over 300 people attended the Call-to-Action Rally at the United
Food and Commercial Workers Union (UFCW) Local 876 Hall
in Madison Heights on February 18th. The rally was organized
to press members of the Michigan Congressional delegation, particularly in the Senate, to pass key components of the progressive
agenda including health care reform, cap and trade energy legislation, immigration reform, and the Employee Free Choice Act.*

*DSA co-sponsored the rally along with 31 other organizations...
Congressmen Sander Levin and John Conyers, Jr. addressed the
audience. In addition, aides to Senators Debbie Stabenow and
Carl Levin and Representatives Dale Kildee, Gary Peters, Carolyn
Cheeks-Kilpatrick, and John Dingell attended the rally.*

*DSA member Al Fishman spoke to the audience about how
the disastrous wars in Iraq and Afghanistan had undermined*

Obama's domestic agenda in a manner analogous to the way in which the Vietnam War undermined President Johnson's Great Society programs.

DSA Executive Board member Dave Ivers spoke about the imperative for a national jobs program… Other speakers included Chris Michalakis, Legislative Director of UFCW Local 876, who spoke about the importance of comprehensive immigration reform.[16]

Chris Michalakis too, was very close to DSA[17] and to the Communist Party USA.[18]

Town Hall with DSA Front Group

In May 2012, Congressman Peters and State Representative Vicki Barnett, together with Marjorie Mitchell from pro-socialised healthcare group Michigan Universal Health Care Action Network (MichUHCAN) hosted a Health Care Town Hall in Farmington Hills to promote President Obama's Affordable Care Act.[19]

Vicki Barnett was very close to DSA for several years. She was endorsed and supported by DSA in her 2008 state legislature race.[20]

The agenda for the March 2009 March Detroit DSA general membership meeting included both a report on MichUHCAN and a state legislative update from state representative Vicki Barnett.[21]

Democratic Socialists of America Greater Detroit Local	March 2009

Agenda for March 7th DSA General Membership Meeting

1. Treasury Report
2. Report on Jobs with Justice—U.S. Social Forum
3. Report on Michigan Universal Health Care Access Network (MichUHCAN)
4. Report on Michigan Alliance to Strengthen Social Security and Medicare
5. Report on Detroit Area Peace with Justice Network
6. Support for Michigan Coalition for Human Rights (MCHR) Annual Dinner
7. Report on Education Committee—next DSA Forum
8. Report on Renegotiate NAFTA Campaign
9. Op-Ed Campaign: What Socialists Really Think
10. Speaker: Deborah Olson on Public-Private Partnerships to Stimulate Employment in Areas of Chronic Unemployment
11. Speaker: State Representative Vickie Barnett—State Legislative Update

Barnett was also a guest of honor at Detroit DSA's November 2013 fundraising event for Mark Schauer.[22]

MichUHCAN itself is a DSA "front group". A quick look at the list of board members confirms that.[23]

+ Longtime MichUHCAN DSA chairman David Green was also a long-serving Detroit DSA chairman

+ MichUHCAN secretary Dave Ivers is also longtime Detroit DSA treasurer

+ Selma Goode, MichUHCAN treasurer was also Detroit DSA secretary

Detroit DSA officers, 2012:[24]

Democratic Socialists of America Greater Detroit	Officers
	Chair: David Green
	Vice Chair: Catherine Hoffman
	Secretary: Selma Goode
	Treasurer: David Ivers
	Executive Board:
	  Reg McGhee, Dave Elsila,
	  Phil Schloop, Lon Herman,
	  Ken Jenkins
		Contact Information
		Mailing Address
		28292 Harwich Drive
		Farmington Hill, MI 48334
		
		Phone Number: 248-761-4203
		E-mail: dsagreen@aol.com

Socialists Deeply Embedded in Michigan

In 2013, DSA-led Progressive Democrats of America assigned activists to deliver their material to almost every US Congressman and several Senators. David Green, chairman of Detroit DSA was assigned as contact for Representative Gary Peters.[25]

In November 2018, longtime activist and Detroit DSA member Rashida Tlaib was elected Congress to replace Detroit DSA member John Conyers.

Rashida Tlaib would become Michigan's third known DSA member to serve in the US Congress.

David Green

Representative David Bonior, once the second ranked Democrat in the House of Representatives was the other.[26, 27]

In September 2020, Rashida Tlaib endorsed Gary Peters' Senate re-election campaign.

Rashida Tlaib ✓
@RashidaTlaib
👤 US House candidate, MI-12

When we needed help exposing the Koch Brothers
illegally dumping of hazardous waste, petcoke, on the
Detroit River, @GaryPeters, stood with us.
#CorporateGreed is hurting our air, land + water & we
need to re-elect Sen. Peters to ensure they are
protected.

freep.com
Endorsement: Michigan needs Gary Peters. So does Washington.
The brainy Bloomfield lawmaker has embellished Michigan's long tradition of
bipartisan leadership in the U.S. Senate

12:50 PM · Sep 30, 2020 · Twitter for Android

Senator Peters clearly has ties to Democratic Socialists of America. To be fair though, it's hard to find an elected Michigan Democrat who doesn't.

COUNCIL FOR A LIVABLE WORLD

Despite having a military background, Senator Peters has been endorsed twice by the defense budget-slashing Council for a Livable World (CLW).

Senator Carl Levin, Gary Peters

In their 2014 endorsement of his first US Senate campaign, CLW noted that Peters would be a suitable replacement for retiring Senator Carl Levin:

> Peters has generally been a supporter of progressive national security policies.
>
> This year, he voted for the McGovern (D-MA) amendment to end the US military role in the Afghanistan war as soon as possible, for the Quigley (D-IL) amendment to cut funds for the B61 nuclear bomb program, for the Nadler (D-NY) amendment to eliminate funding for East Coast missile defense and for the Mulvaney (R-SC) amendment to reduce the Pentagon budget by $3.5 billion.
>
> He also voted against counterproductive Republican amendments to limit missile defense, prevent nuclear arms cooperation with Russia, and cut funding for nuclear non-proliferation programs.
>
> Council for a Livable World believes that Gary Peters will be a worthy replacement for Carl Levin and a solid addition to progressive ranks in the US Senate.[28]

Carl Levin was one of the most far-left Senators ever to serve. He was both an admirer of Michigan DSA leader Millie Jeffrey[29] and a supporter of the Soviet front World Peace Council.

In late September 1975, the World Peace Council sent a delegation on a ten-day tour of the United States of America, where it was "warmly and enthusiastically received".[30] The delegation was led by Romesh Chandra, Secretary General of the World Peace Council and a member of the Communist Party of India.[31]

Delegates included Josef Cyrankiewicz, former communist Premier of Poland, and Chairman of the Polish Peace Committee, British Labour MP James Lamond, Yacov Lomko, Editor-in-Chief of the Moscow News, leading member of the Soviet Peace Committee, and Communist Party USA (CPUSA) member Karen Talbot, a US member of the World Peace Council Secretariat.

At the Detroit airport, the group was met by representatives of local peace organizations and trade unions. A sheriff's escort accompanied the delegates into Detroit where the "keys to the city" were presented to the delegation by Deputy Mayor Malcolm Dade, representing Mayor Coleman Young[32], a long time secret member of the CPUSA.[33]

Senator Carl Levin was a member of the greeting delegation, as were Detroit City Councilors Maryan Mahaffey, and Erma Henderson and Clyde Cleveland.[34]

WPC delegation with members of the Detroit City Council.

Carl Levin, front center, Erma Henderson center, Maryann Mahaffey
fourth from right, Clyde Cleveland third from right

Maryan Mahaffey was herself a pro-Soviet "peace activist"[35] and longtime DSA member.[36]

In the 1940s, Erma Henderson represented Michigan on the national executive of the CPUSA's then-youth wing American Youth for Democracy.[37]

In 1982, Clyde Cleveland was a sponsor of the CPUSA-controlled US Peace Council with Maryan Mahaffey and Erma Henderson.[38]

Senator Levin, a militant US disarmer, was closely tied to the CLW. When Carl Levin died in July 2021, CLW issued a statement:

> *Senator Levin was a good man, terrific progressive and a lifelong advocate of sound arms control policies and smarter Pentagon spending. The Council for a Livable World endorsed him in his first Senate race in 1978 and continued supporting him and working with him until his retirement in 2015.*
>
> *Senator Levin… was a wildly successful chairman of the Senate*

Armed Services Committee, working with liberals and moderates alike to produce progressive defense budgets that sought to realign national security spending with modern threats...in 2012, he helped guide President Barack Obama's New START nuclear arms agreement through the Senate.[39]

Gary Peters also eulogized his "mentor":

When I first began serving in Congress, I would often seek Senator Levin's advice. His guidance was especially important to me as I succeeded him in the US Senate. He was not only a mentor – he was a personal friend, who I looked up to as an extraordinary public servant.[40]

When Carl Levin retired, Gary Peters sought and received the Senator's endorsement.[41]

CLW's 2020 endorsement of Gary Peters was still anti-military but a lot more subtle than usual:

Gary Peters won his Michigan Senate seat in 2014 in a challenging election year for Democrats.

He has a strong national security record. On Afghanistan, he stated, 'In the 17 years since September 11th, the American tax-payer has been asked to bankroll hundreds of billions of dollars of spending on combat, relief, and reconstruction in Afghanistan. What do I tell the people of Flint, Michigan who ask me, 'Why are my taxes paying for clean water in Kabul when I don't have clean water in my own home?'[42]

Still, he must have done enough damage for the CLW to continue investing in him.

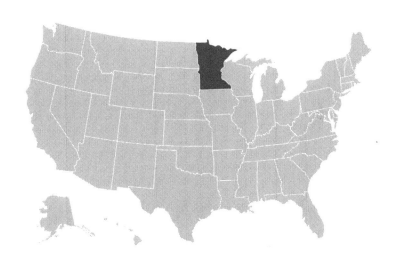

SENATORS FROM THE STATE OF
MINNESOTA

AMY KLOBUCHAR

AMY KLOBUCHAR IS THE SENIOR US SENATOR FROM MINNESOTA

BACKGROUND

A MY KLOBUCHAR WAS born and raised in Minnesota. She graduated from Yale University in 1982 and received her law degree in 1985 from the University of Chicago. Klobuchar worked for a period as legal advisor for former vice president Walter Mondale. From 1999-2006, Klobuchar served as attorney of Hennepin County. She was elected to her office in 2006 after running on the Democratic-Farmer-Labor Party (DFL) ticket.[1] She campaigned for president in 2020.[2]

INFLUENCE

Amy Klobuchar chairs both the Committee on Rules and Administration and the Joint Committee on Printing. She serves as the Vice Chairman of the Joint Committee on the Library. Klobuchar additionally chairs the Subcommittee on Competition

Policy, Antitrust, and Consumer Rights on the Committee on the Judiciary. She also sits on the Joint Economic Committee as well as the Committee on Agriculture, Nutrition, and Forestry.[3]

EARLY SOCIALIST INFLUENCES

Amy Klobuchar grew up in a left-leaning household. Her mother Rose was a schoolteacher and a union activist. Her father Jim was an alcoholic journalist with an affinity for the former Soviet Union.

Red Dad

At the height of the Cold War, Jim Klobuchar spent a week reporting from Moscow. He also covered the murder and funeral of Italian Prime Minister Aldo Mori – killed by Eastern Bloc sponsored Red Brigade terrorists.[4]

Jim Klobuchar also took his daughter Amy on a bike trek, from the Volga River to Moscow. Amy, and future husband John Bessler, later showed a small delegation of their former Soviet hosts around Minneapolis.[5]

Jim Klobuchar also appeared in the movie "The Wrestler"[6] alongside Screen Actors Guild leader and veteran Democratics Socialists of America (DSA) comrade Ed Asner.[7]

College socialism

During her time studying political science at Yale in the early 1980s, Amy Klobuchar came under the influence of several socialist professors.

In her 2015 book, the "Senator Next Door" Klobuchar tells of her political "education" at Yale:

> My interest in politics and policy really blossomed in college. I was particularly inspired by Yale political science professor Robert Dahl...Professor Dahl was sometimes described as the dean of American political scientists and his theories about how American politics worked, opened a whole new world of ideas for me.[8]

Robert Dahl was a Marxist and a long-time member of DSA.[9] Dahl was known for essays such as "On the Theory of Democratic Socialism" (1940); "Workers Control of Industry and the British

Labour Party" (1947); and "Marxism and Free Parties" (1948). The latter was described as a "nuanced critique of Marxist thinking about political parties written on the occasion of the centennial of "The Communist Manifesto".[10]

Robert Dahl

Amy Klobuchar also admired another of her teachers, Professor Charles Lindblom,[11] a founding sponsor of the DSA- aligned maga-zine "The American Prospect",[12] and a fan of the political economy of the late Yugoslav communist leader, Joseph Broz Tito.[13]

Another Klobuchar favorite was Theodore (Ted) Marmor, a national authority on Medicare.

From "A Senator Next Door":

> The last Yale professor who played a major role in my life was the late Ted Marmor. I took Ted's class 'The politics of Medicare' as a junior… The following year he took me and my friend Matt Hamel under his wing. On Sunday evenings Ted conducted weekly tutorial sessions with just the two of us.[14]

Ted Marmor

Professor Marmor was the head of Yale's Center for Health Services, a member of President Carter's Commission on the National Agenda for the 1980s, and a senior social policy advisor to the Mondale presidential campaign of 1984.

In February 2001, Ted Marmor appeared on a panel at the NEXT AGENDA conference in Washington DC.

Co-panelists included The American Prospect founder and DSA-aligned socialist Robert Kuttner;[15] DSA aligned US Senator Paul

Wellstone (D-MN) and Cathy Hurwit from the DSA-controlled Midwest Academy in Chicago.[16]

Ted Marmor has also been a long-time collaborator with healthcare activist Sid Socolar. In 1953, Socolar was accused of being a communist and a "national security risk" by the Senate Judiciary Committee in a report entitled "On Interlocking Subversion in Government Departments".[17]

By the 1990s, Sid Socolar was working closely with DSA.[18]

In April 2009, Ted Marmor appeared on a panel "Defeating the Persistent Attacks on Social Insurance" with Sid Socolar at the DSA-organized Left Forum conference in New York City.[19]

The Don Fraser connection

Amy Klobuchar was very close to far-left Minnesota congressman and former Minneapolis mayor Don Fraser.

Don Fraser

Klobuchar's husband John Bessler had interned for Fraser while in college,[20] and the Fraser and Bessler/Klobuchar families became life-long friends.

Circa 1990, Amy Klobuchar became president of the DFL Education Foundation – a "think tank" that ran independently of the Minnesota Democratic - Farmer - Labor Party. The organization's goal was to promote more "more citizen involvement in politics". Former presidential candidate Walter Mondale chaired the board, while according to Senator Klobuchar, Don Fraser and his wife Arvonne "were the heart and soul of the group".[21]

Don Fraser was undoubtedly a socialist.

In 1972, a coalition of congressmen, radical activists and some communists, spearheaded a drive to relax US government restrictions on Cuba. Representative Don Fraser (DFL-MN) was a congressional sponsor of the seminar.

According to a report on the movement featured in Human Events:

> *Under the auspices of Senator Ted Kennedy (D-MA), and Senator Harold Hughes (D-IA), a two-day conference of 'liberal scholars' assembled in April in the new Senate Office Building to thrash out a new US policy on Cuba...Secretary of the New York State Communist Party, Michael Myerson, was among the observers.*
>
> *One panelist, John M. Cates, Jr., director of the Center for Inter-American Relations matter of factly, remarked during the discussions 'So why are we here? We're here so Sen. Kennedy can have a rationale for our country to recognize Cuba'.*
>
> *The conference was financed by a New York based organization*

called the Fund for New Priorities in America; a coalition of
groups clearly sympathetic to many pro-communist causes.

The Fund was virtually the same group as the Committee for
Peace and New Priorities, a pro-Hanoi group which bought an ad
in November 1971 in the New York Times demanding Nixon set
a Vietnam withdrawal date. Both the Fund for the New Priorities
and the Committee for Peace were located at the same address in
New York.[22]

In 1973, Democratic Socialist Organizing Committee comrade
Lawrence Birns of the far-left New School for Social Research,[23]
Representative Don Fraser of the House Foreign Relations
Committee, and DSA founder Michael Harrington circulated a peti-
tion attacking the anti-communist military government in Chile:

We urge that the people of the world join in pressing upon the
military junta of Chile, the realization that they must abide by the
norms of civilized practices and human decency.[24]

In June 1977, Representative Fraser attended the second bureau
meeting of the Socialist International in Rome.[25]

Don Fraser was also heavily involved in US/Soviet politics – on
the Soviet side.

In April 1982, a group sponsored by the Soviet-friendly, Washington
DC-based Institute for Policy Studies (IPS) visited Moscow, for a
week of high-level meetings with Soviet officials.

The group was led by IPS founder Marcus Raskin and included
prominent IPS official Robert Borosage and then-serving Minneapolis
mayor Donald M. Fraser.

The IPS delegation met at least two Communist Party of the
Soviet Union Central Committee members in Moscow.

From a report by prominent historian of US communism Harvey
Klehr:

Georgi A. Arbatov, head of the Institute of the USA and Canada,
a 'think tank' that provides research and analysis and also cul-
tivates and develops contacts with Americans at the direction of
the KGB and the International Department of the CPSU Central

Committee and Vadim V. Zagladin, first deputy chief of the International Department.[26]

The IPS delegation echoed Soviet foreign policy in calling for US armament cuts as a basis for ending the arms race that was already putting huge pressure on the Soviet socialist economy.

If history is any guide, the proposal would have seen the US cut its military, while Soviets would have simply cheated while covertly increasing their ongoing military buildup.

According to a Washington Post report on the trip:

> *The Americans also reported that Soviet officials said they were prepared to make 'unilateral initiatives' in an effort to stop the arms race. The Soviets were quoted as saying that a proposal by Rep. Albert Gore, Jr. (D-Tenn.) calling for deep cuts in nuclear arsenals could form the basis for future arms negotiations.*
>
> *The Institute for Policy Studies and the Soviet Institute on the USA and Canada, a government think tank, have signed a protocol establishing annual Soviet American conferences to deal with the issues of bilateral relations and disarmament. The first meeting was set for next year in Minneapolis with 40 representatives from each side.*[27]

The Soviet propaganda meeting in Don Fraser's Minneapolis went ahead as scheduled.[28]

Amy Klobuchar has described Don Fraser as her "political mentor". When Klobuchar decided to run for Hennepin County Attorney in 1993, Don Fraser was there for her.

According to a June 3, 2019, tweet from Senator Klobuchar:

> *Former Congressman and Mayor Don Fraser died at age 95. In my first run for office, Don was a campaign co-chair and took to the podium to introduce me. He was a great public servant but also a mentor to the next generation. He got that his public service didn't end with him.*

Amy Klobuchar ✔
@amyklobuchar

Former Congressman and Mayor Don Fraser died at
age 95. In my first run for office, Don was a campaign
co-chair and took to the podium to introduce me. He
was a great public servant but also a mentor to the next
generation. He got that his public service didn't end
with him.

7:02 AM · Jun 3, 2019 · Twitter Web Client

On June 2, 2019, Senator Klobuchar released the following statement honoring the life of her friend Don Fraser:

> *The State of Minnesota has lost a true champion for good. Don
> and Arvonne Fraser were neighbors and friends. Don Fraser was
> always ahead of his time. As a congressman he fought for the envi-
> ronment and human rights and exposed human rights abuses
> around the world… My first job in Democratic politics was as the
> volunteer executive director of the DFL Education Foundation, a
> group Don Fraser founded. His mission? Ideas matter in politics.
> He lived that.*[29]

On October 9, 2004, Don Fraser addressed the Democratic
Socialists of America Mid-West regional conference in Minneapolis.

The event was initiated by the DSA International Commission and the DSA Fund and was cosponsored by Don Fraser and Amy Klobuchar's DFL Education Foundation.[30]

THE WELLSTONE INFLUENCE

If Amy Klobuchar owes her political career to any one person, it is to the late Minnesota Senator Paul Wellstone.

After growing up in Virginia, Paul Wellstone earned a Ph.D. in political science in 1969 at the University of North Carolina with a dissertation entitled "Black Militants in the Ghetto: Why They Believe in Violence". He then moved to Minnesota where he taught political science at Carleton College until 1989.

Senator Paul Wellstone

Wellstone was a radical academic and encouraged his students into leftist politics. Wellstone's student Jeff Blodgett - who would become a political ally to Klobuchar -recalled: "He [Wellstone] helped me get my first job as a community organizer working with family farmers in rural Minnesota."

The FBI first took note of Paul Wellstone when he was arrested on May 7, 1970, at a protest against the Vietnam War at the Federal Office Building in downtown Minneapolis. He would remain under FBI surveillance for more than 30 years.[31]

Wellstone was heavily involved in Jesse Jackson's Rainbow Coalition and served as Minnesota chair for Jackson's 1988 presidential campaign.

Wellstone's upset victory in his 1990 US Senate race essentially evolved out of the far-left Rainbow movement.[32]

Wellstone was also involved in the openly revolutionary New American Movement (NAM), which would later merge into the country's largest Marxist organization Democratic Socialists of America (DSA). In 1979, the NAM published a booklet entitled "Socialist working papers on energy". Contributors included Paul Wellstone and Monty Tarbox, who together wrote "Dangerous Harvest: Tractor Power vs. Power Companies."[33]

After DSA was founded in 1982, Wellstone became very close to the organization – but not publicly. When his socialist ties became an issue in one campaign, Wellstone's staff hid the politically embarrassing connection.

According to Bob Roman of Chicago DSA:

> Wellstone's press secretary was less than truthful when he claimed Wellstone 'knew nothing of the group'. There had been a Youth Section (Young Democratic Socialists) chapter at Carleton College for which Wellstone had been the faculty adviser.[34]

DSA Support

When it came to Wellstone's political ambitions, DSA was right there to assist. There is no doubt that DSA played a major role in electing Wellstone to the US Senate in 1990.

From Democratic Left:

> Twin Cities DSA in Minnesota continues its resurgence with ongoing support of Paul Wellstone's campaign for the Senate seat currently held by Republican Rudy Boschwitz. Local activists are doing literature drops and helping to raise money for this watershed campaign...As a professor at Carlton College, Wellstone has mentored many DSA Youth Section activists...Contributions, made out to Wellstone for US Senate, can be sent to the DSA National Office and will be forwarded to the campaign.[35]

Twin Cities DSA put most of its time and energy in the Fall of 1990 into Wellstone's campaign. They described Wellstone as "explicitly democratic socialist in orientation".[36]

DSA was back to help when Wellstone stood for re-election in 1996. The DSA Political Action Committee endorsed Wellstone, and both local and national DSA put boots on the ground for his campaign.

According to Democratic Left:

> In 1996 Democratic Socialists of America sent six staff members into the field for the final weeks of the campaign. These staff and

> *DSA volunteers "contributed to the re-election of Senator Paul Wellstone, Congressperson Maurice Hinchey (D-upstate NY) and aided in the narrow victory of pro-labor John Tierney (D-MA) over 'moderate' Republican Pete Torkildsen in Massachusetts.*[37]

DSA leader Christine Riddiough was specifically assigned to Wellstone's Senate campaign. She wrote in Democratic Left:

> *Rudy Boschwitz, branded Wellstone 'embarrassingly liberal.' As the campaign intensified, Boschwitz became increasingly negative in his ads. In the last days before the election, he claimed that Wellstone had burned the American flag in the '60s.*
>
> *Before I got to Minnesota the race was neck and neck, but in that last week before the election-coinciding with DSA's active involvement-Wellstone pulled out to a strong lead, finally winning by nine percent. While I was there, I worked with the campaign's superbly organized grassroots efforts. I concentrated on organizing DSA members and members of the gay and lesbian community to round up volunteers for Wellstone. Then I rolled up my sleeves for endless rounds of calls to Wellstone supporters to make sure they got out to vote.*[38]

In 2002, DSA made re-electing Paul Wellstone to a third term its "national electoral project" for the year. Wellstone was originally intending to run for US President, but health issue caused him to opt for another less arduous Senate race. DSA employed some questionable tactics:

> *Together with YDS, DSA's Youth Section, we are mobilizing to bring young people to Minnesota. Minnesota is one of the few states that allow same day voter registration. We will focus our energy on registering young people. Wellstone will need a high percentage of young people to register and vote for him if he is to stave off the campaign that Bush and the Republicans have orchestrated against him. He is the right's number one electoral target.*
>
> *Because we are focusing on issue-based voter registration, this electoral work can be supported by tax deductible contributions and the DSA FUND is soliciting such contributions to support this project.*

> *Contributions are needed to underwrite the costs of transpor-*
> *tation as well as to provide stipends for expenses. DSA members*
> *wishing to contribute should make their check payable to DSA*
> *Fund and return it to...* [39]

A "non-partisan" voter registration drive organized by the Democratic Socialists of America Fund in Minnesota during the 2002 Senate race became the subject of an IRS investigation.

Both DSA and the DSA Fund received letters that indicated their tax-exempt status might be threatened. DSA fretted that "a finding that either organization had engaged in improper partisan activity could have led to fines and penalties that could have included loss of their tax-exempt status".

Of course, DSA blamed their opponents for the problem:

> *In our case, the right-wing Minnesota Taxpayers League charged*
> *that the small non-partisan voter registration drive we organized*
> *actually consisted of an attempt to bring out-of state students to*
> *Minnesota to illegally vote for Democratic Senate candidate Paul*
> *Wellstone. The Drudge Report ran with the charge, and Fox News*
> *spread it further.... Other right-wingers then tried to stir up more*
> *controversy, charging that we organized an illegal partisan voter*
> *registration drive.*
>
> *DSA members around the country contributed thousands of dol-*
> *lars to defray the legal expenses incurred in defending the organiza-*
> *tion from these charges. We retained the firm of... a Washington,*
> *DC firm that specializes in this area of the law.*
>
> *After more than a year of filing, responding and waiting, we*
> *finally have received our closure letters. The IRS has accepted our*
> *2002 returns and our explanation of the voter registration project.*
> *They also said formally that our tax-exempt status was not in*
> *jeopardy.* [40]

Perhaps the "Deep State" is really nothing new.

The Republicans went after Wellstone hard in 2002. After a very close campaign, polls a few weeks before election day showed that Wellstone had pulled slightly ahead of his Republican opponent Norm Coleman. Then, just eleven days before the election, Wellstone's plane crashed near the Eveleth airport, killing the Senator, his wife, Sheila, his daughter Marcia, three campaign staffers and two pilots.[41]

Minnesota voters went on to elect Norm Coleman, but the Wellstone "movement" still dominates Minnesota politics to this day.

'Paul told me I should run for office'

Senator Klobuchar is a creature of the Wellstone socialist movement. She has been an active part of it her entire political career.

Klobuchar was heavily involved in Wellstone's second Senate campaign. travelling on the campaign bus, even standing in for him at a speech he couldn't make.[42]

Nearing the 10th anniversary of Wellstone's death, Minnesota Senators Al Franken and Amy Klobuchar wrote an article in the Star Tribune, entitled "Paul Wellstone's legacy":

Amy Klobuchar and Paul Wellstone

> For both of us, Paul Wellstone was a friend, mentor and hero.
>
> As senators, we've experienced firsthand the lasting personal impression he made in Washington.
>
> As an educator, an activist and a senator, Paul inspired people throughout America. His mission was to bring a voice to the voiceless, power to the powerless and justice to those who've suffered injustice.
>
> Above all, he brought the hope to all of us that, by working together, it's possible to change the world and make tomorrow better than today...[43]

In an October 25, 2017 Facebook post Senator Klobuchar wrote:

> Paul told me I should run for office. He taught me the importance of purpose in politics. He taught me how to campaign.[44]

Wellstone Action

Wellstone encouraged Amy Klobuchar to run for Hennepin County attorney and to seek higher office after that. "Whenever the going was tough" in her campaigns, she said, "I always thought in my mind, 'Well, Paul thought I could do this.'"

After his death, several supporters established a "community orga-nizer" training school named Wellstone Action in his honor. Later named simply "Wellstone" and now "RePower", the organization has trained hundreds of activists, many of whom have run for political office.

Former Iowa Congressmember David Loebsack is a Wellstone Action alumnus, as is current Minnesota Governor Tim Walz. Serving Minnesota Attorney General Keith Ellison is a former Wellstone trainer.[45]

The organization's advisory board was a who's who of the Minnesota and national Left.

It featured such notable names as Minnesota Governor Mark Dayton, Minnesota Secretary of State Mark Ritchie, Minneapolis mayor RT Rybak, Senators Al Franken, Russ Feingold and Tom Harkin, presidential candidates Bill Bradley and Walter Mondale, senior Democratic Party operatives Heather Booth and Donna Brazile, actors Warren Beatty and Robert Redford, folksinger Peter Yarrow, economist Robert Reich, labor leaders Andy Stern, Leo Gerard and Gerald McEntee, Robert Borosage of the far-left Institute for Policy Studies,[46] and DSA members Julian Bond[47] and Frances Fox-Piven.[48]

There is no doubt that the Wellstone movement made Amy Klobuchar a US Senator.

Wellstone Action executive director Ben Goldfarb ran Klobuchar's first Senate campaign and has been active in other campaigns.[49] Former Wellstone executive director Jeff Blodgett, mentioned above, ran all three of Paul Wellstone's campaigns and worked on Amy Klobuchar's successful US Senate campaign in 2006.

In 2008/09, Jeff Blodgett, as executive director of Wellstone Action, studied for a year at the Liberation Road-affiliated Oakland, California-based Rockwood Leadership Institute.[50]

Amy Klobuchar says that Paul Wellstone's ideas remain relevant. "He cared about a lot of issues, but he had a major economic focus…That is still very much in the party — for good reason, because the income gap hasn't really changed…He always stood up for the most vulnerable."[51]

In a 2017 speech on the Senate floor, Klobuchar said that Wellstone made people believe "that getting involved in politics could make a real difference in their lives."[52]

21ST CENTURY DEMOCRATS

In 2018, Minnesota-based Political Action Committee 21st Century Democrats endorsed and supported Amy Klobuchar in her Senate race.[53] Klobuchar has a long relationship with the organization which has a goal "to help bolster progressive policies at all levels of government."[54]

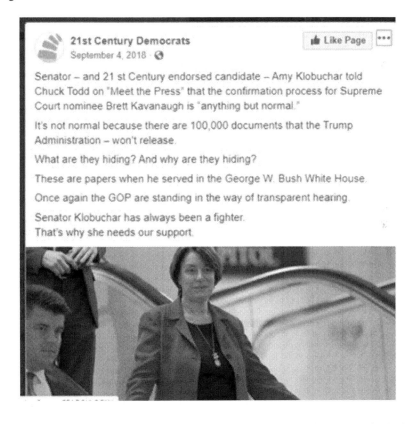

21st Century Democrats was led for many years by Jim Scheibel, a former mayor of St. Paul and a long time DSA comrade.[55] Jim Scheibel knew Paul Wellstone and his wife for more than 30 years.[56]

FAR LEFT FOREIGN POLICY INFLUENCE

Minnesota's main Maoist group, the "FightBack!" faction of Freedom Road Socialist Organization (FRSO), often protests outside Senator Klobuchar's office when she doesn't vote their way.

FRSO is very supportive of several of America's enemies including China, North Korea and Cuba. Like all radical left groups who have allegiance to foreign communists, FRSO consistently works to weaken and defund America's military. Any small reduction in America's military capabilities, or a minor change in US foreign policy in an enemy's favor is a victory for the Maoists.

Women Against Military Madness

In recent years, FRSO has largely taken control of longstanding Minnesota "peace" group Women Against Military Madness (WAMM).

According to the Committee in Solidarity with the People of Syria, writing in 2015:

> *For the last three years, the presence of members of the Freedom Road Socialist Organization, a dogmatic Stalinist sect, on WAMM's board and the influence of their ideology has resulted in increased intolerance from the WAMM board towards anyone with a differing viewpoint.*[57]

Roxanne Abbas of WAMM helped form the Minnesota Peace Project (MPP). Also, MPP Secretary April Knutsen is a former member of the Communist Party USA and its spinoff group Committees of Correspondence.[58]

One of MPP's first items of business was to hold a meeting

Senator Klobuchar with Roxanne Abbass, 2014

"with Amy Klobuchar aides to present the Peace Agenda and to exchange perspectives on the Israel/Palestine conflict."[59]

According to MMP's website, the organization has had several successes with Senator Klobuchar and former Senator Franken.

MPP claims to have influenced Senators Klobuchar and Franken on a range of issues from de-funding America's ally Saudi Arabia to promoting former President Obama's disastrous Iran Nuclear Deal:

> An MPP member worked closely with Senator Klobuchar's office and the Constitution Project to author a bill outlawing torture. Their bill received bipartisan support and was signed into law.
>
> After we explained how Saudi Arabia was using US manufactured arms against Yemeni civilians, Senator Franken co-sponsored a bill to freeze all sales of US arms to the Saudis.
>
> Our persistent advocacy helped convince Senators Franken and Klobuchar to vote in favor of the Iran nuclear deal.[60]

Senator Klobuchar is clearly on very friendly terms with MPP.

> In 2014 seven Minnesota Peace Project members from across the state went to Washington DC to meet with... Minnesota members of Congress or their foreign policy aides. We explored our differences on key foreign policy issues such as military budget, nuclear disarmament, and support for ongoing negotiations on Iran's nuclear program. The team had lengthy second meetings with both Senators' staff.
>
> Due to MPP's perseverance in presenting documentation from recognized authorities, Senator Klobuchar's foreign policy aide announced that Senator Klobuchar's constituent letter on diplomacy with Iran would change; no longer stating that tough sanctions had brought Iran to the negotiation table.
>
> When Senator Klobuchar learned that four MPP leaders were in DC for a conference, she instructed an aide to try to schedule a meeting with them.[61]

MPP even had a group the "K-Team" specifically dedicated to dealing with Senator Klobuchar.

From the MPP website in a section titled "Klobuchar Team Meeting – May 22, 2009":

The K-Team enjoyed a delightful Greek luncheon at…as we discussed strategy for our work with Senator Klobuchar and her staff. A draft of the Senator's positions on the Peace Agenda which has been sent to Klobuchar's MN Chief of Staff, Zach Rodvold and her foreign policy aide, Tom Sullivan, was reviewed and discussed. Rodvold intends to return edits by the end of the day on Friday, May 22.[62]

THE MUSLIM LEFT

Senator Klobuchar enjoys close ties to several leftist Islamic organizations in Minnesota especially local branches of the Council on American Islamic Relations (CAIR) and the Muslim Brotherhood-initiated Muslim American Society (MAS). Both organizations work with local Marxist groups including FRSO.

For example, as recently as September 2019, the Minnesota chapters of CAIR and MAS joined with the FRSO-controlled Anti-War Committee[63] to organize a downtown Minneapolis protest against India's alleged mistreatment of Muslims in Kashmir.[64]

MAS

Senator Klobuchar has been a regular at MAS Minnesota events since the early 2000s, when she was a Hennepin County prosecutor.[65]

Amy Klobuchar attended the annual MAS Minnesota Convention for many years.[66]

MAS Minnesota activists met with Senator Klobuchar for #MuslimHillDay on 2 May 2017.

MAS Minnesota
@MASMinnesota

Follow

Meeting with Senator Amy Klobuchar.
#MuslimHillDay

4:17 PM - 2 May 2017

CAIR

Evidence linking CAIR and its founders to an American support network for Palestinian terror group HAMAS has been released through court action in the Holy Land Foundation terror funding trial of 2008. That evidence prompted the FBI to cut off its outreach with the group. In 2010, the Justice Department said it had seen no "new evidence that exonerates CAIR from the allegations that it provides financial support to designated terrorist organizations."[67]

Yet Amy Klobuchar has no problem with CAIR.

In April 2013, around 400 people turned out for the 6th Annual Banquet of CAIR-Minnesota.

The event, themed "Upholding the Constitution, Defending Civil Liberties," included an awards ceremony, and an "opportunity to learn about CAIR-MN's accomplishments in defense of civil rights over the past year."

Banquet attendees included "community members, leaders of mosques and Muslim organizations, business executives, and interfaith partners". Senator Amy Klobuchar and Congressman Keith Ellison (D-MN) were special guest speakers.

Further, the annual Justice Works award was presented to Minneapolis attorney Jordan Kushner[68] - formerly an activist with the Maoist-leaning Progressive Student Organization.[69]

During the event, Senator Klobuchar told CAIR that she is happy to work with the organization:

> I am proud to serve you in the United States Senate and look forward to continuing our work together in the future.[70]

CUBA CONNECTION

Senator Klobuchar's leftist worldview is most obviously on show in her dealings with America's closest enemy state, Cuba.

The US wisely began to isolate Cuba's communist regime not long after the 1959 insurgency which brought Fidel Castro to power. Economic, cultural and political isolation from the United States has reduced the ability of Cuba to spread communism through Latin America and Africa. It may even have ended communism on the island had not President Obama relaxed restrictions on the communist dictatorship in December 2014.

Amy Klobuchar has done her best to undermine the US sanctions that have kept Cuban communism at least partially contained for over half a century.

In February 2015, Amy Klobuchar hosted the "Modernizing US-Cuba Relations Summit" at the University of Minnesota.

The forum highlighted the "historic opportunity for our country to modernize our relationship with Cuba". Klobuchar was joined by keynote speaker Michael Scuse, the USDA Undersecretary for Farms and Foreign Agriculture Services. There was also a panel discussion with "voices representing Minnesota's agriculture, business, and Latino communities". Senator Klobuchar was described as a "strong proponent of normalizing ties with Cuba and increasing travel and commerce that could create new economic opportunities for American farmers and businesses while improving the quality of life for Cubans."[71]

In March 2015, Senator Klobuchar introduced the "Freedom to Export to Cuba Act of 2015." The bill's introduction followed President Obama's use of executive power in December 2014 to re-establish diplomatic relations and ease travel restrictions on Cuba.[72]

In July 2015, Senator Klobuchar was a guest of honor as the flag was raised over the newly re-established Cuban embassy on 16th Street NW Washington DC.

The raucous and decidedly leftist crowd shouted "Viva Cuba!" to mark the auspicious occasion.

A Washington Post report of the event quoted former Maoist Phyllis Bennis of the Institute for Policy Studies: "It's an amazing moment," she said. In the decades-long effort to normalise relations with Cuba, to stop the US attacks and hostility toward Cuba, we have not had so many victories. Suddenly we have a victory. The flag going up - that's huge."

"I'm excited," said far-left actor Danny Glover, who has joined numerous "cultural delegations" to Cuba. "This is the beginning of another narrative…What's happened in the last 54 years is an insult to our intelligence as human beings and [American] citizens."[73]

Cuba trip

In mid-February 2015, Senators Klobuchar, Claire McCaskill (D-MO) and Mark Warner (D-VA), traveled to Havana Cuba, for four days.

The three Senators "spoke to reporters after talks on the island with Foreign Minister Bruno Rodriguez and Josefina Vidal, Cuba's chief negotiator in talks with the US aimed at normalizing relations".

"I think there is clearly interest in Cuba in lifting the embargo," said Senator Klobuchar. "The issue will be in the US," she continued.

As was revealed in Security Risk Senators Part 1 exposing Senator Hickenlooper of Colorado, Josefina Vidal is both a member of the Central Committee of the Cuban Communist Party and a high-ranking intelligence officer.

Klobuchar emphasized:

> One of the reasons we came on this trip was that we could go back and tell our colleagues what we've seen: That there are more and more people engaged in private sector business, that there is an entrepreneurial spirit here…The people want to see better relations with the US.[74]

Center for Democracy in the Americas

The Senators were accompanied by Sara Stephens of the Center for Democracy in the Americas (CDA) which organized the trip.

Senators McCaskill and Klobuchar in Havana with CDA's Sarah Stephens

The Washington DC-based CDA is one of communist Cuba's most effective allies in the United States. Its main goal is to break the US "blockade" of Cuba by building a Congressional lobby in support of easing restrictions on the island. CDA has arranged multiple Congressional and Senate delegations to Havana in recent years, mostly focusing on far-left Democrats, and occasional Republicans from agricultural states who might be convinced to lobby for greater trade access for American farmers.

CDA is a spin-off of the far-left Institute of Policy Studies.

Julia Sweig, once a CDA board member,[75] was named by US Defense Intelligence Agency top Cuban spy catcher Chris Simmons as a Cuban "Agent of Influence".[76]

Minority Leader Nancy Pelosi and 16 other House Democrats and six US Senators joined President Obama on his historic trip to Cuba March 20-22, 2016. Left wing Politico described the trip as a "symbolic next chapter in his [Obama] attempts to normalize relations with the country".

Senator Klobuchar was, of course, invited along.[77]

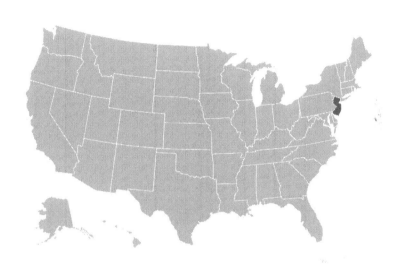

SENATORS FROM THE STATE OF

NEW JERSEY

CORY BOOKER

BACKGROUND

ORY BOOKER (BORN April 27, 1969) received his undergraduate and master's degree from Stanford University, where he also wrote for the student newspaper. He studied abroad at the University of Oxford on a Rhodes Scholarship and graduated from Yale Law School in 1997.[1] From 2006 – 2013, Booker served as mayor of Newark. Before that, Booker served on the Municipal Council of Newark for the Central Ward from 1998 to 2002.

Booker is the junior United States Senator from New Jersey, serving on the Democratic Party ticket.

INFLUENCE

Cory Booker serves on the Committee on Agriculture, Nutrition, and Forestry, where he chairs the Subcommittee on Food and Nutrition,

Specialty Crops, Organics, and Research. Booker also chairs the Subcommittee on Criminal Justice and Counterterrorism for the Committee on the Judiciary. Booker is also on the Committees on Foreign Relations and Small Business and Entrepreneurship.[2]

MARXIST-LENINIST MENTOR

Senator Booker owes his political career to one man – former Marxist-Leninist student activist turned mega-wealthy San Francisco lawyer, Steve Phillips.

LRS at Stanford

Originally from Cleveland, Ohio, Steve Phillips was a leader of the Black Student Union and active in campus Maoist politics at Stanford University in the 1980s.

Steve Phillips

After months of investigation on May 23, 1990, the Stanford Daily senior staff Writer Michael Friedly blew the lid off Stanford's most secretive radical organization: the pro-China League of Revolutionary Struggle (LRS).

The ripples off this expose are still being felt today.

Wrote Friedly:

Over the past three months, The Daily has interviewed dozens of students who have some familiarity with the League. These interviews were part of an investigation of the League which included more than 100 interviews with students, administration officials and nationwide experts. Many students interviewed by The Daily asked not to be identified because they said they are afraid of harassment by League members.[3]

The article went on to detail the League's history of highly secretive political manipulation of certain student groups and its wider influence on student politics.

A secretive nationwide organization called the League of Revolutionary Struggle (Marxist-Leninist) has been a little-known factor in student politics at Stanford for several years, a Daily investigation has found:

Through the selective recruitment of Stanford students into its organization, the League has been able to influence aspects of progressive politics on campus by trying to place its members in leadership positions within the ASSU (Association of Students at Stanford University, the student government), the communities of color and in staff positions. The total number of Stanford students and staff members who are League members is apparently fewer than 30, but these individuals are in positions that allow them to shape student government policies, according to a number of sources who said they have either been recruited by the League or have worked with League members in the ASSU or student of color organizations.

The presence of the League has been in part responsible for dramatic effects at Stanford, ranging from divisions within the communities of color to the pressured resignation of an administrator to parts of the planning of last spring's takeover of University President Donald Kennedy's office.[4]

Friedly also went into the LRS's cultish secrecy and their influence on the Association of Stanford Student Unions (ASSU):

The League, based in the Bay Area but with membership across the country, has been able to recruit Stanford students into its organization in a manner secret enough so that students are not initially told they are being recruited by the League, according to several Stanford students who said they were recruited but did not join the League.

Recruitment of individuals by the League is generally conducted over a long period of time, several years in some cases, according to students who were recruited. Students who are successfully recruited by the League are then able to further the League's goals by running for student offices and helping to determine policies in the ASSU.[5]

In typical Maoist fashion, the LRS focused heavily on racial politics and agitation.

Friedly went on the explain that according to LRS theory, the United States is composed of various "oppressed nations," such as the Afro-American nation in the South, the Chicano nation in the Southwest and the Asian American nation:

The overall goal of the League has been the "liberation" of these nationalities under a socialist state, according to a League publication called 'Peace, Justice, Equality and Socialism' that explains its goals.

Until it can gain enough support to stage a revolution, the League attempts to "organize, agitate and educate the masses" by working with more mainstream groups, according to the publication. By making mass organizations more radical, the League can gain enough support for its

*"protracted revolution" in the United States, the publication states.
Unlike the Communist Party USA, which is a predominantly white
organization, the LRS focuses on mass organizations dealing with
people of color for its support within student and labor movements.*

*At Stanford, the League has tried to work toward its goals with
varying degrees of success in MEChA, a Chicano/Latino student
group; AASA; the Black Student Union and the ASSU through a
student electoral alliance dubbed the 'People's Platform'.*[6]

LRS comrades

Friedly went on to name several alleged LRS activists, including
two staffers of his own newspaper. Friedly quoted student activist
Richard Suh, who was recruited by the League, but eventually balked
at full membership.

> *Former Asian American Student Association chair Richard Suh
> said he was heavily recruited by Elsa Tsutaoka the office manager
> of the Asian American Activities Center. According to Suh, when
> Tsutaoka asked him to apply for membership in the League, Suh
> asked her which Stanford students were members of the League.
> 'You shouldn't ask that question,' was the reply, he said.*
>
> *When questioned by the Daily, Tsutaoka 'denied having any
> knowledge of the League or that she had ever recruited for the
> League'. Added Friedly 'because the recruitment process is secretive
> and individuals refuse to acknowledge that they are members of the
> League, it is difficult to prove whether anyone is a League member.'*
>
> *Council of Presidents (COP) member David Brown and former
> COP member Stacey Leyton are both believed to be members of the
> League, according to a number of sources. Brown refused to com-
> ment. Leyton denied that she was a member or that she had any
> knowledge of the League's membership at Stanford.*
>
> *Although there is no indication that she joined the League,
> COP member Ingrid Nava, who was recently re-elected to a second
> term, was heavily recruited by the League beginning at the end of
> last summer, according to a number of students. Nava refused to
> return numerous phone calls. At the end of last summer, Nava
> lived briefly at a house on Bryant Street in Palo Alto known sar-
> castically by some progressive students as the 'Revolutionary Hotel,'
> where recruitment for the League has occurred, according to sources
> who say they have been recruited.*

> *Tsutaoka and Steven Phillips, a former BSU chair and current Daily multicultural editor who has allegedly recruited for the League, currently live in the house. Phillips recruited Nava beginning in September, according to a student who was also recruited by the League. Phillips said he had no knowledge of the League's involvement at Stanford and has not recruited for the organization.*[7]

Such evasions were standard LRS practice. The flat-out denials were almost certainly lies.

Elsa Tsutaoka was a contributor to Unity,[8] the newspaper of the LRS, and was a close collaborator with Steve Phillips.

Steve Phillips, send from left, Elsa Tsutsaoka right, vote canvassing 1990

In May 1985, Unity published a supplement on the Stanford University South African divestment movement.

The article profiled the activities of several Stanford Out of South Africa (SOSA) activists including Steve Phillips – Black Student Union chair and SOSA liaison committee with the Administration and Stacey Leyton – Students Against Reaganism.

In the interview, Steve Phillips proudly stated that "some of the people who have played roles in organizing SOSA have been folks who've worked with Unity and take a Marxist-Leninist perspective...It's really exciting to see the principles of Marxism-Leninism being successful and making a difference."[9]

Steve Phillips and fellow Stanford activist David Brown were principal organizers of the April 1987 March on Sacramento that mobilized 8,000 people to support "expanded educational opportunities for students of color."[10]

In 1990, Steve Phillips contributed an article on Nelson Mandela to the July 9, 1990 issue of the LRS's Unity and another article "keeping hope alive in 1990" in the November 26 issue.

After the LRS dissolved in late 1990, Unity January 28, 1991, issued a statement: "A call to build an organization for the 1990s and beyond." It listed more than 100 activists working to build a new group from the ashes of the LRS – the Unity Organizing Committee. The League wasn't dying. It was reincarnating.

Among those committed to building the new organization were:

+ David Brown, former student body co-president Stanford University
+ Stacey Leyton, West Coast organizer United States Students Association
+ Ingrid Nava, student body co-president Stanford University
+ Steven C. Phillips. writer, education activist San Francisco

David Brown went on to work in education and is today Chief of Staff at the Office of Democratic Party leader and Alameda County Supervisor Wilma Chan – herself a former LRS leader.[11,12]

Ingrid Nava is a labor lawyer, Associate General Counsel at SEIU Local 32BJ, New York.[13]

Stacey Leyton went on to clerk for Supreme Court Justice Stephen Breyer and currently serves as a Lawyer Representative to the Northern District of California.[14]

Steve Phillips, Influencer

Steve Phillips is now a self-described "national political leader, civil rights lawyer, and senior fellow at the Center for American Progress…" According to his biography at the Center for American Progress, Phillips has "appeared on multiple national radio and television networks including NBC, CNN, MSNBC, Fox News and TV One. He is a columnist for The Nation and a regular opinion contributor to The New York Times."

In 2014, he was named one of "America's Top 50 Influencers" by Campaigns and Elections magazine.[15]

And he is a would-be political kingmaker.

The Sandler connection

Soon after leaving Stanford, Steve Phillips married fellow Stanford graduate Susan Sandler, daughter of far-left billionaires Herb and Marion Sandler. The Sandlers made their $2.4 billion fortune through the sale of their company, Golden West Financial Corporation, to Wachovia Bank. The Sandlers invested $1.3 million into their Sandler Foundation, which supports mainly leftist causes such as Center for American Progress and ProPublica.[16]

Both Steve Phillips and Susan Sandler have played roles in the "Democracy Alliance",[17] a semi-secret network of the leftist ultra-rich including George Soros, Norman Lear of People for the American Way, Democratic Party mega-donor Tom Steyer, and others.

Now more than 150 members strong the highly secretive Democracy Alliance has donated billions of dollars to Democratic Party and leftist causes in the last 15 years.[18]

Phillips has been very influential inside the Democracy Alliance because he has brought a unique strategic vision that many of the more money-focused members lacked.

Re-visiting the Rainbow

And it all goes back to Jesse Jackson's famous "Rainbow Coalition" of the 1980s.

Jesse Jackson ran for president twice, in 1984 and 1988, with an idea way ahead of its time.

The Rainbow Coalition strategy was to unite "progressive" white voters with leftist black, Latino,

Asian-American, Native American, and gay activists into a multi-colored electoral coalition. In 1988, Jackson got 6.9 million votes and won 11 states in the Democratic primary with this strategy.[19] Steve Phillips was a delegate to Jackson's 1984 and 1988 campaign conferences and took a year off from college to serve as the California student coordinator of Jackson's 1988 campaign.[20]

Today, minorities are a much larger proportion of the population, and some, particularly Asian-Americans, have trended more Democratic since the mid-1990s. Through his New York Times best seller "Brown is the New White" and multiple op-eds and speeches, Phillips has been working hard to convince leading Democrats and his Democracy Alliance "partners" to stop wasting money on white "swing voters". Phillips points to the multiracial "Rainbow Coalition" alliance that put Barack Obama in the White House – and he should know as he played a major role in that victory.

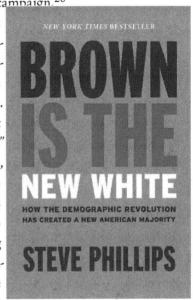

Steve Phillips has created several organizations including PowerPAC and PowerPAC+ to fund "candidates of color" around the United States; and Democracy in Color to propagandize his message to a wide audience.

PowerPAC, certain wealthy leftist donors and "grassroots" socialist groups worked together to play a decisive role in the close-fought 2007-2008 Obama campaign. Phillips explained in a June 2008 Huffington Post article:

> Contrary to earlier reports about the demise of independent efforts this cycle, the work in 2008 will be robust, vibrant, and more coordinated than ever before. In 2008, the progressive movement is taking on an unprecedented collaboration of grassroots groups to raise $100 million that will mobilize millions of new voters and

engage them in effective organizations that will be around long after November 4.

Major donors across the country are as inspired as everyone else about this important moment, and significant investments are being made to make the most of this opportunity. In addition to widespread non-partisan work, many of these efforts will support progressive candidates up and down the ticket, helping elect Barack Obama, picking up Senate seats, flipping state legislatures and permanently reshaping the electoral landscape in key states across the country.

The Democratic primaries illustrated our country's hunger for a progressive agenda as millions of new and previously disengaged voters expressed their desire for change at the polls. Young people and African Americans and Latinos voted in record numbers across the country (1 million new Latino voters turned out in California alone.)

PowerPAC, an organization whose primary purpose is to advocate for social justice policies and increase voter participation for people of color, was fortunate to participate in this historic moment. We were the first group on the air in South Carolina in January with get-out-the-vote radio ads targeting African American voters. We partnered with churches, labor and community-based organizations to increase Black voter turnout in 14 states with a focus on the South, including Alabama, Tennessee, Maryland and Virginia. In California and Texas, we contacted over one million Latino voters to make sure that they were educated and prepared to make their votes count.

Following our successful work in the primaries, PowerPAC is moving to expand our efforts and collaborate with other independent grassroots groups to build a permanent progressive infrastructure that will not only have a tangible impact on this campaign cycle, but will continue to work for positive change long after the last campaign posters have come down...

Through an effort dubbed the Jimmie Lee Jackson Project, PowerPAC will collaborate with groups like the NAACP, National Coalition on Black Civic Participation, the Pushback Network, and others to coordinate non-partisan registration, education, and mobilization efforts of African American voters during the General Election. Jimmie Lee Jackson was a 24-year-old civil *rights demonstrator whose death at the hands of Alabama State Troopers led to the Selma-Montgomery march and passage of the Voting Rights Act in 1965. Our coordinated Black voter drive will register and mobilize one million new Black voters through a $10 million, multi-state mobilization in states such as Virginia, North Carolina, Mississippi, and Georgia.*

PowerPAC will also collaborate with the major grassroots mobilization efforts led by America Votes and its 30-plus partner organizations, representing the largest progressive issue-based organizations in the country. In a national collaborative table and a series of collaborative tables in 14 states, these groups are dividing up constituencies and coordinating communication and mobilization efforts to educate voters about the national and down-ticket races.

Working from a common voter file, long-standing groups like the Sierra Club will contact 700,000 members and other voters concerned about environmental issues; the Campaign for Community Change will organize immigrant advocates and workers; Emily's List and Planned Parenthood will carry the message to female voters; and the United States Student Association, Young Democrats of America and League of Young Voters will mobilize the millennial generation.

A confluence of factors has created a once-in-a-generation opportunity to reorder priorities and reshape public policy for decades to come. To seize this opportunity, progressive leaders, donors, and activists alike all must rise to the challenge.

In his (primary) victory speech on June 3rd, Senator Obama closed by saying, "Generations from now, we will be able to look back and tell our children that this was the moment when we began to provide care for the sick and good jobs for the jobless." In order to convey that message to future generations, we need a massive mobilization now of Americans from all backgrounds who hunger for change. At PowerPAC, we are proud to join with our allies to do our part to make the most of this historic moment.[21]

It is doubtful that without Steve Phillips' access to big money and his update of Jesse Jackson's Rainbow Coalition strategy that we ever would have had a President Barack Obama.

Steve Phillips has also partnered with the hard left to deliver minority votes to the Democratic Party. Phillips and his Democracy

Alliance partners have spent millions funding radical voter registration organizations and "get out the vote" efforts in states with large minority populations. Many of these organizations are led by former members of the disgraced Association of Community Organizations for Reform Now (ACORN) or are supporters of Liberation Road, a successor to a faction of the former LRS.

In 2013, Phillips and his wife were major funders of a study which led to the formation of LeftRoots, a satellite organization of Liberation Road with a mission to promote "21st Century socialism".[22]

The US left made a big mistake in running Hillary Clinton for president after Barack Obama termed out. Black turnout dropped to such an extent that Donald Trump was able to carry the day.

In the 2020 election cycle Steve Phillips dismisses "Trump voters in the Midwest," in favor of mobilizing "people of color and progressive whites" who outnumber conservative whites. Therefore, according to Phillips, the Democrat's road to victory is not to chase white "Trump voters," but to inspire "progressives" by using the "Obama formula" – that is the Rainbow Coalition strategy:

> This notion that we should chase the Trump voters in the Midwest is illogical. That focuses on a shrinking sector of the population. The Obama formula—inspire people of color and progressive whites to turn out in large numbers—is how you win elections.[23]

'New American Majority'

Steve Phillips' update of the Maoist Rainbow Coalition strategy is openly racial in nature. Policy is secondary to racial or ethnic demographics when it comes to winning elections.

According to Phillips' book "Brown is the New White", the US "minority" population has grown to the point where more than 25% of the electorate are now what he terms "progressives of color". Phillips adds that number to the locked-in hard-core white Democrat voting "progressives" to get a "New American Majority."

This alliance properly mobilized could rule the US forever after one more Democratic presidential victory.

Phillips explained in a speech to the City Club of Cleveland on January 10, 2014:

In terms of US politics, people have always thought that there were too few progressive whites to matter. But with the growth of the Latino, Black, and Asian populations, that is no longer the case. The closest statistical measure we have for political ideology in this country is the Presidential exit poll. Going back to Jimmy Carter's election, we see that anywhere from 34% to 48% of whites have voted for the Democratic candidate for President

That's an average of 41% of Whites voting Democratic. And, so, back to our arithmetic, 64% of the country is White, and 41% of those Whites are progressive, that means that progressive Whites make up 26% of the entire country. If you add that 26% to the 36% who are people of color, you get 62%, a clear majority of the United States.

Now, the other response I hear when we do these numbers is that not all people of color are progressive. Believe me, I know. I often shake my head wondering what some of these conservative people of color are thinking. But, back to exit polls, the data shows that the vast majority of people of color vote Democrat. In the last election, 80% of people of color voted Democratic. 80% of the entire People of Color population is 29% of the entire country's population. If you add that 29% to the 26% of the country that are the white progressives, you get 55%. 29% + 26% = 55%. That is the new majority in America.

This demographic and mathematical theorem has now been tested and proven twice at the national level in the 2008 election and 2012 re-election of President Obama.[24]

Steve Phillips' math alters slightly over time, but the principle remains constant.

Compare Steve Phillips' New American Majority and his electoral strategy to this 1989 document on electoral politics from the League of Revolutionary Struggle's theoretical journal "Forward":

The Jackson campaign also pointed the way towards a progressive electoral strategy, which the left needs to develop as part of its immediate political program. Concretely, this means developing strategies to expand and shift the electorate and breaking the so-called conservative electoral "lock" in the South and Southwest, which has upheld the right-wing edge in the last four presidential elections.

> *People of color now approach 30% of the US population. The changing demographics in the US will make oppressed nationalities the majority in California and Texas by the turn of the century, and they will comprise a steadily increasing proportion of the population as a whole.*
>
> *With increased voter registration and participation, Black, Latino, Asian, poor white and other historically disenfranchised voters can constitute a new, progressive electoral majority. This new electoral majority, with its base in the South and Southwest and key Northern industrial areas, can make the critical difference in future elections. It provides the electoral basis for reversing the right-wing direction of American politics.*
>
> *Electoral work is thus an important aspect of our work to build the mass movement against the right, and for democracy and social progress.*[25]

Is Phillips' "New American Majority" simply an update of the LRS's "new electoral majority"?

To old Maoists like Steve Phillips, mobilizing "minority voters with progressive policies and high profile "candidates of color is the key to winning a one-party socialist America.

If the Democrats hadn't foolishly run Hillary Clinton in 2016, we would already be there.

PHILLIPS/BOOKER CONNECTION

Steve Phillips has helped the careers of most of the leading "candidates of color" who sought the 2020 Democratic presidential nomination. Phillips likes to keep his options open but his favorite protégé is undoubtedly Senator Cory Booker of New Jersey.

Booker's 'Sugar Daddy'

Cory Booker went to Stanford University, receiving a Bachelor of Arts in political science in 1991 and a Master of Arts in sociology the following year. Booker ran The Bridge Peer Counseling Center, a student-run crisis hotline, and organized help from Stanford students for youth in mainly black East Palo Alto, California.[26]

Booker's time at Stanford overlapped with Steve Phillips and another LRS "hang around" named Aimee Allison. The three were friends at Stanford and work together to this day.[27]

Steve Phillips and his wife Susan Sandler have backed Cory Booker's political career every step of the way – from his Newark mayoralty run, to his US Senate race to his 2020 presidential bid. Phillips has used his family and business connections to raise money for all of Booker's elections – especially from the left-leaning elites of Silicon Valley.

According to Vox writer Theodore Schleifer:

> *To understand Booker's love/hate relationship with Silicon Valley, look no further than how he's handling the Bay Area's most prominent outside group so far, this primary: the super PAC set up by his Stanford classmate, Steve Phillips.*
>
> *Phillips and I are sitting in a corner of The Battery, the posh hangout for the tech elite in San Francisco. Phillips isn't in tech — he's a lawyer by trade, and a political operative by practice — but he is a key Booker emissary to the world of tech's mega wealthy.*
>
> *He's introduced Booker to the likes of billionaire Salesforce chief Democratic donor Marc Benioff (at Obama's second inauguration) and to Google super-executive David Drummond. And while Phillips has his detractors in the Democratic fundraising world who think him more flash than substance, according to some Democratic sources, he's got the ability to raise big money thanks to his marriage into the family of Herb Sandler, one of the Democratic Party's biggest donors in recent cycles. He's prioritized mobilization above persuasion, working on behalf of candidates of color like Obama, Stacey Abrams, and even Kamala Harris.*
>
> *His new group, Dream United, is the only candidate-specific super PAC up and running so far in the 2020 primary. Phillips claims $4 million in commitments to back Booker.*
>
> *'[Booker] was seen as the senator of Silicon Valley'*
>
> *'He was seen as the senator of Silicon Valley," Phillips argued. "There's this cultural connection that's a little bit deeper with him.'*[28]

Ironically Booker's strong business ties have been a hindrance to political ambitions. Despite backing Democratic Socialists of America-driven programs like the Green New Deal and Medicare for All and having a leftist voting record comparable to Senators Kamala

Harris, Bernie Sanders, and Elizabeth Warren, Cory Booker has always been viewed with suspicion by much of the US Left.

Steve Phillips addressed this problem head-on in a December 2012 blog post "The Progressive Case for Cory Booker".

The Progressive Case for Cory Booker

Posted by Steve Phillips on December 20, 2012

Every progressive person in America should support Cory Booker's campaign for U.S. Senate. Lest there be any confusion on the Left, allow me to make the case for why this needs to be a priority for all progressive-minded people.

Every progressive person in America should support Cory Booker's campaign for US Senate. Lest there be any confusion on the Left, allow me to make the case for why this needs to be a priority for all progressive-minded people.

First, let me make clear that I come out of the Left. I've studied Marx, Mao, and Lenin. In college, I organized solidarity efforts for freedom struggles in South Africa and Nicaragua, and I palled around with folks who considered themselves communists and revolutionaries (the non-violent type), and I did my research paper on the Black Panther Party. My political baptism was the Jesse Jackson 1984 Presidential campaign, and I've drawn my inspiration from Malcolm, Martin, and Mandela rather than Democratic Party triumvarite of Kennedy, Carter and Clinton.

So it is with that background and perspective that I consider the candidacy of Cory Booker. And I believe every progressive in America should enthusiastically support Cory...

Progressives will never be able to compete directly with the money and power that flows from the beneficiaries and protectors of the current capitalist system. But whereas they have concentrated capital, we have the power of numbers in that economic, political, and social change is in the best interest of the vast majority of the American people (99% anyone?). Historically, however, it's been prohibitively expensive to physically connect and organize similarly-situated, but geographically dispersed, people. Social media has the potential to change that and level the playing field, and the power of technological tools is one of the best hopes for advancing small "d" democracy. With his 1.3 million Twitter followers, and his savvy integration of new and old media, Cory is one of the most sophisticated political leaders using cutting edge technology tools. All progressives can learn from his example and join his cause to build our collective network for change.

Some progressives have criticized Cory for being too cozy with the hedge fund crowd and too tepid in supporting organized labor... A couple observations in that regard. First, having served on an urban school board for eight years (in San Francisco), I know firsthand the political complexity of trying to look out for the interests of low-income children of color when those children have little political power. I had to make some decisions that my friends in labor didn't approve of, but I believe I did the right thing for the children, and that doesn't make one "anti-union." Second, although Cory is friends with some deep-pocketed business leaders, he has used those relationships to try to help low-income children. No one else has inspired Mark Zuckerberg to drop $100 million, and for Zuck's first large grant to be to help the children of Newark speaks volumes about Cory's persuasiveness.

At the end of the day, though, Cory's network does span a broader ideological spectrum than many of us have historically been comfortable, and I'd just say that that's all the more reason to create a strong left flank in Cory World so that the Wall Street crowd doesn't exert disproportionate influence. We should do for Cory what's been hard to do for Obama -- create a strong left pole that both provides accountability and room to operate effectively.

As frequently happens with successful movements for change, the standard bearer has a hard time remaining the crusader once he or she wins office. Obama is now the President (thank God), but he is no longer the principal embodiment of a grassroots movement for change. Obama is the establishment, and that's good thing. But now we need new vehicles to champion change over the next several years, and Cory Booker's campaign is one of the best vehicles for that kind of movement that I have seen in many years. Progressives from coast to coast should enthusiastically embrace and back his candidacy.[29]

Steve Phillips' ambitions for Cory Booker ran well past a US Senate seat. Phillips always saw Booker as someone who could carry on the Jesse Jackson-Barack Obama legacy.

According to Buzzfeed:

Pac+, a San Francisco-based group that focuses on mobilizing black and latino voters — and which is looking for new leaders for President Obama's coalition of young and minority voters — has in the past backed figures like California Attorney General Kamala Harris and Obama, on whose behalf it raised about $10 million in 2008. The group's founder said it will spend between $1 and $2 million in the run-up to the New Jersey special election this October.

'Here we are talking about the post-Obama world, and where the Obama coalition is going to go,' the group's founder, Steve Phillips, told BuzzFeed. 'We think that Cory is one of the people who is best positioned to advance that movement.'

Philips said his wife Susan Sandler — whose family members are among the largest liberal donors in the country — would seed the group with a $100,000 check. Pac+, where the Booker project will be housed, is a hybrid political action committee and so-called Super PAC, with one arm that can make unlimited expenditures and another that can contribute directly to federal campaigns.

Phillips said the project will be called "Help Cory Win…

Phillips said he sees Booker as the "young leader who can capture the imagination of an ascendant coalition," he said, citing Booker's engagement with issues like urban poverty and economic inequality.

"He is the most unapologetic and eloquent spokesperson about poverty in this country right now," said Phillips. "I have not heard anybody talk about poverty in that way since Jesse Jackson's 1988 Democratic convention speech."[30]

Steve Phillips put his PAC+ resources at Cory Booker's service in his successful run for New Jersey's open US Senate seat.

Truly honored to have @CoryBooker keynote the
@PowerPAC_Plus Conf. #Winin2014

12:39 PM · Jun 25, 2014 · Twitter for iPhone

After the election, Phillips wrote an appeal to his "progressive" friends to rally around the new Senator:

From Steve Phillips' blog Political Intelligence:

> Now that Cory Booker has been elected to the United States on Senate, I would like to take this opportunity to urge all of my friends in the progressive movement to work with Cory to create the kind of country we all want to see.
>
> Our team at PAC+ has been excited about the possibilities and potential of Cory's leadership for years. In 2012, Cory asked us to crunch numbers for him to assess a path to victory in a state-wide race, and our data crunchers put together charts, graphs, and maps highlighting the critical counties to focus on in order to pre-vail. We followed that up with one of the first polls on the Senate

race in January of this year. When he first said he was exploring the race, we emailed tens of thousands of progressives across the country urging them to join the cause.

Before he was able to fully ramp up his campaign, we put together the first public piece highlighting his record as Mayor, and when the special election was called, we put together an independent expenditure campaign that contacted 120,000 voters. And we leveraged all of our relationships to help raise more than $100,000 for his campaign.[31]

Although acknowledging that Cory Booker is not an orthodox communist, Phillips made it clear that the Senator was still well to the left and deserved "progressive" support. Remember this was written in 2013. Steve Phillips was probably just as surprised as anyone at just how "relevant" Bernie Sanders would later become.

To be clear, Cory Booker is not Karl Marx. Nobody is. Bernie Sanders, bless his heart, is the only avowed socialist in Congress, and his impact is limited at best.

Cory is a different kind of political leader, and the progressive movement hasn't known what to make of him. Unsure how to judge things such as his relationships with corporate leaders and his complex position on education reform, many have defaulted to wariness and skepticism. Whereas previous political leaders have sought a "third way" that looks far too much like a new face to conservative Democratic politics, I believe Cory is attempting to transcend traditional categories to build alliances that advance the progressive agenda.

I have sat in small-group meetings with Cory and top corporate executives in America and listened to him talk to them about criminal justice reform, addressing poverty, and supporting teachers' unions (yes, you heard that right; supporting teachers' unions)

Just as he is open to conversation with Wall Street leaders, he is open to conversation with progressive activists, so I would strongly urge you to join in in order to help hold him accountable. At worst, you'll be a counterweight to the more conservative forces in his orbit (like most national leaders, his supporters span a broad ideological spectrum). At best, you'll help strengthen a movement that can solidify the progressive majority in America.[32]

In June 2014, PowerPAC+ convened a "Race Will Win the Race" conference at the National Press Club in Washington DC - the event focused on winning elections through racial identity politics.

Senator Booker addresses 'Race will win the race'

Cory Booker, Steve Phillips and Susan Sandler addressed the event,[33] as did former student radical turned Phillips staffer Andy Wong[34] and former Stanford comrades turned PowerPAC+ board members Aimee Allison, Ingrid Nava and Julie Martinez-Ortega.[35]

Anti- 'America First'

Steve Phillips' and Cory Booker's race-based political agendas are as Anti-American as can be.

It is not hard to see why in July 2019, Senator Booker lashed out at President Trump:

> *The reality is this is a guy who is worse than a racist. He is actually using racist tropes and racial language for political gain. He is trying to use this as a weapon to divide our nation against itself...*[36]

In other words, President Trump's "America First" policies have proven so popular among many black and Latino Americans that they are peeling away from the Democratic Party in historic numbers. Steve Phillips must have known that if President Trump was re-elected, millions more minority voters would switch parties, turning the whole Rainbow Coalition strategy into dust.

On November 29, 2019, MarketWatch posted an interesting report:

> A super PAC formed to support Cory Booker's Democratic presidential campaign is shutting down.
>
> The group's founder, San Francisco lawyer Steve Phillips, indicated in a news release Wednesday that Dream United had struggled to raise money.[37]

Cory Booker's presidential campaign was a disaster. Maoist socialist identity politics couldn't compete with President Trump's vision individual liberty, jobs, lower taxes and economic growth.

CORY BOOKER AND VAN JONES

Steve Phillips isn't the only socialist Cory Booker likes to pal around with.

Cory Booker is a close friend of political commentator and former Obama "Green Jobs Czar" Van Jones. The two have known each other since their Yale law School days in the early 1990s.

Cory Booker wrote a review of Van Jones' book "Beyond the Messy Truth: How We Came Apart, How We Come Together."

Van Jones, Cory Booker, October 2015

> Van Jones is a light in the darkness when we need it most. Beyond the Messy Truth breaks with the tribalism of today's politics and offers us a way forward. In the tradition of the great bridge builders of our past, Van's love for this country and all its people shines through.

Booker and Jones have worked closely together on what the left calls "criminal justice reform" and what most people call "let the criminals out early programs."

To Marxists, people don't commit crimes because they are "bad" or irresponsible, but because they are oppressed by "racism" and "capitalism," so it is a revolutionary duty to keep people out of jail, almost regardless of what they have done.

And Van Jones has long been a Marxist– albeit a slick and very personable one.

In 1992, while studying at Yale, Van Jones interned at the Lawyers Committee for Human Rights in San Francisco where he acted as a legal observer during the trial of policemen charged with assaulting Los Angeles man Rodney King.[38]

"Not guilty" verdicts in the King case led to mass rioting-and arrests.

Van Jones told the East Bay Express how he was radicalized by his own jail experience:

> I met all these young radical people of color - I mean really radical, communists and anarchists. And it was, like, 'This is what I need to be a part of... I spent the next ten years of my life working with a lot of those people I met in jail, trying to be a revolutionary... I was a rowdy nationalist on April 28th, and then the verdicts came down on April 29th... By August, I was a communist.[39]

In 1994, Van Jones formed Maoist collective, Standing Together to Organize a Revolutionary Movement (STORM), which "held study groups on the theories of Marx and Lenin and dreamed of a multiracial socialist utopia".[40]

Over several years STORM dissolved with many members going on to work in non-profit leadership usually in the orbit of the Freedom Road Socialist Organization (now Liberation Road).

Jones moved into leadership with the Ella Baker Humans Rights Center and Green for All. He became a TIME Magazine 2008 Environmental Hero, one of Fast Company's 12 Most Creative Minds of 2008, and the New York Times Bestselling author of The Green Collar Economy, which was endorsed by Nancy Pelosi and Al Gore. In recent years he has become a CNN commentator and the Co-Founder of Rebuild the Dream.[41]

But even with all the mainstream influence, Van Jones has never left the Left.

Over the years Jones has maintained ties to supporters of the Maoist-leaning Liberation Road left. In 2013, he was consulted by former STORM member Steve Williams in the Steve Phillips funded program that set up a Liberation Road satellite group LeftRoots.[42]

When Steve Phillips released Brown is the New White in 2015, Van Jones was ready with an endorsement:

> Steve Phillips has provided a vital roadmap to a more hopeful, more inclusive America. Let's pay attention to this important book as we gear up, in 2016, to use our votes to make real change.[43]

In April 2016, the Ford Foundation hosted a discussion with Steve Phillips about how America's "shifting racial demographic landscape and its underlying disconnects are shaping this polarized election season".

Van Jones moderated the discussion and revealed in conversation that he had known Steve Phillips as an activist in the 1980s, and also when Phillips served on the San Francisco School Board in the early 1990s.[44]

Van Jones, Steve Phillips Ford Foundation

Van Jones, Cory Booker and Steve Phillips are old radicals pretending to be moderates for mainstream audiences. They are the modern face of Maoism.

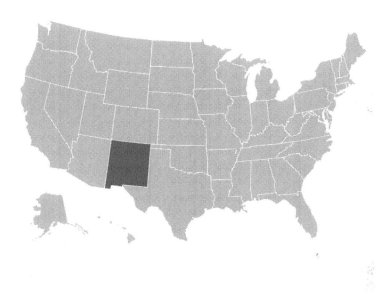

SENATORS FROM THE STATE OF
NEW MEXICO

MARTIN HEINRICH

MARTIN HEINRICH IS THE SENIOR US SENATOR FROM NEW MEXICO

BACKGROUND

ARTIN HEINRICH WAS elected in 2012 on the Democratic Party ticket. He previously served two terms in the US House of Representatives and before that, as Albuquerque City Councilor. Heinrich received a B.S. in Mechanical Engineering from the University of Missouri and worked as a contractor on directed energy technology.[1]

INFLUENCE

Martin Heinrich is the vice chairman for the Joint Economic Committee. He also chairs the Subcommittee on Military Construction, Veterans Affairs, and Related Agencies for the Committee on Appropriations. Heinrich additionally sits on the Committee on Energy and Natural Resources, as well as the Select Committee on Intelligence.[2]

COMMUNIST AND SOCIALIST ROOTS

In the early part of his political career, Senator Heinrich was closely involved with several factions of New Mexico's communist and socialist communities.

Communist Support

Martin Heinrich first ran for Albuquerque City Council to support a minimum wage spearheaded by the Albuquerque Living Wage Campaign – which was led the radical "community organizing group" ACORN.[3]

Heinrich claims he ran for City Council specifically to raise the minimum wage. "It was the reason why when I ran for city council. I carried the legislation to raise the minimum wage."[4]

According to American Crossroads:

> When Martin Heinrich was on the Albuquerque City Council, he got a call from everyone's now-defunct 'community organizing' group, ACORN. They wanted a favor – raise the minimum wage, and he was all too quick to respond. In fact, less than a week after ACORN called Heinrich, he tried to force through their minimum wage rule over the objections of the city council.
>
> Then he tried to take it to the voters, who sided with Albuquerque's small businesses in rejecting the law. ACORN pushed hard, but small businesses and working-class voters in Albuquerque stood up and said no.
>
> Heinrich, never one to let the voters make decisions on their own, went back to the city council, and dictated a new minimum wage law. Since Martin got his way, Albuquerque has lost 17,740 jobs."[5]

Emil Shaw, center

But ACORN wasn't the only far-left group behind Heinrich.

Among key supporters of the campaign were Gerry Bradley of New Mexico Voices for Children[6] and Albuquerque Democratic Socialists of America[7] and Emil Shaw,[8] president of the New Mexico Alliance for Retired Americans (NMARA),[9] and state chair of the New Mexico Communist Party.[10]

In October 2007, Emil Shaw wrote about Martin Heinrich in the Communist Party USA publication People's World:

> *New Mexico is offering new opportunities to trounce the Republican*
> *right next year.*
>
> *GOP Rep. Heather Wilson...said she would not run for re-*
> *election to the House. This gives the Democrats an open shot*
> *not only for the Senate seat but also Wilson's 1st Congressional*
> *District slot.*
>
> *Martin Heinrich, former Albuquerque City Councilor and*
> *active participant in the local labor-community fight for a liv-*
> *able wage, has announced his candidacy for Wilson's House*
> *seat....Also running is Michelle Lujan Grisham, former state*
> *health secretary and protégé of Gov. Bill Richardson. A political*
> *newcomer, she has also projected an antiwar and people's agenda.*[11]

On October 12, 2012, the 14,000-member strong NMARA announced their endorsement of Martin Heinrich for US Senate. NMARA Field Staffer Terry Schleder said:

> *Martin Heinrich understands New Mexicans and will continue to*
> *fight to keep Seniors and the Middle Class strong. His record of*
> *opposing cuts to Social Security, Medicare, and Medicaid is a win-*
> *ning one for retirees and aging workers who would lose-out under*
> *the GOP plan to privatize programs that make our state healthier*
> *and economically secure.*[12]

The NMARA president at the time was long time Albuquerque Communist Party supporter Pablo Trujillo.[13]

Pablo Trujillo

Henrich and SWOP

Senator Heinrich also has close ties to influential Albuquerque-based "community group" South West Organizing Project (SWOP).

Founded in 1980 by long-time Albuquerque activist Richard Moore, SWOP has roots in the Chicano/Maoist movements of the 1960s and '70s and the radical Black Berets.

New Mexico Black Berets

The late Betita Martinez, a former New Mexico activist, laid out the history in Monthly Review:

> In 1974, self-identification with the socialist vision reached a high point. That was the year Richard Moore went to Cuba with another Beret leader, Joaquín Lujan. Marvin Garcia…went with a group to China.
>
> A major meeting took place to discuss strategy in the face of what we saw as heightening repression. Over fifty seasoned activists came from all over the state. In a dialogue about our long-range goals, someone asked what socialism was. I explained some basic points and added it was a stage on the way to communism but not the final goal, communism. At that point a Chicana cried out, 'Well, in that case, we're communists!' and everyone clapped to my and others' amazement.
>
> The major, crucial exception to that (isolation) was travel to Cuba, going back to El Grito and now the Venceremos Brigade. Richard Moore served on the Brigade's National Committee and went to Cuba every year through the 1970s.
>
> That experience is why he could say, as he did recently, 'we didn't pull any punches about being for socialism then. We might use slightly different language with grassroots folk, but the ideas were there. We were not afraid of saying so.'[14]

In 1974, these New Mexico activists received a series of recruitment pitches from national Marxist-Leninist formations.

Explains Betita Martinez:

> *The only formation to attract serious interest was the August 29th Movement, founded in 1974 and named after the historic August 29, 1970, Chicano Moratorium against the Vietnam War, in Los Angeles.*[15]

In 1978, the Maoist-leaning August 29th Movement dissolved into the League of Revolutionary Struggle, parts of which later merged with Freedom Road Socialist Organization (FRSO). In 2019, FRSO re-named itself Liberation Road. SWOP remains in the Liberation Road orbit to this day.

Betita Martinez continues:

> *Today, the left tradition can be seen in New Mexico, for example, in the battle against environmental racism where the enemy is so clearly capitalism. The SouthWest Organizing Project of Albuquerque (SWOP) and the Southwest Network for Environmental and Economic Justice (SNEEJ), with headquarters in that city, confront capitalism and imperialism constantly.*
>
> *Richard Moore of the Black Berets was cofounder of SWOP and coordinates SNEEJ. In the homeland of the atomic bomb and crucial military bases, New Mexican radicals also confront militarism firsthand on many levels including environmental racism. Chicanos/as and other Latinos in New Mexico, as elsewhere, have a long way to go to develop a strategy and tactics for social transformation."*[16]

In May 2021, President Biden appointed New Mexicans Jade Begay and Richard Moore to the first White House Environmental Justice Advisory Council.[17]

SWOP is a client of New Mexico activist and political consultant Alicia Maldonado.[18]

In the early 2000's, Maldonado created "several organizations to tackle the diverse needs of the

Jade Begay, with Judith LeBlanc Communist Party USA and Deb Haaland Secretary of the Interior 2019

community including a for-profit political consulting firm, Soltari Inc., with the goal of getting local progressive [sic] elected to office". One of their early successes was Martin Heinrich - Soltari Inc. ran his first political race for Albuquerque City Council.[19]

Alicia Maldonado is a consultant with RoadMap,[20] a FRSO/ Liberation Road affiliated consultancy group.

RoadMap was founded by Elsa Rios, once an organizer with a pro-Cuba Marxist-Leninist group, the Puerto Rican Socialist Party (PRSP).[21]

Alicia Maldonado's fellow RoadMap consultants include Bill Fletcher, Jr. and Bill Gallegos[22, 23] both of FRSO/Liberation Road,[24] Makani Themba,[25] formerly with the Communist Workers Party,[26] and Shiree Teng,[27] a former member of the League of Revolutionary Struggle.[28]

Michael Montoya ran political programs for SWOP. He was also a field organizer for the successful 2008 Martin Heinrich for Congress campaign.[29]

In 2003, Martin Heinrich was still a graduate student, and was only just starting to consider a run for District Six's vacant city council seat.

From The Nation:

> Javier Benavidez, a fellow student and long-time political activist from the city, volunteered for his campaign. 'Like a lot of us at that school, he was focused on smart growth and community development,' he remembers.
>
> Heinrich won that election and spent the next few years working on labor issues, conservation politics—transport policy, and other themes that endeared him to local progressives. 'He was seen as a real fighter for working people. Very active when it came to labor disputes, the minimum wage, helping neighborhoods with crime issues, and smart growth,' says Benavidez, who Heinrich hired on as his policy analyst.[30]

Javier Benavidez also served as Martin Heinrich's speechwriter and Communications Liaison for Congressman Heinrich before becoming a long-term CEO of SWOP.[31]

Benavidez spent time with SWOP as a teen, interned with SWOP in the early 2000s, was arrested for protesting the Iraq war with SWOP comrades, and served on the organization's board for several terms.[32]

In 2015/16, while CEO of SWOP Javier Benavidez trained for a year at the Oakland-based Rockwood Leadership Institute.[33] Rockwood is essentially a school for radicals. It trains many ACORN and Liberation Road-aligned comrades, and has been led at times by bona fide Maoists, including the aforementioned Shiree Teng.[34]

Javier Benavidez being escorted from a Trump rally November 2016

While SWOP is essentially a Maoist-leaning organization, it does also have some conventional communist connections.

New Mexico Communist Party chair Emil Shaw was an active SWOP member until his death in 2010.[35]

Shaw's wife Rose served on the National Committee of the Communist Party USA[36] and on the editorial board of the SWOP newsletter for many years.[37]

COUNCIL FOR A LIVABLE WORLD CONNECTIONS

Senator Heinrich is very supportive of the "disarm America" agenda of the far-left Council for a Livable World (CLW).

In 2012, the CLW endorsed and helped fund Martin Heinrich's US Senate race.

The CLW said of Heinrich:

> *Heinrich supports ratification of the Comprehensive Nuclear Test Ban Treaty and the Kissinger-Schulz-Nunn-Perry vision of moving toward a world free of nuclear weapons. He also opposes building a new generation of nuclear weapons...*
>
> *Additionally, Heinrich has pressed President Obama to begin withdrawing US troops from Afghanistan. Congressman Heinrich received a perfect 100% on the Council's voting scorecard.*
>
> *If Martin Heinrich is elected to the US Senate, he will be positioned to be an active leader on our issues for many years.*[38]

CLW hosted an event January 21, 2013 at the Phoenix Park Hotel ballroom in Washington DC to celebrate the second inauguration of President Barack Obama and Vice President Joe Biden and feature endorsed candidates in the 113th Congress.

A number of "prestigious guests" attended the event, including Senators Martin Heinrich, Tammy Baldwin, Angus King and Bernie Sanders, as well as US Representatives Suzan DelBene, Lois Frankel and Mark Takano and United Steel Workers International President Leo Gerard.

CLW Board member Robert K. Musil introduced Senator Heinrich.

Wrote CLW:

> *Senator Heinrich, who is well known for his environmental and clean energy advocacy, spoke about the importance of grassroots support. Over 1,300 council contributors gave more than $100,000 to Senator Heinrich's campaign with an average gift of $75.*[39]

CLW endorsed Senator Heinrich when he came up for re-election in 2018:

> *In the Senate, Heinrich has maintained a progressive record, scoring a 100% on key votes in 2015—16. He is a strong supporter of the New START agreement, the Iran nuclear deal, ratification of the Comprehensive Test Ban Treaty, and a robust non-proliferation programs budget.*[40]

Russia, China and Iran are now growing increasingly aggressive in the face of the Biden Administration's military and foreign policy weakness. Senator Heinrich must shoulder some of the blame for this.

EARTH FIRST! AND OTHER RADICAL ENVIRONMENTALISTS

While Martin Heinrich presents himself as a moderate conservationist, his circles have long included radical environmentalists who endorse and engage in violence ostensibly to save the planet. Not only does Heinrich have deep ties to Earth First! leaders who have engaged in domestic terror activities, the Senator from New Mexico also continues to support and collaborate with militant activists.

Earth First!

Earth First! was a domestic terror organization most active in the 1980's and 90's. Their tactics included "tree spiking" or hammering metal rods into trees that were set to be cut by loggers. In 1987, 23-year-old logger George Alexander was a victim of this tactic:

> *He was nearly three feet away when the log hit his saw and the saw exploded. One half of the blade stuck in the log. The other half hit Alexander in the head, tearing through his safety helmet and face shield. His face was slashed from eye to chin. His teeth were smashed and his jaw was cut in half.*[41]

Earth First! was unapologetic in this behavior, using the slogan "No Compromise in Defense of Mother Earth." There was a "close alliance" between Earth First and the Industrial Workers of the World (IWW), who refer to themselves as "Wobblies". IWW started as a mishmash of "radical working-class anti-capitalists" in 1905, with the goal of establishing a giant union of workers from all walks of life to ultimately "abolish wage slavery [Capitalism] altogether".[42]

David Foreman

One of the founders of Earth First! was David Foreman, a convicted criminal[43] who provided excruciatingly detailed plans, including diagrams and photos, for destroying property and otherwise sabotaging perceived threats to the environment in the 1985 book "Ecodefense: A Field Guide to Monkeywrenching".[44]

David Foreman (Screenshot)

The book gives advice for tree spiking: "Drive the nail almost all the way into the tree," advises the author, "[C]ut the head off with the bolt cutters. Then, drive the now headless nail the remainder of the way into the tree."

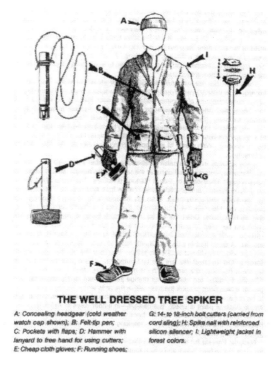

THE WELL DRESSED TREE SPIKER

A: Concealing headgear (cold weather watch cap shown); B: Felt-tip pen; C: Pockets with flaps; D: Hammer with lanyard to free hand for using cutters; E: Cheap cloth gloves; F: Running shoes; G: 14- to 18-inch bolt cutters (carried from cord sling); H: Spike nail with reinforced silicon silencer; I: Lightweight jacket in forest colors.

Image from "Ecodefense: A Field Guide to Monkeywrenching"

Tracy Stone-Manning

One of the domestic terrorists who engaged in tree spiking was Tracy Stone-Manning, who was an editor of the Earth First! Newsletter.[45] The Daily Caller described Tracy Stone-Manning's direct involvement in a tree-spiking case, making her a "target of the federal government's investigation":

> *Stone-Manning received legal immunity to testify in the 1993 criminal trial over the matter that she sent an anonymous and threatening letter to the Forest Service warning that a local forest had been sabotaged with tree spikes. Her testimony led to the conviction of a man she identified as her former roommate and friend.[46]*

Stone-Manning sent the ominous letter to the Forest Service signed by pseudonym "George Hayduke", the fictional hero of environmental activist Edward Abbey's 1975 novel, "The Monkey Wrench Gang". Hayduke is referenced repeatedly in Earth First! Newsletters.

This is the letter:

```
To Whom It May Concern:

This letter is being sent to notify you that the Post Office
Sale in Idaho has been spiked heavily.

The reasoning for this action is that this piece of land is
very special to the earth.  It is home to the Elk, Deer, Mountain
Lions, Birds, and especially the Trees.

The project required that eleven of us spend nine days in
God awful weather conditions spiking trees.  We unloaded
a total of five hundred pounds of spikes measuring 8 to 10
inches in length.  The sales were marked so that no workers
would be injured and so that you assholes know that they are
spiked.  The majority of trees were spiked within the first
ten feet, but many, many others were spiked as high as a hundred
and fifty feet.

I would be more than willing to pay you a dollar for the sale,
but you would have to find me first and that could be your
WORST nightmare.

Sincerely,


George Hayduke


P.S.  You bastards go in there anyway and a lot of people
      could get hurt.
```

Letter from Biden Bureau of Land Management Nominee Tracy Stone-Manning

Despite her involvement in domestic terror, Joe Biden nominated Stone-Manning for Director of the Bureau of Land Management, Department of the Interior. Senator Martin Heinrich enthusiastically supported the move. "Tracy Stone-Manning is qualified, focused, and ready to get to work," he tweeted in part.[47]

Heinrich also supported Stone-Manning in a press release dated July 22, 2021:

> Stone-Manning has worked with ranchers and conservation advocates, hunters and mountain bikers, and unions and Tribal leaders, making her well-suited to lead the BLM. She has earned broad support, and I am confident she will be confirmed as BLM director very soon so that she can get to work in this important role...[48]

Stone-Manning, like many radical leftists, is preoccupied with the idea of "overpopulation". Speaking derisively of humanity, the activist wrote in 1991 that people were "breeding our weapons [children]" and stated it was necessary to "wage war on overpopulation".[49]

In his 1991 book, "Confessions of an Eco-Warrior", David Foreman likewise referred to humanity as "humanpox" and stated that "...human overpopulation is the fundamental problem on Earth today."[50] Foreman, along with fellow Earth First! comrades Nancy Morton (also Foreman's wife) and Todd Schulke were board members of the group "New Mexico Wilderness Alliance", which was founded by Martin Heinrich.[51]

Nancy Morton has been a significant donor to Martin Heinrich. Todd Schulke has also donated thousands to Heinrich's campaigns.[52, 53, 54, 55]

Center for Biological Diversity

Todd Schulke went on to be co-founder of the Center for Biological Diversity (CBD), which files lawsuits using the Endangered Species Act to shut down human activity in the name of environmental protection.

Schulke's comrade Kieran Suckling is also a CBD co-founder and former member of Earth First!.[56, 57] Kieran Suckling, who stole "a pair of boots and some bedroom slippers" from Walmart in 1994,[58] now enjoys a very large salary as Executive Director of CBD.[59] Suing the federal government is quite lucrative, particularly when the government is sympathetic to one's cause.

Kieran Suckling has made it his mission in life to completely eradicate ranches. In an article titled "No People Allowed" at the New Yorker in 1999,[60] Suckling said: "You cannot ranch economically in the desert without devastating the ecology." The Center for Biological Diversity follows in the footsteps of Earth First! In 1991, the New York Times reported:

> Ranchers say environmental groups are actually pushing for an end to livestock grazing on public lands, not just a reduction. They point to the slogan of the environmental group Earth First: 'Cow free by '93.'[61]

Like Tracy Stone-Manning and David Foreman, Suckling is not a fan of people. In an interview at his alma mater, the liberal arts college Holy Cross, Suckling explained in part:

...we are destroying nature at an increasing pace due to rapid advances in technological power, the relentless speed of capitalism, the industrial outlook of more communist leaning societies, and a universal inability to address unsustainable human overpopulation. The world is in a race between rapidly expanding ecological consciousness and rapidly expanding, technologically powered population growth.[62]

On April 27, 2017, Kieran Suckling addressed an event sponsored by "Refuse Fascism", a front group for the Revolutionary Communist Party.

Kieran Suckling at Revolutionary Communist Party 'Teach In' (screenshot)

The "Teach In", titled "Fascism in America: Can It Happen Here? Is It Happening Here? What is the Danger the Trump/Pence Government Poses?",[63] also featured such luminaries as:

- ✦ Sunsara Taylor, Revolutionary Communist Party Leader and Refuse Fascism co-initiator
- ✦ Jay W. Walker, Steering Committee of the New York chapter of Refuse Fascism.
- ✦ George Prochnik, author, New Yorker contributor
- ✦ Rita Dentino, Exec. Dir., Casa Freehold of National Day Laborer Organizing Network

♦ Andy Zee, Revolutionary Communist Party mainstay
and Refuse Fascism co-initiator, Revolution Books
NYC spokesperson

The day before Kieran addressed the Revolutionary Communist Party, he tweeted his support to Senator Martin Heinrich. "A public lands leader as always," he gushed.[64]

Kierán Suckling
@KieranSuckling

Thank you @MartinHeinrich. A public lands leader as always.

Martin Heinrich ✓ @MartinHeinrich · Apr 26, 2017
I'm standing up against Pres Trump's EO that puts our National Monuments like #OMDP #RGDN & #BearsEars at risk. #MonumentsForAll

5:47 PM · Apr 26, 2017 · Twitter for Android

28 Retweets   **1** Quote Tweet   **86** Likes

The CBD brags on their website that they "resisted the Trump administration in every way possible — especially in the courts." The Center filed 266 lawsuits against the former president and claims to have "won 9 out of every 10 resolved cases".[65]

SENATORS FROM THE STATE OF
NEW YORK

CHUCK SCHUMER

CHUCK SCHUMER IS THE SENIOR US SENATOR FROM NEW YORK

BACKGROUND

CHUCK SCHUMER WAS born and raised in Brooklyn, New York. He graduated from Harvard Law School in 1974 and was elected to the New York State Assembly that same year, with the help of New York State Representative Stephen Solarz.[1] Schumer was elected in 1980 to represent the 9th congressional district, where he served for eighteen years. In 1998, Chuck Schumer was elected to the Senate.[2]

INFLUENCE

Chuck Schumer sits on the Select Committee on Intelligence, and the Committee on Rules and Administration. Chuck Schumer is the Senate Majority Leader.[3]

SOCIALIST AND COMMUNIST CONNECTIONS

Chuck Schumer, like most leftist New York Democrats, has mixed and mingled with socialists and communists throughout his career.

Major Owens

In 1982, Major Owens ran in the primary to contest the New York City Congressional seat vacated by the retiring leftist Shirley Chisholm. His main opponent was the Democratic Party leadership's favored candidate Vander Beatty. Owens prevailed, helped with the endorsements of Councilwoman Ruth Messinger, Congresswoman Bella Abzug and Congressman Chuck Schumer.[4]

Four years later, Major Owens openly identified as a member of Democratic Socialists of America (DSA).[5] Ruth Messinger was already a DSA comrade.[6] Bella Abzug was active in Communist Party USA (CPUSA) fronts including the Labor Research Association,[7] the US Free Trepper Committee,[8] and Women Strike for Peace (WSP).[9]

Radical leftists often travel to communist countries. Abzug and her comrades were no different. In 1972, the militant leftist went with a WSP delegation to Paris to meet with Viet Cong and North Vietnamese representatives. In a subsequent Congressional hearing, 10 out of the 12 top officers of WSP took the Fifth Amendment when asked about CPUSA membership.[10]

David Dinkins

In 1990, as part of the New Democratic Coalition, Chuck Schumer personally endorsed the New York mayoral campaign of DSA comrade David Dinkins.[11]

The New Democratic Coalition was a "coalition of progressive Democrats" which included New York City Democratic Socialists Organizing Committee member Ronnie Eldridge,[12] DSAer and City Councilor Ruth Messinger and DSA Congressmembers Major Owens and Jerry Nadler.[13]

Ex-Communist Workers Party leader Margaret Chin was on the list,[14] as were several CPUSA supporters including State Assembly member Richard Gottfried,[15] Women Strike for Peace activist Frances Boehm,[16] City Councilor Miriam Friedlander[17] and Representative Bella Abzug.

Righteous Persons Foundation

In February 1995, a private party was held in New York to celebrate Margery Tabankin who had been recently chosen to head Steven Spielberg's Righteous Persons Foundation.[18]

The gathering was a socialist love fest.

Marjery Tabankin herself was a veteran of Students for a Democratic Society[19] and had meetings with Fidel Castro and terrorist leader Yasser Arafat.[20] She was also included in a "major donor letter" for inviting wealthy Southern California socialists to join the DSA's exclusive "Upton Sinclair Club."[21]

Attendees included Reverends Jesse Jackson and Al Sharpton, along with socialist and future New York Governor David Paterson[22] in addition to DSA members Ruth Messinger and David Dinkins.

DSA supporters Mark Green[23] (formerly a speechwriter for Presidential candidate Gary Hart),[24] Warner Records chairman Danny Goldberg (another Upton Sinclair Club invitee)[25] and Chuck Schumer rounded out the gathering. The talk focused on how "liberals could take the political spotlight back from the conservatives".[26]

Committees of Correspondence

Unsurprisingly the Communist Party USA spin-off "Committees of Correspondence for Democracy and Socialism" supported Chuck Schumer electorally.

From the CoC's Correspondent:

> Fifty members of the Metro NY CofC turned out on Oct. 24 to discuss the 1998 elections in the context of the fight to defeat the

right… The following statement was adopted: 'The New York Metro Committees of Correspondence urges the defeat of all reactionary candidates and the election of Charles Schumer and Carl McCall, and a vote for Peter Vallone on the Working Families Party line, and further that this position be communicated to the membership in an immediate mailing.'[27]

Schumer Co-Sponsors Communist Party's Spending Bill

In March 1997, then-Congressman Schumer was a co-sponsor of legislation written and promoted by the Communist Party USA. H.R. 950, the "Job Creation and Infrastructure Restoration Act of 1997" was introduced in the 105th Congress on March 5, 1997, by Congressman Matthew Martinez of California.

From a New York State Communist Party memo, March 16, 1997:

The primary purpose of this emergency federal jobs legislation was to provide much needed jobs at union wages to crisis ridden cities by putting the unemployed to work rebuilding our nation's infrastructure (schools, housing, hospitals, libraries, public transportation, highways, parks, environmental improvements, etc. $250 billion is authorized for emergency public works jobs over a five-year period.[28]

If the bill had ever passed it would have been a huge financial boon for CPUSA-controlled labor unions and their Democratic Party friends. Unfortunately, the left's relentless push for massive spending bills designed to benefit cronies and encourage dependence on the federal government continues to this day.

At the time, the bill's main promoters were Los Angeles Labor Coalition for Public Works Jobs and its only affiliate, New York Coalition for Public Works Jobs,[29] which was headed by CPUSA member Bill Davis.[30] Both organizations were essentially CPUSA front groups.

Furthermore, Evelina Alarcon was the national Communist Party USA coordinator for the Martinez Jobs Bill,[31] while also serving as chair of the Communist Party's Southern California District.[32]

THE IAPAC CONNECTION

Hassan Nemazee

Senator Schumer is extremely close to the Iranian American Political Action Committee (IAPAC), which was co-founded by disgraced Iranian American businessman Hassan Nemazee. Nemazee began raising "sizable sums for the Democratic National Committee" in the mid-nineties. Controversy followed the Iranian American activist, but he held onto power within the party, clawing his way up the ranks.

During the Monica Lewinsky scandal, Nemazee collected tens of thousands of dollars for former president Bill Clinton's legal defense fund. His loyalty earned him a nomination as ambassador to Argentina. Before he could be confirmed, however, an article at Forbes revealed that the Iranian "had magically turned himself into an 'Hispanic' by acquiring Venezuelan citizenship in order to fulfill the minority-ownership requirement of a California public pension fund."[33]

While his nomination was withdrawn, Nemazee still was favored by the democrats. He served in John Kerry's failed 2004 presidential campaign, and in 2006, he served under Chuck Schumer as the "national finance chair" of the Democratic Senatorial Campaign Committee (DSCC).

Hassan Nemazee had a finance leadership role in Hillary Clinton's 2008 presidential campaign. While he was serving in this capacity, he joined a delegation arranged by former president Jimmy Carter's National Security Advisor Zbigniew Brzezinski.

Brzezinski, a Council on Foreign Relations leader, and supporter of normalization of relations with Beijing,[34] endorsed Clinton's opponent Barack Obama during the 2008 campaign. Hassan Nemazee joined the delegation to meet with leaders in the Middle East, including Bashar al-Assad, president of Syria.[35] At the time, it was alleged that Assad was "facilitating the travel of Al Qaeda terrorists into Iraq," and "had a role in the assassination of Lebanon's president, Rafik Hariri." The delegation "raised questions about Hillary Clinton's support for Lebanon's democracy movement."

A year later, the gig was finally up. Obama and the Democratic National Committee pledged to "return or donate"[36] campaign contributions from Hassan Nemazee after he "was charged in 2009 with orchestrating a scheme that defrauded banks of nearly $300 million." He began serving a twelve-year sentence but was released early under former President Trump's "First Step Act" in 2019.[37]

IAPAC and Democrat Allies

Chuck Schumer got into IAPAC from the ground floor. IAPAC was launched July 22, 2003, at the Phoenix Park Hotel in Washington, DC. The reception was attended by three United States Senators: Ted Kennedy (D-MA), Tom Carper (D-DE) and Chuck Schumer. During the event, Senator Schumer affirmed his "commitment to work with and engage Iranian Americans in the political process and the need to combat racism in American society."[38]

While IAPAC claims to be a strictly domestically focused organization, it works closely with pro-Tehran lobby group National Iranian Action Council (NIAC).

Immigration and Political Power for Iran

The Iranian American Bar Association (IABA) launched its "Unity Campaign" on November 21, 2002, aimed at bringing together Iranian Americans as a "formidable, influential force on civic life." IABA invited Hassan Nemazee and the President of NIAC Trita Parsi to speak at the event. The goal was to lobby against immigration policies aimed at securing America, as part of a process of increasing Iranian political power in the US. Specifically, the Iranian activists were disputing the Enhanced Border Security and Visa Entry Reform Act, which was signed into law by then-president George W. Bush.[39]

As Iran was quite rightly listed as a "state sponsor of terrorism" by the US State Department, it was clearly in the Mullahs' interests to fight the legislation. Another topic of the evening was a bill that would ban all visas to Iranians.[40] Senator Schumer worked closely with IAPAC on these issues.

Relaxing immigration requirements is always a goal of leftist organizations. In 2003, IAPAC met personally with Senator Schumer, who then served as Chairmen of the Senate Judiciary Sub-committee on Immigration, to discuss the "immediate impact of the implementation of the Section 306 of the Enhanced Border Security & Visa Enter Reform Act."

From the IAPAC website:

> IAPAC spoke to Senator Schumer about the unfairness and short
> sightedness of the legislation and presented to him specific recom-
> mendations drafted by the Iranian American Bar Association on
> how Section 306 should be interpreted. Senator Schumer agreed
> to hold and chair a meeting with the Department of Justice, the
> Department of State and the Central Intelligence Agency to discuss
> the regulations that will be applied regarding the implementation
> of Section 306.
>
> In addition, IAPAC asked for and received a press release
> from Senator Schumer regarding visa policy for non-immigrants.
> Senator Schumer summed up his concerns by stating that "we do
> not want our non-immigrant visa policy to impose an undue hard-
> ship on American citizens, including Iranian Americans, many of
> whom have made and continue to make outstanding contributions
> to the economic and social life of our country.[41]

Senator Schumer did not let up on the immigration issue or his
friends at IAPAC. On July 22, 2007, the organization held its annual
New York City reception. The featured speaker was Senator Chuck
Schumer, who told of his work securing visas for Iranian nationals
travelling to the US.

Senator Schumer at the July 2007 IAPAC event in New York

From the IAPAC website:

> Schumer went on to acknowledge some of the immigration-related
> concerns of the Iranian American community. He explained that
> the US government must do everything in its power to prevent the
> entry of terrorists into our nation. At same time America should
> not exclude those individuals who want to come to the United
> States to do good, Schumer said. He gave examples of how constit-
> uent representatives in his office have dealt with a number of cases
> of Iranian nationals who had difficulties securing visas, including
> a top-ranking executive from Deutsche Bank Group who was a
> German citizen of Iranian descent.[42]

Senator Schumer received money from IAPAC during the 2004,
2010,[43] and 2016[44] election cycles.

THE COMMUNIST WORKERS PARTY'S ASIAN AMERICANS FOR EQUALITY

Senator Schumer works closely with Asian Americans for Equality
(AAFE).

Asian Americans for Equality is a 501 (c) (3) non-profit organization based in New York City. Founded in 1974 in Manhattan's
Chinatown, AAFE "has transformed in the past four decades to
become one of the city's leading housing, social service and community development organizations."[45]

In 2016, AAFE was described as "the largest developer of affordable housing in Lower Manhattan, having preserved or developed
eighty-six buildings with more than seven hundred apartments since
1989."[46]

AAFE's Communist Roots

AAFE was founded by the Communist Workers Party (CWP). A
Maoist organization, CWP was notorious for its slavish support for
Communist China and North Korea.

From City Magazine:

During the 1980s, the CWP was acquiring a local power base in Chinatown, in the form of a community group calling itself Asian Americans for Equality. The latter did not avow its connection with the CWP, but for years the two groups shared an office and phone number, and CWP veterans had a way of turning up as Asian-Americans for Equality leaders, notably in the form of its president from 1982 to 1986: Margaret Chin.

Asian-Americans for Equality resembles a familiar type of New York activist group, collecting grievances and brokering deals. In 1985 it made the news when it, charged that federal regulators had committed a "racist" act in closing the Golden Pacific National Bank. When the Chinese-language press raised questions about possible links between Asian-Americans for Equality and the bank's owner, reporters from five of the papers received threats.[47]

CWP also had a well-earned reputation for violence. It stormed the Democratic Party National Convention in 1980[48] and its newspaper Workers Viewpoint regularly called for attacks on police.

In the mid-80s, the CWP morphed into the New Democratic Movement (NDM) and began penetrating the New York business community and local government. The goal was power, influence and access to lots of taxpayer money to further the revolution.

CWP member Ben Connors, wrote an article for the party's The Expert Red in February 1985, on the change in party tactics from one of traditional Marxist-Leninist agitation, to a conscious program of infiltrating America's institutions:

> Organizing other leftists like ourselves seemed sufficiently impor-
> tant at the time. We came to learn however that it was indeed
> important, but hardly sufficient. It was time to assume leadership
> over the whole society…Rather than storm City Hall, we are don-
> ning tuxedoes, and preparing to enter through special invitation.
> We are learning to use our skills in ways that are proving far more
> dangerous to the ruling class, and far more beneficial to the masses
> to whom we have dedicated lives of service.
>
> These days we not only organize but will also begin to deliver.
> We will not be content to petition the state legislature, we want
> to be the state legislature. It is truly an exciting time to be an
> American revolutionary.[49]

From City Magazine:

> At a convention in mid-1985, the CWP formally dissolved itself, in
> its place arose a new organization, the New Democratic Movement,
> devoted to establishing 'local power bases.' Jerry Tung, general sec-
> retary of the former CWP, explained the idea to the assembled
> faithful. '[O]nce you get people elected or appointed to office; you
> can award contracts to friends.... When you can raise money for
> political purposes, when you do it in the right place in the right
> atmosphere, and look right, and the [mainstream] party bosses are
> there, then that money makes them take you seriously.'[50]

From business and local government to the highest reaches of the
Democratic Party was an easy leap for the CWP/NDM.

From City Magazine:

> It would not seem easy for a left-wing sectlet to build a serious
> power base in Chinatown, then as now one of the most politically
> conservative neighborhoods in New York City. Instead, the CWP
> alumni played what can in retrospect be seen as a brilliant cross-
> town gambit. The Village Independent Democrats, the venerable
> liberal club, had fallen on hard times. As former CWP members
> flooded into the Village Independent Democrats they brought cash
> and credit to help it wage its political battles.[51]

This communist penetration was soon attacked by prominent
Democratic Party liberal, the late Adlai Stevenson:

> In 1987 he (Stevenson) wrote an open letter to Village Democrats,
> urging them to reject the local district leader candidates of the Village
> Independent Democrats, which had chosen to make common cause
> with CWP-style extremism. An outraged New York City political
> establishment mobilized, like antibodies, to expel the alien intruder:
> in this case not the CWPers, but Adlai Stevenson. The Village
> Independent Democrats sent out a response charging Stevenson
> with 'red-baiting' and 'resuscitat[ing] the work of Joe McCarthy.'
>   The letter was signed by such eminences as Congressman Ted
> Weiss, since-indicted State Senate Minority Leader Manfred
> Ohrenstein, City Council member (later Manhattan Borough
> President) Ruth Messinger, and Manhattan Borough President
> (later Mayor) David Dinkins.[52]

As noted previously, Ruth Messinger and David Dinkins were both Democratic Socialists of America comrades. Representative Ted Weiss had connections to the Soviet-controlled World Peace Council.[53]

Soon AAFE was on its way to the higher reaches of New York City politics:

> *Asian Americans for Equality began to go big time. Its annual banquets in Chinatown garnered greetings from not only an array of Democratic officeholders, but also such Republicans as Senator Alfonse D'Amato and Representative Bill Green. Since the mid-Eighties, AAFE has taken in more than $2 million in grants from the State Department of Social Services and Division of Housing and Community Renewal and from the Lower East Side Area Policy Board, a funnel for federal monies.[54]*

While no longer as explicitly pro-Beijing as it was in CWP days, there is no doubt that AAFE leans towards Communist China.

Pictured below are Representative Nydia Velazquez (D-NY), AAFE's Margaret Chin and Representative Carolyn Maloney (D-NY), marching with US and Communist Chinese flags at the 2011 Lunar New Year Parade in Chinatown.

Margaret Chin in CWP days

In January 2014, after winning a tough re-election campaign New York City Councilmember Margaret Chin of AAFE "showed off her own strong political ties" at an inauguration event in Chinatown.
From AMNY:

> *Chin was also praised — always professionally, but sometimes on a deeply personal level — by Sen. Chuck Schumer, House Representatives Jerry Nadler and Carolyn Maloney, State Assembly Speaker Sheldon Silver, Borough President Gale Brewer, and State Sen. Daniel Squadron.*
>
> *'What we can say about Margaret is this: No one put a silver spoon in her mouth, and no one plucked her up and put her into high office,' said Schumer, who, among other things, would go on describe Chin as a 'tiger' when it came to her persistence in securing disaster recovery aid after Hurricane Sandy.*
>
> *'Margaret, you have earned all this,' Schumer declared.*[55]

Securing Taxpayer Dollars for Asian Americans for Equality

Senator Schumer has attended multiple AAFE events and has helped secure considerable taxpayer funding for the organization.

Charles Schumer
Senate Majority Leader

It gives me great pleasure to congratulate Asian Americans for Equality on your 48th Annual Lunar New Year Gala. I was born in the Year of the Tiger, so this celebration is extra special to me.

May you all have a happy and successful New Year, and may it bring the healing and the prosperity that we need to pick ourselves back up from the challenges we've experienced these past two years. The Asian American community represents the best of New York and our nation, and I will continue to fight for you in the Senate.

Senator Schumer sends greetings to AAFE's annual gala, March 2022

On November 21, 2010, Senator Schumer and New York State Senator Daniel Squadron "urged the Lower Manhattan Development Corporation (LMDC) to commit funding from the Lower Manhattan Redevelopment Fund to complete the East River Waterfront Park project".

Schumer, who secured $20.4 billion in funding to help rebuild lower Manhattan in the aftermath of the September 11 attacks, fought to use a portion of those funds for the East River Waterfront Park project, endorsed by the Asian Americans for Equality.

Christopher Kui, Executive Director of AAFE said:

> AAFE would like to thank immensely the hard work of Senator Chuck Schumer and State Senator Daniel Squadron in fighting for funds that would enable our waterfront to realize its greatest potential. A waterfront park at Pier 42 would give residents of the Lower East Side, Chinatown and East Village access to quality open space so needed in our community.[56]

Over One Million Dollars to AAFE Since 2017

Since 2017, Senator Schumer has doled out over a million taxpayer dollars to AAFE.

In May 2017, Senators Schumer and Kirsten Gillibrand (D-NY) announced $4,804,166 in grants for New York state community development organizations in the national NeighborWorks network.

'Access to affordable housing is essential for the health of our families and the economic strength of our communities,' said Senator Schumer. 'This funding, from NeighborWorks America, will strengthen neighborhoods, remove blight, and provide safe, quality housing for New York families. I will continue to fight for and deliver funds to New York that help provide families and children with safe and affordable housing options.'[57]

AAFE received $290,000 of taxpayer money from that grant.

On March 22, 2019, Senators Schumer and Gillibrand announced $1,593,500 in federal funding for New York City and Long Island community development organizations in the national NeighborWorks America network. In that case, AAFE's share was $285,000.[58]

on February 22, 2021, Senators Schumer and Gillibrand announced $5,395,000 in NeighborWorks America grants for 16 community development organizations "to bring local solutions to affordable housing challenges across New York". AAFE received a more respectable $465,000 of that money.[59]

Dream of Equality Awards

On March 16, 2017, AAFE celebrated its 43rd Annual Lunar New Year Banquet in Manhattan's Chinatown.

In a long-standing tradition AAFE presented its annual Dream of Equality Awards to favored "community activists" and political allies.

From the AAFE website:

We were pleased to present Dream of Equality Awards to four distinguished members of our community. They included: US Sen. Charles E. Schumer; Javier Valdes, co-executive director of Make the Road New York; Yvonne Stennett, executive director of Community League of the Heights; and New York State Supreme Court Judge Doris Ling-Cohan.[60]

Past recipients of AAFE' s Dream of Equality Awards include:

+ David Paterson – socialist, and former New York
  Governor
+ Bill Perkins - former New York State Senator and
  DSA member[61]
+ Jean Quan – former Oakland, California Mayor and
  CWP member[62]
+ Reverend Jesse Jackson
+ Michio Kaku – scientist. Former Worker's Voice
  Organization (forerunner to CWP) leader[63]
+ Andrew Cuomo - former New York Governor
+ Mario Cuomo - former New York Governor
+ John Liu - former Comptroller of the City of New
  York
+ Cushing Dolbeare – former housing activist,
  Democratic Socialist Organizing Committee leader [64]
+ Geraldine Ferarro – former US Democratic vice-presi-
  dential candidate

Esteemed company indeed.

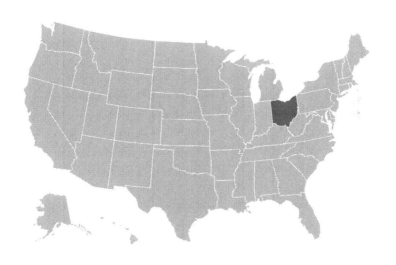

SENATORS FROM THE STATE OF
OHIO

SHERROD BROWN

SHERROD BROWN IS THE SENIOR US SENATOR FROM OHIO

BACKGROUND

S HERROD BROWN, BORN in 1952, was elected as senator in Ohio since 2006 on the Democratic Party ticket. He received a bachelor's degree in Russian Studies from Yale. He also speaks Russian and has been described as a "Russophile".[1] He has a Master's in Education (1979) and a Master's in Administration (1981) both from Ohio State University. Brown served in the Ohio State House from 1975-1983 and was Ohio Secretary of State from 1983-1991.[2]

He is married to Pulitzer Prize-winning columnist Connie Schultz.[3]

INFLUENCE

Sherrod Brown chairs the Committee on Banking, Housing, and Urban Affairs, where he also sits on the Subcommittees on Foreign Policy; Financial Institutions and Consumer Protection; Housing, Transportation, and Community Development; National Security and International Trade and Finance; and Securities, Insurance, and Investment. On the Committee on Finance, Brown chairs the subcommittee on Social Security, Pensions, and Family Policy and sits on the subcommittees on International Trade, Customs, and Global Competitiveness; and the subcommittee on Taxation and IRS Oversight.

Sherrod Brown also sits on the Committee on Veterans' Affairs, as well as the Committee on Agriculture, Nutrition and Forestry, where he sits on the subcommittees on Commodities, Risk Management, and Trade; Conservation, Climate, Forestry, and Natural Resources; and Rural Development and Energy.[4]

RADICAL ROOTS

Sherrod Brown's interest in far-left politics first manifested in high school.

Brown was elected student council president, then used his platform to protest the Vietnam War and to advocate for "black studies". In 1970, Brown organized a rally for the first Earth Day in his hometown Mansfield, Ohio.[5]

Sherrod Brown, front, back to camera

After he received his degree in Russian studies at Yale, the Democratic Party recruited him to run for Ohio state representative. At 22 years of age, Sherrod Brown became the youngest state representative in Ohio history.[6]

In April 2020, Senator Brown commemorated the 50th anniversary of the first Earth Day with a digital town hall organized by Cleveland activist Yvonka Hall.[7]

Unsurprisingly, Hall works closely with Molly Nagin[8] of the Ohio Communist Party and with Democratic Socialists of America.[9]

Emily Brown, Radical Mom

Sherrod Brown likely inherited his socialist views from his radical mother Emily Brown – a stalwart of the Mansfield Ohio left.

Emily Brown died in 2009, aged 88. According to her Plain Dealer obituary she became president of the Richland County Medical Society auxiliary, the Mansfield YWCA and the Ohio Council of YWCAs. She and husband Charles helped found the local Habitat for Humanity.

She was also elected to the county Democratic committee and served on the party's Richland County central and executive committees.

Emily Brown started life as Mary Emily Campbell in another Mansfield - in Georgia.

She earned a bachelor's degree from Wesleyan College in Macon, Georgia, then taught high school English in Georgia and Florida.

During World War II, somehow, she transformed from a humble southern schoolteacher to an assistant supervisor for the US Foreign Economic Administration in Washington DC.[10] Who recommended her for this position? One of her professors perhaps?

According to the Plain Dealer, in this role she "supervised classified documents".[11]

The testimony of former Soviet spies Elizabeth Bentley and Whittaker Chambers, as well as the broken Soviet codes revealed in the famous Venona Project transcripts, have proven that most wartime US government agencies were deeply penetrated by Soviet agents.

The Foreign Economic Administration supervised foreign aid to wartime allies including the famous Lend-Lease program to the Soviet Union. The agency was a very important target for Soviet intelligence.

Known Soviet spies working the Foreign Economic Administration during WW2 included:

- Michael Greenberg - Board of Economic Warfare, Foreign Economic Administration, specialist on China. Communist Party USA member.
- Allan Rosenberg - Foreign Economic Administration, Perlo spy group.
- Frank Coe – Assistant to the Executive Director of the Board of Economic Warfare, Assistant Administrator, Foreign Economic Administration, Silvermaster spy group.
- Laughlin Currie – Administrative Assistant to President Roosevelt, Deputy Administrator Foreign Economic Administration, Silvermaster spy group.
- Bela Gold (aka William Gold) – Senate Subcommittee on War Mobilization, Office of Economic Programs in Foreign Economic Administration, Silvermaster spy group.[12]

Mao Tse Tung, Frank Coe

Michael Greenberg was an identified Communist Party USA (CPUSA) member.[13]

Frank Coe was named seven times, under oath, as a party member.[14] He would later wind-up living in Beijing, where he loyal served the Chinese Communist Party until his death in 1980.[15]

So, Mary Campbell, an idealistic young left-wing schoolteacher gets parachuted into a highly sensitive US government wartime agency dealing with aid to the Soviet Union. She handles "classified documents". Several of her colleagues, including two senior administrators, are identified communists and Soviet spies.

After the war, Mary Campbell - now known as Emily Brown - becomes an open leftist activist in Ohio. She produces an equally leftist son who studies Russian in college. He later becomes a far-left US Senator who develops his own deep ties to the CPUSA. At one point he seriously considers running for US President.[16]

Are there any grounds for concern here?

SHERROD BROWN AND THE COMMUNIST PARTY

Senator Brown has been close to Ohio Communist Party USA activists for decades.

Molly Nagin and the Tamir Rice tragedy

Molly Nagin, club organizer of the Cleveland Ohio Communist Party USA (CPUSA), gave a speech on July 16, 2022 at the Rice Butterfly Memorial Ceremony, at Cudell Recreation Center in Cleveland, Ohio.[17]

Molly Nagin addresses ceremony

Nagin's speech was ostensibly used to commemorate the life of Tamir Rice, a black boy, killed by police on November 23, 2014, aged 12. Much of Nagin's speech was used to condemn "capitalism" and to advocate for leftist political changes through greater voter participation.[18]

Nagin's speech was reproduced on the CPUSA website.

> *Unlike Tamir Rice, the cops who took his life did not act as individuals that day. They did not act alone. They acted on behalf of the City of Cleveland. They also acted on behalf of a larger system, one that Tamir had absolutely no part in building at all, as he was a twelve-year-old child. That system is called capitalism.*
>
> *I also hope that everybody here is registered to vote. We need a county prosecutor who will fight to ensure Tamir's case is reopened.*

We need a county executive and council who will fight for non–law enforcement crisis response, and an end to all New Jim Crow policies and institutions, including the county jail.

To do this, we not only need to vote, we need to build electoral coalitions, and we need to run for office. Start small, run for precinct captain, build from there…In 2020, the Tamir Rice Foundation partnered with Cleveland VOTES and the Ohio Student Association to celebrate Tamir's 18th birthday with a voter education drive.

The #WeVoteForTamir was born, and this election year we must continue to vote for Tamir, and for every life that did not matter to this society still striving to realize democracy.

Ella Baker once referred to quantitative changes [as]..'the spadework.' The thankless minutiae of community organizing that leads to the revolution of society.[19]

Tamir Rice was carrying a replica toy gun at the time of his death and had allegedly been pointing it at passersby. When police arrived, Tamir was fatally shot when an officer believed he was trying to draw the "gun".[20]

Despite the facts, Tamir Rice's tragic death soon became a focus of activism for the CPUSA in Ohio and nationally.

Molly Nagin and Tamir Rice's mother Samaria appeared together at the CPUSA's 2019 100th anniversary convention in Chicago.

Samaria Rice, mother of Tamir Rice, right, with Molly Nagin, a Communist Party activist from Ohio, at the CPUSA 100th anniversary convention in Chicago. | Al Neal / PW

The CPUSA website People's World exploited the issue for years.

Coalition backs Tamir Rice's mother in pushing Justice Dept. to re-open case

May 17, 2021 | 9:51 AM CDT | BY TIM ZELINA AND MOLLY NAGIN

People's World article by Molly Nagin

After the death of Tamir Rice, his family and some Cleveland activists including Molly Nagin established the Tamir Rice Foundation to combat "racism" and to advocate for "police reform."

Molly Nagin became Secretary[21] and the Vice President of the Tamir Rice Foundation. She also personally designed the Tamir Rice Memorial Butterfly Garden.[22]

Senator Brown also joined the Tamir Rice bandwagon.

In April 2021 ,Senator Brown wrote to Attorney General Merrick Garland urging the Department of Justice to "immediately reopen its civil rights investigation into Tamir Rice's death:"

> *Justice delayed is justice denied, and accountability for Tamir Rice's death has been delayed for more than six years. Therefore, we strongly support the request of Samaria Rice, the mother of Tamir Rice, that DOJ reopen its investigation into her son's case.[23]*

Though no police were ever charged, Senator Brown has publicly labelled the killing a "murder".

Sherrod Brown ✔ @SenSherrodBrown · Jun 25, 2020   ···
Today would have been **Tamir Rice**'s eighteenth birthday.

But he was murdered by police in a Cleveland park at the age of twelve.

Our hearts break for the young man he might have been and the future he
might have had. #TamirRice

More than 250 people attended the July 2022 memorial opening ceremony, including Senator Brown and his wife and journalist Connie Schultz, and far left Ohio State Senator Nickie Antonio.[24]

In August 2012, Senator Antonio had addressed the funeral of Ohio Communist Party veteran Judy Gallo.[25]

Senator Brown addressed the memorial event, alongside Molly Nagin.[26]

The Ohio Communist Party is perfectly willing to exploit the tragic death of a 12-year-old boy for political gain. So, it appears, is Senator Brown.

Rick Nagin connection

Rick Nagin, CPUSA National
Committee April 2018

Sherrod Brown at least partially owes his US Senate career to Molly Nagin's father, Ohio Communist Party head Rick Nagin.

In 1990, the office of Ohio Secretary of State Sherrod Brown gave a certificate of recognition to Rick Nagin, chairman of the Ohio Communist Party.

Nagin collected the award for registering more than 2,000 voters during his losing campaign for Cleveland City Council.[27] Rick Nagin returned the favor in 2006, through working in the Ohio labor movement, to elect Sherrod Brown to the Senate.

In 2006, Rick Nagin was a paid political coordinator for the AFL-CIO Labor campaign which supported Senate candidates Sherrod Brown and Ted Strickland.[28]

Rick Nagin, addressing a June 25, 2006 meeting of the CPUSA national committee in New York, explained:

> ...the labor movement and other progressive forces are using a ballot referendum to raise Ohio's minimum wage to reach out to voters in rural and southern Ohio, a bastion of the Republican Party. The referendum could prove decisive in Rep. Sherrod Brown's drive to oust Republican Sen. Michael DeWine.[29]

Sherrod Brown and the communist steelworkers

By the early 1990s, Sherrod Brown was working closely with the Lorain branch of the Ohio Communist Party.

In 1992, after losing his Ohio Secretary of State position, Sherrod Brown moved to Lorain, Ohio, 30 miles west of Cleveland on the shores of Lake Erie. That year he successfully contested Congressional District 13 to become the Congressman for the area.

Bruce Bostick

This move brought Brown into close contact with large numbers of unemployed steelworkers and the Lorain Communist Party.

After mass steel industry layoffs in the 1980s, Lorain communists set about organizing the unemployed workers.

Lorain Communist Party stalwart Bruce Bostick gave some background in an April 2020 People's World article:

> The Lorain Communist Party club played the key role in establishing and running a storefront coalition grouping, the Unemployed Crisis Center... They were able to concretely help thousands of unemployed workers and, as a side benefit, recruited new folks to the CPUSA.

> *The Lorain Communist Party club's main work had been in the steel union, USWA Local 1104, with 8,000 members...*
>
> *When a major cutback, with big layoffs, hit our local, it caused cutbacks throughout the surrounding community of local shops, businesses, and public services... The party felt they had to react, to do something to help out.*
>
> *The club pushed the union to stand up and fight by setting up an official Unemployed Workers Committee.*
>
> *Working at Mt. Zion, we set up a 'Crisis Center' that was able to begin filling in some gaps in needs that laid-off workers had.*
>
> *Of course, there would be no UCC if not for the Communist Party club. Unions would not have moved to represent laid-off workers if not for the club...*
>
> *UCC was a place we discussed socialism, the possibility of a new society run by workers, where there would be no layoffs. One time, we even had a Soviet worker, in the US representing their labor movement, drop in to talk.*[30]

The Unemployed Crisis Center (UCC) was still active well into the 1990s. Enter Sherrod Brown.

Bostick continues:

> *Relationships were developed between unions and rising authentic community leaders, especially... David Flores. Flores was a leader that had been a steelworker... He pushed hard for upgrading less-developed, mainly Hispanic areas... The Campedo area was heavily Puerto Rican and was without sidewalks or sewer development.*
>
> *We worked to support the drive, led by Flores, to upgrade this area. Flores, along with then Rep. Sherrod Brown, became long-range future leaders fighting for labor and minority communities.*
>
> *Now-Sen. Sherrod Brown was then our congressman. He would report to us on any legislative developments, allowing us to mobilize crowds to pack the hall and speak on issues.*[31]

Was Sherrod Brown, effectively, a spy inside Congress for the Lorain Communist Party?

In a 2007 article in People's World, Bruce Bostick commented on Sherrod Brown's election to the US Senate.

> *Conventional wisdom, at least according to political pundits in Ohio, was that Sherrod was 'too liberal' to beat incumbent senator DeWine.*
>
> *Sherrod Brown…soundly defeated DeWine, running a strong campaign based on 'mainstream progressive values.'*
>
> *Organized labor was the main force fueling this upsurge against the GOP and the ultra-right.[32]*

In 2012, Bruce Bostick served on the board of the Ohio Alliance for Retired Americans Education Fund.[33]

Around the same time, former Ohio Communist Party chairman Wally Kaufman[34] was vice president of the communist-dominated Ohio Alliance for Retired Americans.[35]

In 2012, the Ohio Alliance for Retired Americans endorsed Sherrod Brown's US Senate campaign.[36]

Bruce Bostick is also a long serving member of national executive of the communist-dominated Steelworkers Organization of Active Retirees (SOAR).[37]

According to Bruce Bostick, the Ohio Alliance for Retired Americans and SOAR organised a rally held on April 27, 2015 at the Old Stone Church in Cleveland to protest for the need to strengthen the White House Commission on Aging.

Senator Brown was scheduled to address the rally.[38]

Communist affinities

Senator Brown likes communists and communists like him.

Then-Congressman Brown wrote a commentary on Medicare privatization for the St. Louis Post-Dispatch December 11, 2003.

It was reprinted by permission of the author, in the CPUSA's People's World of December 19, 2003.

Laborfest

The main branch of the Cleveland Public Library hosted "Laborfest: a multimedia celebration from videos and PowerPoint presentations to live drama and music" on February 23, 2013.[39]

Audience members were welcomed by Harriet Applegate (Executive Secretary of the North Shore Federation of Labor),[40] who incidentally was Rick Nagin's guest at the Ohio Communist Party convention the following year.[41]

Speakers were Professor Ahmed White, Colorado School of Law; Professor Patricia Hills, Boston University; and Dr. M. Melissa Wolfe, Curator of American Art at the Columbus Museum of Art.[42]

The whole event was communist-themed.

Charles Pervo of the Ohio Alliance for Retired Americans filed a report for People's World:

> Mr. White covered the infamous 'little steel' strike of 1937... (he used the phrases 'class struggle' and 'class consciousness' positively and freely and observed openly contributions made by Communists and 'fellow travelers').
>
> Ms. Hills spoke on Art and Politics in the Popular Front: The Union Work and Social Realism of Philip Evergood. She displayed works and covered the life of several other labor/New Deal artists, including William Gropper, Louis Lozowick, and Hugo Gellert. Many artists of the period gravitated to the CPUSA, and to the John Reed Clubs.
>
> Ms. Wolfe presented the life and works of Joe Jones - a worker/ artist... Ms. Wolfe: 'What did it mean to be a Communist artist, as Jones clearly decided he would be?... To be a Communist artist during the Third Period of the Communist Party - between 1928 and 1935 - meant that you were a class-conscious worker whose production - art - acted as a weapon to incite a revolution that would end Fascist structures of power and give workers control of their production... [43]

People's World also noted that Senator Brown and his wife - "the well-known progressive writer Connie Schultz" - also attended.[44]

In 2018, Ohio Communist Party member Aleena Starks was active in the Democrats of Cuyahoga County and Friends of Sherrod Brown.[45] She was leading a team "making calls and organizing neighbors to get involved in electing Sherrod in November."[46]

She was also a field organizer for the Ohio Democratic Party.[47] All while remaining an active communist.

Communist Party USA
@communistsusa

Our comrades, Aleena Starks and Rick Nagin, handing out literature and recruiting new members at the Cleveland #Pride Festival. Long live the #LGBT community and the CPUSA!

4:59 PM · Jun 1, 2019 · Twitter for iPhone

The 27th Wanshou Forum - jointly organized by the International Department of the Communist Party of China Central Committee and Renmin University of China - was held on February 28, 2019, in Beijing.

The theme of the forum was "Building a Community with a Shared Future for Mankind and Development of Socialism in the World."[48]

The Communist Party USA contribution to the Forum was delivered by Aleena Starks.[49]

Aleena Starks, center

Aleena Starks told the assembled communists:

> *Racism has been and continues to be the greatest weapon the ruling class has to divide the struggles of the American people. Racism has become structural and is clearly reflected in unemployment rates, college graduation rates, wage disparity and especially incarceration rates.*
>
> *Thank you for inviting our Party to participate in learning about the many important developments in your country. I bring greetings from our Party's National committee, wishing you all the best in establishing socialism with Chinese characteristics.*

Aleena Starks is a true Democrat. Just like Senator Brown.[50]

SOCIALIST CONNECTIONS

Senator Brown also has a history with the Marxists of Democratic Socialists of America (DSA).

He was described in a Dissent magazine interview with long time long DSA comrade Michael Kazin[51] as "perhaps the most class-conscious Democrat in Washington."[52]

Ohio DSA members campaigned for Brown in his successful 2006 Senate race.

From Democratic Left:

> *Although the 2006 election had been, at least initially, character-*
> *ized as a referendum on Iraq and GOP scandals, trade policy was*
> *in many ways the sleeper issue.*
>
> *Former Representative, now Senator Sherrod Brown is the*
> *most visible symbol of this change… A longtime critic of 'free*
> *trade' agreements, frequently characterized as far left and out of*
> *the mainstream, Brown handily defeated the relatively moderate*
> *but free-trade proponent Mike DeWine…*
>
> *Trade was also an issue in the narrow loss of Mary Jo Kilroy*
> *to Deborah Pryce. Local DSAers worked in both the Brown and*
> *Kilroy campaigns.[53]*

Mary Jo Kilroy was a DSA member.[54] Though unsuccessful in 2006, she was narrowly elected to Congress in 2008 with DSA help.[55]

In 2010, Senator Brown and Representative Kilroy formed a team to tout "Obamacare" to Ohio union members and retirees.[56] They also both supported repealing the "don't ask, don't tell" policy to allow homosexuals to serve openly in the US military.[57]

The partnership dissolved when Kilroy was defeated after only one term.

PDA and 21st Century Democrats

The DSA-dominated Progressive Democrats of America (PDA) also worked hard to elect Sherrod Brown.

In 2006, PDA bragged: "PDA wins included Rep. John Hall, D-NY, and Sen. Sherrod Brown, D-OH."[58]

21st Century Democrats also backs leftist candidates in Congressional and US Senate races.

The organization was led for many years[59] by former St. Paul, Minnesota Mayor and DSA comrade Jim Scheibel.[60]

21st Century Democrats has strongly supported Sherrod Brown, from his first Congressional race and his 2012[61] and 2018 US Senate races.[62]

Brown with PDA OHIO, April 2009

From the 21st Century Democrats website:

> *A longtime ally, 21st Century Democrats provided Brown active support in his Senate election in 2006. One of our first endorsees, we first helped this true progressive win his House seat in 1992.*[63]

Midwest Academy

Every year, the DSA-dominated, Chicago-based Midwest Academy holds an awards dinner to honor standout "progressives."

The 2017 event was held December 17th at the Sphinx Club in Washington DC.

Senator Brown received the "prestigious" Progressive Leaders Award.

From the Midwest Academy Facebook page:

> *The Midwest Academy is proud to honor Senator Sherrod Brown with the Progressive Leadership Award at our Academy Awards! As a champion for working people, Senator Brown has been at the frontlines from the fight for labor union rights to guaranteeing that healthcare is affordable and accessible to all!*[64]

Other Awardees were Leo Gerard, International President of the United Steel Workers, Steve Phillips of Democracy in Color and Jessica Pierce, Director of Special Fellowships Movement Voter Project.

Leo Gerard is a Canadian labor unionist with strong ties to Democratic Socialists of America.

One of Gerard's most notable recruits into the leadership of the United Steel Workers was former Democratic Socialist Organizing Committee comrade Ron Bloom,[65] who would later serve as President Obama's "Car Czar."[66]

Leo Gerard at 2007 Chicago DSA dinner

Steve Phillips of course is mentioned throughout this book.

A former Stanford University Maoist turned mega wealthy San Francisco lawyer, Phillips was being honored for his role in winning an Alabama US Senate seat for Democrat Doug Jones in 2016.[67]

Jessica Pierce has been working with organizations such as Wellstone Action, Midwest Academy, and the Center for American

Progress. Throughout her career, she has "personally trained more than 20,000 people".[68]

Pierce also served as National Chair at Black Youth Project 100; part of the Freedom Road Socialist Organization (FRSO)-dominated Movement for Black Lives.[69]

In 2013, she travelled to Jackson, Mississippi with a team led by FRSO activists including Cazembe Jackson[70] to help elect socialist mayor Chokwe Antar Lumumba.

Cazembe Jackson left, Jessica Pierce right

DSA-aligned 'progressive'

DSA certainly sees Sherrod Brown as part of their long-term vision of moving America to the far left.

From a Fall 2012 Democratic Left article titled "Democracy Endangered: DSA's Strategy for the 2012 Elections and Beyond:"

> *Democratic socialists must work to build a multi-racial coalition of working people, the unemployed, indebted students and the fore-closed that is capable of forcing politicians to govern democratically.*
>
> *The first task of a movement to defend democracy is to work for maximum voter turnout in the 2012 election.*
>
> *Building such a mass social movement for democracy is DSA's major task; the 2012 elections are only a tactical step on that*

strategic path…DSA and other progressive forces should work to increase the size of the Congressional Progressive, Black and Latino caucuses and to elect pro-labor candidates to state legislatures.

The election this year of Tammy Baldwin (D-WI) and Elizabeth Warren (D-MA), along with the re-election of Sherrod Brown (D-OH) and Bernie Sanders (I-VT), would increase the number of progressive voices in the United States Senate.[71]

In 2009, Senator Brown endorsed Bob Creamer's book "Listen to Your Mother: Stand Up Straight - How Progressive Can Win".

Creamer was a member of DSA's predecessor New American Movement and a co-founder of the Midwest Academy.[72] He is also married to one-time DSA comrade Jan Schakowsky (D-IL).[73]

ACORN, COMMUNISTS, SOCIALISTS AND MAOISTS

Senator Brown has worked for years with the Ohio affiliates of a nationwide network encompassing CPUSA comrades and some Liberation Road-affiliated revolutionaries: the former Association of Community Organizations for Reform Now (ACORN).

Health Care for America Now

Much of this network origi-nally coalesced around the cam-paign for socialized healthcare.

From Rick Nagin of the People's World, April 2009,

Repeatedly chanting 'Yes, We Can,' some 600 labor, retiree and community activists loudly voiced determination to win health care reform this year at a rally April 17, in Cleveland Heights sponsored by Health Care for America Now.

The crowd…cheered Sen. Sherrod Brown as he outlined plans for a 'public option' in legislation expected to be introduced soon in Congress. Brown is seen as the lead Senator in the fight in Congress for health care reform.

'I would love to see a single payer system,' Brown said, refer-ring to a national health care program without private insurance

companies... The conservative era is over. We now have the oppor-
tunity for a national health care reform."

The US, Brown said, has entered a 'new progressive era' similar
to the New Deal of the 1930's and the Great Society of the 1960's.
'The government is on the side of middle-class people," he said, and
high on the agenda is an overhaul of the failed health care system.[74]

Speaking alongside Senator Brown were Robyn Hales, president of
Northeast Ohio Alliance for Hope (NOAH); Becky Williams, presi-
dent of SEIU local 1199; and Brian Rothenberg, executive director
of Progress Ohio and a coordinator of Ohio HCAN and Marjorie
Mosely, co-chair of the Association of Community Organizations for
Reform Now (ACORN).

Health Care for America Now was basically ACORN and its
allied organizations, working together to push the Obama agenda
forward.

At the time, the Health Care for America Now field director was
Margarida Jorge, the self-proclaimed "chief architect of the 47-state
field program that helped win the Affordable Care Act."[75]

Margarida Jorge, Executive Director

Margarida Jorge is the Executive Director of Health Care for American Now (HCAN). She was
a co-founder of the campaign in 2008 and chief architect of the 47 state field program that
helped win the Affordable Care Act. Margarida brings nearly three decades of experience to
health care advocacy from national and state work. Margarida currently lives in Washington,
D.C.

Immediately prior to this, Margarida George had served on the
District Executive Board of the Missouri/Kansas District of the
Communist Party USA.

May Day Greetings from
the Missouri/Kansas
District of the
Communist Party, U.S.A.
Honoring Comrades —
Past & Present — and
Wishing Workers of the
World a Happy May Day!

From the members of the MO/KS District and its executive board:
Jim Wilkerson, Zenobia Thompson, John Pappademos, Glenn Burleigh,
Margarida Jorge, Quincy Boyd, Tony Pecinovsky

MO/KS District Communist Party • 438 N. Skinker • St. Louis, MO 63130
314-776-7732 • moks@cpusa.org

People's Weekly World, April 28, 2007, page 4

Ohio Organizing Collaborative

In Ohio, ACORN and Health Care for America Now overlap considerably with the Ohio Organizing Collaborative (OOC) and its constituent local affiliates.

The OOC was formed in 2007 by Kirk Noden of Health Care for America Now. Its mission is to organize citizens to "build power and combat social, racial and economic injustices in communities across Ohio".[76]

Senator Brown works very closely with OOC.

On August 16, 2010, Senator Brown joined the Mahoning Valley Organizing Collaborative in Youngstown to "discuss legislative efforts aimed to combat childhood hunger and promote access to nutritious foods in Ohio schools and underserved communities."

"The Mahoning Valley Organizing Collaborative is proud to stand shoulder-to-shoulder with Senator Sherrod Brown to release the results of our recent Health Equity Campaign Report, which proves beyond the shadow of a doubt why the Healthy, Hunger Free-Kids Act is so important for our Valley's future," said Executive Director of the Collaborative Kirk Noden.

The same year, Noden spent several months training at the Liberation Road-connected Rockwood Leadership Institute in Oakland California.

On January 14, 2013, Senator Brown met with twelve Ohio Organizing Collaborative leaders from Akron, Canton, Dover and Youngstown. The discussion focused on Social Security, Medicare and Medicaid. OOC leaders and Senator Brown discussed the possibilities of working toward Medicaid expansion in the state.[77]

Senator Brown with OOC leaders, January 2013

The Senator continues to confer with OOC on a regular basis.

 Ohio Organizing Collaborative @OHorganizing · May 29, 2014   ...
Members of Alliance for Senior Action &MVOC/ON Grassroots
Ambassadors present Sen. **Sherrod** Brown with Thank you card

 Ohio Organizing Collaborative   ...
@OHorganizing

Join us for a conversation with Sen Sherrod Brown this Wed at 11 am via zoom. Hear from policy and legal and advocacy experts on Ohio's current state of unemployment and learn how you can take action for other unemployed Ohioans. RSVP today! zcu.io/1eb8

12:09 PM · Oct 19, 2020 · Zoho Social

In recent years, OOC has become closely aligned to the Ohio Student Association bringing in a stronger Liberation Road influence into the organization.

When Senator Brown was given a "Progressive Leadership" award in December 2017 by the Midwest Academy, OOC leaders Molly Shack and DaMareo Cooper sent a video message congratulating him. The group said they "looked forward to working with you [Brown] in 2018."[78]

Molly Shack front left DaMareo Cooper, front right

Revolutionaries

To be clear, OOC is a revolutionary organization.

In 2017/18 DaMareo Cooper, Executive Director of OOC; Prentiss Haney, Executive Director, Ohio Student Association (and OOC leader) and Amanda Hoyt, OOC State Campaign Director were all "Leadership Now: Ohio Fellows" at the Liberation Road/ACORN linked Rockwood Leadership Institute.[79]

In 2016, OOC Civic Engagement Director Molly Shack and OOC People's Justice Project State Organizing Director Aramis Malachi-Ture Sundiata travelled to communist Cuba.

In 2018, Aramis Malachi-Ture Sundiata attended the national conference of the ultra-militant, pro-Russia African People's Socialist Party (APSP).

On July 29, 2022, the APSP's headquarters in St. Louis, Missouri and St. Petersburg, Florida, were both raided by the FBI.

The federal indictment issued to AFSP leaders charges Russian national Aleksandr Ionov with working with Russian intelligence agencies to recruit "members of US political groups as foreign agents of Russia within the United States."[80]

AFSP's leader Omali Yeshitela does have direct ties with Aleksandr Ionov and his organization Anti-Globalization Movement of Russia.

Alexander Ionov, left Omali Yeshtela right

These are Senator Brown's people.

COUNCIL FOR A LIVABLE WORLD

When reported Soviet agent Leo Szilard established Council for a Livable World to weaken the US military, Sherrod Brown was probably just the kind of candidate he had in mind.

Sherrod Brown was first elected to the US Senate in 2006 "with Council for a Livable World's enthusiastic support".[81] CLW endorsed Senator Brown again in 2012, praising his leftist views and his anti-military voting record:

> First-term Senator Sherrod Brown is the most prominent elected Democrat in Ohio. An unabashed progressive, he is one of the most articulate and respected spokespeople for progressive causes in the United States, especially on universal health care, labor, reproductive rights, responsible gun ownership and gay marriage.
>
> Totally committed to nuclear arms control and responsible national security policies, Brown has the voting record to match.

On the two most recent Council for a Livable World Nuclear Arms Race Voting Records, he achieved a perfect 100%

Brown was a strong proponent this past December of the New START nuclear arms reduction treaty, helping to beat back amendments designed to undermine the treaty.

Council for a Livable World believes that Sherrod Brown has been an influential addition to the US Senate. The nation needs him there for the next term. He is a committed progressive and a hard worker.[82]

The Council supported Senator Brown again in 2018, this time citing his support for President Obama's lapsed "Iran Nuclear Deal" and engagement with North Korea:

Senator Brown is a strong supporter of the Iran nuclear agreement and has criticized the Trump's administration decision not to certify the deal. He has also urged talks with a nuclear-armed North Korea, saying, 'This is no time for bluster or empty threats.'[83]

No time to defend America from its enemies either, apparently.

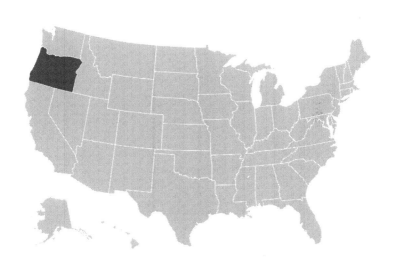

SENATORS FROM THE STATE OF

OREGON

RON WYDEN

BACKGROUND

RON WYDEN SERVED as a member of congress from 1981 before becoming senator in 1996 on the Democratic Party ticket. Before his career in public service, Wyden taught gerontology to university students, and co-founded the Oregon chapter of the activist group Gray Panthers in 1974.

Ron Wyden received his bachelor's degree from Stanford University. He received his law degree from the University of Oregon School of Law in 1974.[1]

INFLUENCE

Ron Wyden chairs the Committee on Finance. He also chairs the Subcommittee on Water and Power on the Committee on Energy and Natural Resources. Wyden is the Vice Chairman of the Joint Committee on Taxation. Additionally, Wyden sits on both the Senate Committee on Intelligence and the Committee on the Budget.[2]

PARENTS

Ron Wyden was born in Wichita, Kansas in 1949. His mother Edith was a librarian at Stanford University, and his father Peter was an author and journalist. Both of Wyden's parents fled Nazi Germany as children with their families in the 1930s. Edith came to America from Nazi Germany after a period in Iraq in 1939,[3] and Peter was 13 years old when his Jewish parents fled Germany for New York in 1937. Wyden's parents divorced in 1959.

Cuban dictator Fidel Castro with Peter Wyden[4]

After his service in the US Army's Psychological Warfare division in World War II, and a period working as a journalist, Peter Wyden (born Peter Weidenreich) became an author of numerous books. His book "Bay of Pigs: The Untold Story," may have been his most famous. The Washington Post[5] interviewed the elder Wyden in 1979 about the book, and he was also quoted[6] that same year about his six-hour interview with Cuban dictator Fidel Castro:

> *He was very proud — for a good reason. How many island countries have licked the United States of America? Nobody. Look at it objectively, no ideology attached. He won. It was the most spectacular defeat of the United States in this century.*

PROMOTING CUBA

Speaking of Cuba, Peter Wyden's son has often used his role as senator to push pro-Cuba policy. He visited Cuba in 2006 with then-Senator Ben Nelson ostensibly "for a first-hand look at the prison at Guantanamo Bay."[7] Notably, both Wyden and Nelson were endorsed by the nuclear disarmament group, a Council for a Livable World (see later in this profile).

In 2009, Wyden joined democrat senators Jeff Bingaman, Maria Cantwell, Tom Harkin, Mary Landrieu, Blanche Lincoln, Mark Pryor, and Debbie Stabenow in sponsoring legislation to promote "more agricultural exports to Cuba."[8]

The bill, sponsored by then-Senate Finance Committee Chairman Max Baucus, was not the first pro-Cuba legislation sponsored by Baucus. In 2007, Baucus also fought for the so-called "Promoting American Agricultural and Medical Exports to Cuba Act," which did not receive a vote on the Senate floor. But in 2009, Baucus was likely buoyed by then-president Barack Obama, who sought to "seek a new beginning"[9] with the communist dictatorship. As an aside, the former president used identical language i.e., "seek a new beginning" in a speech in June 2009 in reference to America's relationship with Muslims.[10]

Again in 2009, Ron Wyden signed onto a letter written by Senator Mary Landrieu addressed to then-treasury secretary Timothy Geithner "promoting US small business exports/activities in Cuba." The letter specifically references Obama's "series of changes to US policy towards Cuba."[11] Senators Byron Dorgan, Jeanne Shaheen, and Maria Cantwell also signed the letter.

Throughout his presidency, Obama was aggressive about promoting a "normalization of relations" with the island nation. Senator Ron Wyden was always supportive of the effort. On December 17, 2014, the president made a statement[12] declaring in part:

> In the most significant changes in our policy in more than fifty years, we will end an outdated approach that, for decades, has failed to advance our interests, and instead we will begin to normalize relations between our two countries [America and Cuba].

That same day, Ron Wyden tweeted his support. "Opening relations with Cuba is good for the Cuban people & America's economy," he declared.[13] Wyden was so inspired that he released a statement[14] praising the former president. "I applaud the President for today's announcement and for taking these historic steps to normalize relations with Cuba," Wyden said in part. He continued:

> For more than a half-century, the United States has sought to isolate Cuba diplomatically and economically and bring down the Castro regime. By any metric, that policy has failed. At some point, policy makers must put aside personal ideology, look at the historical record, and reassess. In my judgment, that point is now.

In 2018, Ron Wyden joined a delegation to Cuba led by "longtime normalization advocate"[15] Senator Patrick Leahy, which was used seemingly to downplay Havana Syndrome, which has directly affected "diplomats and C.I.A. personnel around the world"[16] and to bash President Donald Trump's restrictions on Cuba.

Senator Gary Peters and Representatives Jim McGovern, Susan Davis and Kathy Castor were also in the delegation, which met with then- Cuban dictator Raúl Castro. "[Trump's] embargo makes no sense and the reversal of the policies that Presidents Barack Obama and Raul Castro negotiated doesn't help the United States or Cuba," Senator Patrick Leahy reportedly stated during a press conference at the US Embassy in Havana.[17]

In early 2021, Ron Wyden introduced the "US-Cuba Trade Act of 2021," which would remove sanctions on Cuba. Senators Patrick Leahy, Dick Durbin and Jeff Merkley cosponsored the legislation.[19]

Most recently, Wyden praised Biden administration efforts to lift Trump's restrictions on Cuba. This, particularly in wake of continued repression of the Cuban people, as well as the suspected involvement of the Cuban government in Havana Syndrome.

"This is an important first step in changing our country's outdated, harmful policy of isolation," Ron Wyden declared on social media on May 18, 2022. "I'll continue pushing my legislation in Congress to establish normal trade relations with Cuba, which is key to charting a new diplomatic course," he continued.[20]

DIRECT SOCIALIST CONNECTIONS

Maggie Kuhn and the Gray Panthers

RON WYDEN URGES SENIORS TO GET ACTIVE
Here with Maggie Kuhn, Grey Panthers founder
[21]

Ron Wyden has mentioned his role in starting the Oregon chapter of the Gray Panthers on numerous occasions throughout his career.[22,23,24] During a congressional tribute to the late Gray

Panthers founder Maggie Kuhn in 1995,[25] Wyden said that Kuhn "was the inspiration for the Oregon Gray Panthers". Wyden worked closely with Maggie Kuhn for several years in his role as co-director, then as director of the organization.

Wyden did not mention that Maggie Kuhn "helped organize the college chapter of both the League of Women Voters and the Young Socialists League" at her alma mater, the College for Women of Case-Western Reserve.

Kuhn's first job out of university was with the deceptively named "Young Women's Christian Association," which, as Kuhn stated in a 1983 interview,[26] was "very radical" and "always stocked with social-ists." "It was a very powerful influence in my life," she explained.

Like most dedicated socialists, Maggie Kuhn managed to visit communist countries throughout her life. In July 1986, Kuhn was a "member of the Philadelphia delegation to the Soviet Union spon-sored by the Philadelphia/Leningrad Sister Cities Project."[27] A decade earlier in 1976, the elderly activist "was chosen [as] a tour leader for travelers to China by the US-China People's Friendship Association."[28, 29]

Wyden also failed to note that Maggie Kuhn was a longtime member of America's largest Marxist organization: the Democratic Socialists of America (DSA). In fact, the vision for the Gray Panthers was *specifically* aligned with "DSA's analysis of the current society" and included the promotion of a healthcare system taken over by the federal government, a long-time socialist effort.

30

During an in-depth interview with Maggie Kuhn published in the DSA publication Democratic Left in 1989,[31] the long-time socialist explained that "DSA's analysis of the current society is very important to me and to the Gray Panthers..." The "priorities" of the Gray Panthers, she said, included "the demilitarization of our society, and establishing a national health care program."[32]

Wyden was enthusiastic about the radical vision of the Gray Panthers. In the 2012 book "Gray Panthers", author Roger Sanjek reveals that Ron Wyden was one of a "handful of congressmembers" rallying for a "national health-care system" at the White House during a demonstration in 1990.[33] At the time, "a hundred panthers visited legislator's offices" to promote Single Payer.

Maggie Kuhn was involved in the beginnings of Medicare, a known stepping stone to a complete government takeover of healthcare (Single Payer is recently and euphemistically referred to as "Medicare for All"). Ron Wyden's comrade Maggie Kuhn "helped plan and then chaired the section on national agencies for the first White House Conference on Aging, a convocation which recommended what four years later became Medicare."[34]

Maggie Kuhn: An Inspiration in The Struggle for Social Justice

Democratic Left, May/June 1989, Page 10

"Maggie is truly an American hero," Wyden gushed during his speech.

Reuben Lenske

Ron Wyden eulogized the Russian-born Reuben Lenske, an activist attorney closely associated to the communist party front: the National

Lawyers Guild. The Portland Federal Bureau of Investigation, as well as the intelligence branch of the Portland, Oregon police department "stated that they have reason to believe that Mr. Lenske is a communist."[35]

Reuben Lenske was one of the "earliest supporters" of Ron Wyden, who "burst into prominence in 1980 with a stunning upset in the Democratic primary for the US Congress".[36] Lenske and his wife would remain significant donors to Senator Wyden until Lenske's death in 2002.

A good indication of radical leanings in the early 1950's was support of Communist Party members Julius and Ethel Rosenberg, who were convicted and executed for passing top secret atomic weapon information to the Soviets during World War II. Reuben Lenske supported[37] a Communist-backed effort to discredit the government's investigation into the Rosenbergs, as well as Morton Sobell who was also imprisoned for being a Soviet spy but was released in 1969.

Lenske was a strong supporter of far-left activist Supreme Court Justice William O. Douglas. When Douglas granted an albeit short-lived stay of execution to Julius and Ethel Rosenberg, several republicans - and democrats - introduced impeachment resolutions which were ultimately unsuccessful.[38] Lenske was inspired by the Justice, who was appointed by Franklin D. Roosevelt. So much so that he served as chair of the committee to get Douglas on the Oregon ballot for president in 1952.

In 1954, Lenske defended Herbert Simpson, a truck driver who was charged with communism before the House Un-American Activities Committee. But the most sensational case of his career was the probably the trial of William Mackie, a housepainter who was charged in 1960 with "membership of a subversive organization."

The Immigration Service had said at Mr. Mackie's deportation hearings that he had attended more than 30 meetings of the Albania Section, a Communist Party cell operating in Portland in the late 1930's. Lenske fought the case all the way up to the Supreme Court but lost on a 5-4 vote.

Lenske's defense of accused communists - combined with letters to the editor criticizing US policy toward Cuba, Laos and China - came back to haunt him. In 1959, spurred by a secret FBI dossier on his alleged communist sympathies, the Internal Revenue Service launched a lengthy probe into his affairs. Lenske was convicted of tax evasion to the tune of $6,000 and sentenced to two years in jail.

Lenske later testified during a hearing on his tax evasion that in addition to belonging to the Communist Party USA-initiated "National Committee to Abolish the House Un-American Activities Committee," he had sued the city of Portland "for the denial of the use of the city auditorium to a communist speaker." He also "advocated the recognition of China and its admission to the United Nations".[39, 40]

"Whether it was fighting for the rights of the persecuted or the defenseless, Reuben always took on their causes as his own," Ron Wyden declared in a eulogy for Reuben Lenske, who passed away at age 102. "He was willing to stand up and speak out for them when others kept silent," Wyden continued.[41]

In the early 1960's, Reuben Lenske's son Aryay Lenske and his roommate - Communist Party USA member Mike Myerson - were key promoters of the student demonstrations against House Un-American Activities Committee hearings. Aryay Lenske later became executive secretary[42] of the National Lawyers Guild, "the foremost legal bulwark of the Communist Party."[43]

As an addendum, Morton Sobell quickly returned to communist activism once he was released from prison in 1969. He went to Cuba and Vietnam, and visited Moscow with his wife Helen, "where he was greeted as a hero by the KGB."[44] Like the Rosenbergs, he long maintained his innocence. He finally admitted to having been a spy in 2008, ten years before his death at the age of 101. "Now I know it was an illusion," Sobell said of communism in 2008. "I was taken in."[45]

COUNCIL FOR A LIVABLE WORLD

In 1972, Wyden worked on the reelection campaign of his "mentor"[46] Wayne Morse, who he believed "epitomized...issues of social justice and economic fairness."[47]

Like his mentor, Ron Wyden's Senate run was supported by the Council for a Livable World, an organization dedicated to disarming

America. The group was founded in 1962 by long-time socialist activist and alleged Soviet agent, Leo Szilard. Both Wayne Morse and Ron Wyden are listed on the Council's website along with other elected officials on a page titled "Our Legacy in Congress: Who We've Helped Elect."[48]

In 2012, Ron Wyden officially honored the Council for a Livable World on their fiftieth anniversary in the Congressional Record.[49] Wyden said in part:

> The Council for a Livable World believes, like I do, that the United States must work toward a 'world free of nuclear weapons.' They expressly advocate for deep reductions, and the eventual elimination, of nuclear weapons.

RON WYDEN'S RELENTLESS EFFORT TO DISARM AMERICA

As one would expect, Ron Wyden has a long history of doing the bidding of the Council for a Livable World by fighting against the US military and efforts to protect America.

Sustainable Defense Task Force

In 2010, for example, the Oregon senator joined an effort along with far-left Massachusetts democrat Representative Barney Frank and libertarian-leaning Texas republican Ron Paul dubbed the "Sustainable Defense Task Force" to slash the military budget.[50] A letter initiated by Wyden, Frank and Paul insisted "in the strongest terms that any final [President's Deficit Reduction] Commission report include among its recommendations substantial reductions in projected levels of future spending by the Department of Defense."

The resulting task force led by disarmament activists produced a report titled "Debt, Deficits, & Defense: A Way Forward,"[51] which was naturally touted by the Council for a Livable World.[52]

The "main body" of the report was drafted by Carl Conetta of the "Project on Defense Alternatives," which was founded in 1991 by Conetta and fellow task force member Charles Knight.[53]

During his time at university, Carl Conetta was a very active and vocal member of the Revolutionary Student Brigade, the youth wing of the pro-Beijing Revolutionary Communist Party. Conetta referred to himself and his peers as "revolutionary communists" in 1977.[54] "Yes, we are revolutionary communists," Conetta declared in an article titled "RSB [Revolutionary Student Brigade]: Justifiable Reformers" published in the Connecticut Daily Campus on Wednesday, October 5, 1977.

He continued:

> [We are] 'revolutionary' because we want to put an end to things like unemployment, poverty, discrimination, war and economic crisis once and for all; 'communist' because we want to build a society where the masses of working people can take control of the society that they built in common and make it serve their common needs rather than the needs of a handful of wealthy parasites.

Conetta's comrade and fellow task force member Charles Knight is a long-time member of Democratic Socialists of America.

55

As the author explained in a report at Breitbart News in 2012:

> Connetta and Knight's organization is the lead project of the Boston based Commonwealth Institute.
>
> Interestingly, four of the Institute's seven board members have been identified members of Democratic Socialists of America – Charles Knight, Richard Healey, Guy Molyneux and Cynthia Ward. A fifth, S. M. Miller has at least been a long time D.S.A. affiliate. Richard Healey is the son of the famous, late California communist Dorothy Healey, and is a former staffer with the Institute for Policy Studies. Healey also serves on the board of

> *Rosenberg Fund for Children, which is run by the sons of executed Soviet 'Atom Bomb spies', Julius and Ethel Rosenberg.*
>
> *One notable former board member of the Project on Defense Alternatives was Dr. Philip Morrison, Professor, Emeritus, Massachusetts Institute of Technology, who died in April 2005. Morrison had been a Communist Party USA member, a Manhattan Project scientist and was long suspected of being a Soviet spy – code names: 'Relay' or 'Serb.'*[56]

"Any serious effort to reduce the deficit has to be willing to examine the defense budget for wasteful spending," Ron Wyden stated at the time as quoted on his website.[57]

Wyden also quoted Carl Conetta in his press release:

> 'We strongly urge the Commission to consider our recommendations for making significant cuts to defense as part of their analysis,' said Carl Conetta, Co-Director of the Project on Defense Alternatives (PDA) at the Commonwealth Institute. 'These savings can be realized not only through targeting waste and mismanagement at DoD, but also through a frank assessment of current US military goals and strategies, which in many cases involve outdated assumptions that leave the United States spending money on commitments as well as weaponry that are no longer necessary for our national security.'

Warning to President Donald Trump

Senator Ron Wyden and Illinois Representative Bill Foster spearheaded a campaign in June 2020 to stop President Donald Trump from pursuing nuclear testing after "a decades-long moratorium" in the wake of alleged discussions on the matter, according to the Washington Post.[58] Notably, Bill Foster is yet another "Council for a Livable World" candidate.[59]

The president's proposal cited an ongoing threat from Russia and China, who were reportedly "conducting low-yield nuclear tests" at the time.

"We are deeply concerned by recent reports that you are considering a resumption of explosive nuclear testing, something the US has not done since 1992," Wyden and Foster wrote. "We urge you in the strongest terms to reject this awful idea both because it is technically unnecessary and because it would represent a dangerous provocation," they continued.[60]

The Council for a Livable World tweeted a supportive article about Wyden and Foster's letter on June 9, 2020.[61]

JEFF MERKLEY

JEFF MERKLEY IS THE JUNIOR US SENATOR FROM OREGON

BACKGROUND

J EFF MERKLEY HAS been serving as senator in Oregon since 2009 on the Democratic Party ticket. He received his undergraduate degree from Stanford and earned his graduate degree in Public Policy at Princeton's Woodrow Wilson School of Public and International Affairs. After graduation, Merkley worked as a national security analyst at the Pentagon and at the Congressional Budget Office before returning to Oregon in 1991 to lead the Portland branch of Habitat for Humanity. He was also president of the World Affairs Council in Portland. In 1998, Merkley entered the Oregon House of Representatives, and became Speaker of the House in 2007.[1]

INFLUENCE

Jeff Merkley chairs the Subcommittee on Chemical Safety, Waste Management, Environmental Justice, and Regulatory Oversight on the Committee on Environment and Public Works. He also chairs the Subcommittee on Interior, Environment, and Related Agencies on the Committee on Appropriations. Merkley also sits on the Committee on Rules and Administration, the Committee on the

Budget, the Committee on Environment and Public Works, and the Committee on Foreign Relations.[2]

MARK HATFIELD CONNECTION

Jeff Merkley's public service career began as a 19-year-old intern with Oregon Republican Senator Mark Hatfield. Merkley was elected as a Democrat to Hatfield's old Senate seat 33 years later. Senator Merkley makes much of his close relationship with his old boss. In 2007, Merkley asked Hatfield to swear him in as speaker of the Oregon House. When Merkley came to the US Senate chamber, he asked for Senator Hatfield's old desk.[3]

Senator Merkley paid tribute to Senator Hatfield, who died in August 2011, in a eulogy to the US Senate. Merkley described Senator Hatfield as a "mentor".

Merkley said of Hatfield:

> *He inspired many to public service, encouraging them to work to do what is right rather than what is convenient or popular.*[4]

While conservative on issues such as abortion, on defense and foreign policy issues, Senator Hatfield was consistently to the left of most Democrats. Indeed, Merkley's mentor had no qualms at all with working with the pro-communist Left.

National Conference on Nicaragua

Along with several other radical groups, the Communist Party USA-controlled US Peace Council organized a National Conference on Nicaragua in 1979 to ensure that the Marxist rebel Sandinistas took control.

Three Congressmen and two Senators lent support to this Conference: Ron Dellums (a member of Democratic Socialists of

America),[5] Tom Harkin, and Walter Fauntroy in the House and Ted Kennedy and Mark Hatfield in the Senate.[6]

Institute of Policy Studies

Senator Hatfield was also very active with the Institute of Policy Studies (IPS), despite its consistent alignment with Soviet foreign policy goals.

The Washington School, founded by the IPS in 1978, was an important means of influencing Congress and the Democratic Party. Courses were held at the school on defense, foreign affairs, and domestic policies, taught by IPS officers and staffers, and other American or foreign radical "experts."

Many members of Congress and staffers attended the schools. Several legislators also taught there, including DSA comrades Ron Dellums and John Conyers,[7] and lone Republican Mark Hatfield.[8]

IPS celebrated its 20th anniversary with an April 5, 1983, reception at the National Building Museum attended by approximately 1,000 IPS staffers and former staff. Among those serving on the IPS 20th Anniversary Committee were Senators Chris Dodd (D-CT) and Gary Hart (D.-CO), with an endorsement provided by Senator Mark Hatfield (R-OR).[9]

Degrading America's Military

Through his career, Senator Hatfield worked consistently to undermine and defund the US Military, and US military operations.

According to Laurence Arnold of Bloomberg:

> In 1970, Hatfield partnered with Democratic Senator George McGovern of South Dakota to propose legislation that would have set a deadline for the end of US military operations in Vietnam. Strongly opposed by President Richard Nixon, the so- called McGovern-Hatfield amendment was defeated, 55 to 39...
>
> As chairman of the Senate Appropriations Committee for the first six years of Ronald Reagan's presidency, he succeeded in diverting $100 billion from Reagan's military buildup to social programs. He joined Democrats in mocking Reagan's plans for the space-based missile-defense system known as Star Wars...
>
> He opposed development of the mobile, multiple-warhead nuclear MX missile, which he deemed 'a monument to madness.'

In 1986 he criticized as an 'immoral act' the US bombing raid on Libya."[10]

In 1979 during the Strategic Arms Limitation Treaty (SALT II) debate, Senator Hatfield introduced an amendment that called for a "strategic weapons freeze"

Senator Mark Hatfield

As tensions between Soviet Union and the United States increased, and weapons numbers increased on both sides, Hatfield and other legislators "heard from their constituents", who "sought a way off the escalatory ladder and were calling for a 'nuclear freeze' with the Soviet Union on the testing, production, and deployment of nuclear warheads and delivery systems".

President Ronald Reagan understood that Soviets would likely cheat on any agreement to gain an advantage over the United States, as they had done with virtually every previous agreement.

According to the Arms Control Association:

We heard from people at every stop who knew about the nuclear freeze proposal and wanted us to support it. 'Why not?' they asked. We found that question difficult to answer, Hatfield and Senator Edward Kennedy (D-Mass.) later explained in their 1982 book Freeze! How You Can Help Prevent Nuclear War. 'A new arms control initiative was needed to offer leadership in Congress and respond to the growing public concern,' they wrote.[11]

President Reagan publicly stated that "the originating organization" for the freeze was the communist World Peace Council; and that the first person to propose it was Soviet leader Leonid Brezhnev.[12]

But Representative Markey was a big supporter of the Nuclear Weapons Freeze Campaign and a close friend of campaign spokeswoman Randall Forsberg.[13]

The Soviet Union is gone, but Putin's Russia and the Chinese Communist Party remain better armed than ever. Certain US Senators still promote US nuclear disarmament.

On February 27, 2014, Senators Ed Markey (D-MA) and Jeff Merkley (D-OR) introduced S. 2070, the Smarter Approach to Nuclear Expenditures (SANE Act) of 2014. The bill would "save US taxpayers about $100 billion over ten years by scaling down, delaying, or canceling a variety of nuclear weapons programs and facilities."[14]

Markey and Merkley's SANE Act was named for disarmament legislation promoted in the 1980s by SANE, A Citizens' Organization for a Sane World, which worked very closely with the Nuclear Weapons Freeze Campaign.[15]

COUNCIL FOR A LIVABLE WORLD

Like his mentor Mark Hatfield, Jeff Merkley works very closely with the pro-US Disarmament organization Council for a Livable World (CLW).

In 1970, the FBI internally published a top-secret memo entitled "Contacts Between Representatives of the Soviet Union and Members or Staff Personnel of the United States Congress Internal Security – Russia".

The memo stated:

> A review of information we have developed through our coverage of Soviet officials and establishments in Washington, D. C., has disclosed a continuing interest by representatives of the Union of Soviet Socialist Republics (USSR) to maintain contacts with and cultivate members or staff personnel of the U. S. Congress. There appears below a compilation of such contacts which have come to our attention from January 1, 1967, to date:'

UNITED STATES DEPARTMENT OF JUSTICE

FEDERAL BUREAU OF INVESTIGATION

WASHINGTON, D.C.

July 28, 1970

CONTACTS BETWEEN REPRESENTATIVES OF THE
SOVIET UNION AND MEMBERS OR STAFF PERSONNEL
OF THE UNITED STATES CONGRESS
INTERNAL SECURITY - RUSSIA

A review of information we have developed through
our coverage of Soviet officials and establishments in
Washington, D. C., has disclosed a continuing interest by
representatives of the Union of Soviet Socialist Republics
(USSR) to maintain contacts with and cultivate members or
staff personnel of the U. S. Congress. There appears below
a compilation of such contacts which have come to our
attention from January 1, 1967, to date:

	Senators	Representatives	Staff Employees
1967	77	33	265
1968	34	23	224
1969	53	10	239
1970 to date	18	6	104

Based on a review of the information disclosed
through our coverage, it appears that Soviet officials are
making more contacts with the following Congressmen or members
of their staff than with other U. S. Legislators:

Senator Edward W. Brooke of Massachusetts
Senator Allen J. Ellender of Louisiana
Senator J. W. Fulbright of Arkansas
Senator Mark O. Hatfield of Oregon
Senator Edward M. Kennedy of Massachusetts
Senator Michael J. Mansfield of Montana
Senator Eugene J. McCarthy of Minnesota
Senator George S. McGovern of South Dakota
Senator Walter F. Mondale of Minnesota
Senator Edmund S. Muskie of Maine
Representative James G. Fulton of Pennsylvania
Representative Robert L. Leggett of California
Representative Donald W. Riegle, Jr., of Michigan

Group 1
Excluded from automatic
downgrading and

DECLASSIFIED

The list did not imply that any of the listed Congressmembers were cooperating with the Soviets, but almost all those listed were on the left on foreign policy and defense issues.

Of those listed, Senators Mark Hatfield of Oregon and Edward Brooke were Republicans. Others listed included future Presidential candidates Ted Kennedy of Massachusetts, Eugene McCarthy and Walter Mondale (both of Minnesota), Ed Muskie of Maine and George McGovern of South Dakota - all Democrats.

Of the Senators listed on the FBI's Soviet contacts memo, six Democrats (Fulbright, Kennedy, McGovern, Muskie, Mondale and Riegle) and the Republicans Brooke and Hatfield were elected with the help of the far-left Council for a Livable World (CLW).

Senator Hatfield was one of a handful of Republicans supported by the Council for Livable World. When the Senator died in 2011, CLW posted a tribute to Mark Hatfield's immensely destructive career:

When Ronald Reagan was elected in 1980, he launched a massive military buildup and abandoned the SALT II nuclear arms treaty. Senator Mark Hatfield was the only Republican Senator to oppose the enormous Reagan military expansion...

Hatfield also led the fight against neutron weapons. In 1984, as chairman of the subcommittee that funded Department of Energy warhead production, he killed the plan to produce 155 mm neutron artillery shells. He was active in the fight against the MX missile, in fact offering the first amendment to kill the new system in 1979 when few were concerned about the issue.

Then there was the fight against the production of deadly new nerve gas weapons requested by President Reagan. Working with Sen. David Pryor (D-AR) and a bipartisan pair in the House, the two Senators fought the Reagan Administration to a draw for several years.

In 1992, Hatfield helped lead the fight that stopped United States nuclear testing. His amendment with Sen. Jim Exon (D-NE) calling for a nine-month US testing moratorium was approved 55 – 40. After President George H.W. Bush signed the legislation, the United States ended nuclear explosive testing. The moratorium has been in place for nearly 20 years.[16]

The Council has funded and endorsed several Merkley campaigns. The Senator also regularly attends CLW events.

In October 2009, Senator Merkley keynoted a CLW fundraiser at the Cambridge Massachusetts home of Abby Rockefeller and Lee Halprin – both incidentally long-time funders of Democratic Socialists of America.[17]

council for
A LIVABLE WORLD

Please join Abby Rockefeller and Lee Halprin at a party to benefit
Council for a Livable World and the
Center for Arms Control and Non-Proliferation!

Wednesday, October 21
104 Irving Street • Cambridge, MA 02138
6:30 – 8:30 pm

At the party, Oregon Democratic Senator Jeff Merkley, a nuclear policy expert, and Sarah Sewall of Harvard Kennedy School, a foreign policy adviser to Barack Obama, will lead the discussion

Sponsor: $1,000 (includes two tickets to event)

During the event, Merkley led a discussion with Sarah Sewall of Harvard Kennedy School, a foreign policy adviser to President Barack Obama.

On June 6, 2012, Council for a Livable World, along with its sister organizations "Center for Arms Control and Non-Proliferation" and CLW's "PeacePAC", celebrated the 50th Anniversary of their founding by Leo Szilard.

To mark the anniversary, six sitting senators joined CLW in an afternoon national security forum held in the US Capitol to "speak on the issues [the] Council has been working on for 50 years". Senators Jeff Merkley (D-OR), Jack Reed (D-RI), John Kerry (D-MA), Tom Udall (D-NM), Carl Levin (D-MI) and Ben Cardin (D-MD) all "spoke eloquently on these pressing issues".[18]

From the CLW website:

> Council for a Livable World has a long and close relationship with each of the Senators. They have all been leading advocates in the Senate for sensible national security policies, such as reducing the dangers posed by weapons of mass destruction, reigning in the bloated defense budget, and bringing an end to the War in Afghanistan.
>
> Senator Merkley praised the Council's work on the New START treaty and advocacy for a swift drawdown of US troops in Afghanistan. Senator Merkley has been a Senate leader on this issue. He focused in particular on his work on Afghanistan, noting that the legislative efforts of those opposed to the war have given space to the President to drawdown troops more quickly than he otherwise might have."[19]

From the Council for a Livable World website:

> Council supporters rallied behind Merkley's bid for the Senate, and since his election in November 2008, he has not disappointed. Senator Merkley has consistently earned a perfect 100% rating on Council for a Livable World's scorecard. In the Senate, Merkley has pushed for expediting troop withdrawal from Afghanistan and coordinated with the Council to gather signatures urging the President and Congress to bring the troops home by the end of

2014. Sen. Merkley also strongly opposes indefinite military deten-
tion and was a solid supporter of New START.[20]

As an aside, the START treaty was extended "with no conditions" for five years under Joe Biden in March 2021, as reported at the Center for Strategic and International Studies (CSIS).

> *As one of its first decisions regarding security policy, the Biden administration agreed to extend the New Strategic Arms Reduction Treaty (START) for five years with no conditions.*[21]

The CLW also endorsed Merkley's 2020 US Senate race:

> *Senator Merkley has been one of the Senate's foremost leaders on arms control and nuclear weapons issues. He has either sponsored or cosponsored virtually all bills the Council tracks and speaks out on these issues frequently.*[22]

Soviet agent Leo Szilard established CLW to inflict maximum possible damage on US military capability and preparedness. He would have been quite proud of Senators Hatfield and Merkley.

MERKLEY'S SOCIALIST CONNECTIONS

For many years Jeff Merkley has been close to the US socialist move-ment and to the Bernie Sanders campaigns that arose from it.

Gretchen Kafoury

Merkley was particularly close to well-known Portland socialist politician Gretchen Kafoury. An icon on the Oregon Left, Kafoury spent 20 years in elected office, serving in the Oregon legislature (1977-1983), on the Multnomah County Commission (1985-1990), and on the Portland City Council (1991-1998). She was a champion of "social and economic justice" and a leader in the "affordable housing" move-ment. Kafoury was also a member of first the Democratic Socialist Organizing Committee (DSOC),[23] then served on the steering com-mittee of Portland Democratic Socialists of America.[24]

Jeff Merkley was a leader of low-income housing advocacy

organization Habitat for Humanity during the period Kafoury and her DSA comrades were pushing the "affordable housing" movement.

In January 2013, Senator Jeff Merkley, Gretchen Kafoury - a veritable "who's who" in affordable housing got together to launch a new housing project "Gray's Landing."

Gretchen Kafoury, center, Senator Merkley, right

In 2014, Gretchen Kafoury's old comrade and fellow "housing activist" Steve Rudman[25] initiated an ActBlue fundraiser for Merkley's Senate campaign.

Screenshot of ActBlue Fundraiser

On March 14, 2015, Oregon's Senator Jeff Merkley made the following statement after Gretchen Kafoury passed away:

I'm deeply saddened by the passing of my friend, Gretchen. She was the heart and soul of Portland's affordable housing community. She cared deeply about those who were struggling to get a simple, decent roof over their head, and did everything she could to make that happen, inspiring us all.[26]

21st Century Democrats

The progressive political action committee "21st Century Democrats" based in St. Paul Minnesota has endorsed and funded Jeff Merkley in nearly every election cycle since 2008. He is certainly one of their favorite candidates. 21st Century Democrats focuses on hard-left candidates. For many years the organization was chaired[27] by former St. Paul Minnesota mayor and DSA comrade Jim Scheibel.[28]

From a 21st Century Democrats Jeff Merkley endorsement:

The 21st Century Democrats, a national grassroots organization that supports candidates who fight for working families in the tradition of Paul Wellstone, endorsed Jeff Merkley's campaign for US Senate. Founded to give progressive and populist candidates the support they need to win elections, 21st Century Democrats has grown to become one of the largest political action committees in the nation.

Jeff Merkley has been a leader for progressive values in Oregon and a fighter for working families. 21st Century Democrats enthusiastically supports Jeff's campaign because Jeff brings the courage and skill needed to take our nation in the right direction.[29]

In recent years Senator Merkley has affiliated himself closely with the Bernie Sanders movement and its radical nationwide support network Our Revolution.

Merkley was the only US Senator to endorse Bernie Sanders in 2016,[30] a move that endeared him to DSA comrades. Our Revolution is essentially a front for DSA, though in some areas the Communist Party USA also participates.[31]

Jeff Merkley is a regular at Our Revolution events all over the country – mixing with socialists and communists wherever he goes.

Here he is with California DSA and Our Revolution comrades Brandon Harami[32] and Zenaida Huerta:[33]

Our Revolution endorsed and supported Jeff Merkley in his 2020 US Senate race.[34]

It was the least they could do.

THE PHILIPPINES CONNECTION

For more than 70 years, the Communist Party of the Philippines (CPP) has been fighting a protracted "People's War" against the Philippines state.

Originally a hardline Maoist party, the CPP has split many times into an "alphabet soup" of sometimes competing, sometimes cooperating revolutionary organizations. While the rump of the CPP is still fighting a guerilla war in the countryside, a diverse revolutionary movement has deeply penetrated unions, political parties, churches and civil society.

For many years now, the revolutionary movement has spawned an array of foreign support groups among the overseas Filipino communities and the wider revolutionary left.

The goal of these groups is to funnel overseas money and support into the Philippines revolutionary movement, and to mount slander campaigns against whichever government happens to be in power in Manila at the time. This constant barrage of attack is designed to weaken the Philippines government internally and cause splits between the government in Manila from friendly overseas countries such as Australia, New Zealand, Canada and particularly the United States.

Senator Jeff Merkley is now involved in this movement.

International Coalition for Human Rights in the Philippines

One of the most important international solidarity networks for the Philippines revolution is the International Coalition for Human Rights in the Philippines (ICHRP).[35] Jeff Merkley has aggressively supported their efforts in destabilizing the government.

The organization was founded out of a gathering held in Quezon City, Philippines in July 2013, attended by 168 delegates from 26 countries. At the first ICHRP General Assembly, delegates elected Peter Murphy of Australia to lead the organization going forward.[36] Murphy is a long-time Philippines "solidarity" activist and a life-long socialist.

Peter Murphy joined the Communist Party of Australia in 1975, eventually becoming a National Committee member from 1989 until the party's dissolution in 1991.[37] Murphy and a group of party die-hards went on to establish the Sydney-based SEARCH Foundation, of which Murphy served as secretary for some years.[38]

According to its website, the SEARCH Foundation "maintains international solidarity with democratic and revolutionary move-ments in Timor-Leste, the Philippines, Zimbabwe, Iran, and in Latin America."[39]

Prior to leading ICHRP, Murphy served as secretary of Philippines Australia Union Link.[40] He then served on the "International Coordinating Committee of International League of Peoples' Struggle", an international communist network chaired by Communist Party of the Philippines founder Jose Maria Sison.[41]

Merkley's ties to the US branch of the ICHRP

One hundred leftist activists from dozens of cities across the US rallied on December 9, 2017 to launch a national campaign against "fascist dictatorship in the Philippines" and form the US branch of the International Coalition for Human Rights in the Philippines (ICHRP-US).

The US head of the ICHRP is iconic Bay Area activist Pam Tau Lee.[42] A life-long Maoist, Pam Tau Lee has been involved in a succession of socialist groups including I Wor Kuen, US-China Friendship Association, Chinese Progressive Association,[43] League of Revolutionary Struggle,[44] and LeftRoots[45] since the early 1970s.

Participants of the ICHRP-US gathering "vowed to strengthen their advocacy for human rights in the Philippines, including Senate Foreign Relations Committee member Senator Jeff Merkley".[46] Senator Merkley was quick to fire off a congratulatory letter, vowing to oppose Philippines President Duterte's "campaign of murder."[47]

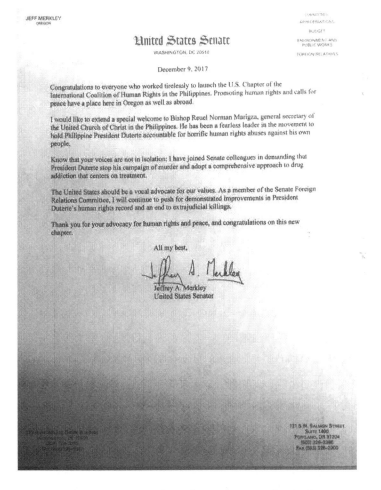

In May 2018, Filipino political activists embarked on an anti-Duterte propaganda tour along the US West Coast.

According to the Willamette Week:

> Since Philippine President Rodrigo Duterte was elected on an anti-drug platform, police have shot thousands of people suspected of using and dealing drugs in alleyways without question.
>
> 'We are exposing the atrocities of the Philippine and US government, especially because the US is intervening in terms of funding our military forces and Philippine national police,' Fritzi Magbanua, one of the guest speakers at the rally, told WW. 'The US is funding us with weapons such as drones and guns, and we don't need that.'
>
> The organizers did get a letter of support from a powerful ally. With his seat in the US Senate Committee for Foreign Affairs, US Sen. Jeff Merkley (D-Ore.) has met with Filipino organizers about policy changes and appeals.[48]

Jagjit Nagra, a field representative from Merkley's office, gave a statement on behalf of the senator:

> Thank you all for coming out today to stand out for an important cause. The International Coalition for Human Rights in the Philippines does important work supporting peace and justice in rejecting the terror and human rights abuses that Philippine President Duterte has perpetrated against his own people.
>
> As you know I have previously joined my Senate colleagues in demanding that President Duterte stop his violence and anti-drug campaign of murder and adopted comprehensive approach to drug addiction that centers on treatment instead of vigilantism.
>
> Using my seat on the Senate foreign relations committee, I will continue to press President Duterte on his human rights record and call on him to end his campaign of extrajudicial killings across the board. I know this is a frightening time. I will continue to work with my colleagues in demanding that the Trump administration join us in condemning instead of rewarding President Duterte's human rights abuses and violations. Thank you for all that you do. I look forward to working with you in the future as well.[49]

In early April 2018, members of ICHRP-Pacific NorthWest, Drew Elizarde-Miller of People Organizing for Philippine Solidarity, and Alma Trinidad of the Malaya Movement and an at-large member of the ICHRP-US National Coordinating Committee, met with Merkley aide Jagjit Nagra.

Left to right: Drew Elizarde-Miller, Jagji Nagra, Alma Trinidad

From the IHCRP-US Facebook page:

> *The US International Coalition for Human Rights in the Philippines representatives pleaded with Merkley's office to throw further support behind the efforts of ICHRP and the Stop the Killings Campaign.*[50]

Later the same month ICHRP introduced Senator Merkley to Filipino tribal activist Fritzi Junance Magbanua in his Washington DC office.

*Junance Mabanua [sic], Lumad indigenous teacher of the Save Our
Schools Philippines met with Senator Jeff Merkley this morning.
Thank you, Senator Jeff Merkley, for your leadership on human
rights in the Philippines #StoptheKillings #SolidarityisOurDuty.*

Fritzi Junance Magbanua

In April 2019, members of ICHRP-PNW and Malaya Movement
"met with the offices of Senator Ron Wyden (D-OR) and Senator Jeff
Merkley to demand justice for the victims of the tyrannical Duterte
regime and call for a Senate hearing to expose the role US military aid has in perpetuating egregious human rights abuses against
Filipino people".

 ICHRP PNW is with **Fredi Mikay** and **Raymond De Vera Palatino**.   •••
April 18, 2019 · ❸

Members of ICHRP PNW and Malaya Movement met with the offices of Senator Ron Wyden (D,
OR) and Senator Jeff Merkley (D, OR) to demand justice for the victims of the tyrannical Duterte
regime and call for a Senate hearing to expose the role US military aid has in perpetuating
egregious human rights abuses against Filipino people. We were joined by two guest from the
Philippines who shared about the exploitative conditions of Filipino workers, the rapid decline of
press freedoms under Rodrigo Duterte, and their experiences organizing on the frontlines for the
interests of workers and the urban poor. Ed Cubelo is the Chairman of the Metro Manila chapter
of Kilusang Mayo Uno, and Mong Palatino is the founder of the Kabataan Party Playlist and is the
current Chair of Bayan Metro Manila.

No Red Tagging

On July 3, 2020, the Philippines government passed the Anti-Terrorism Act which made it easier to target "legal" organizations covertly aiding the revolutionary movement. The Filipino Left promptly condemned this crack-down on supporters of communism and terrorism" as "red-tagging."

Senator Jeff Merkley personally reached out to Philippines Ambassador Jose Manuel Romualdez, who wrote an op-ed to counter the Senator's criticisms.[51]

In August 2021, leftist Democrat Senators led by Ed Markey (D-MA) and including Jeff Merkley wrote to the Biden administration to condemn "at the highest levels" the alleged "continuing pattern of human rights violations" under the Duterte administration.

The senators condemned the alleged "red-tagging" of individuals and groups "falsely accused of terrorism and communism, in an effort to stifle criticism and freedom of expression."[52]

In May 2022, Merkley and several others again attacked "red-tagging" in a letter to the US State Department, after the election of new Philippines President Ferdinand Marcos, Jr.:

> By publicly naming and threatening people who are advocating for basic rights such as land reform, labor rights, or environmental protection, the government puts them under threat of harm and violence, they wrote. This practice is abhorrent. We encourage the United States to vociferously push back against this practice and work with the new Philippine administration to stop its use and make amends to those who have been harmed.[53]

The letter also criticized incoming President for the alleged sins of his father, the late President Ferdinand Marcos, Sr.:

> The election of Ferdinand Marcos Jr., even though expected, is undoubtedly jarring and traumatic to those who experienced the violence, rampant corruption, and cronyism of his father and namesake who brutally ruled the country for two decades… we must discourage the new Philippines administration from following in the steps of the Marcos Sr. dictatorship or the current president or engaging in revisionist history.[54]

In February 2022, a coalition of eleven Oregon leftist groups, including ICHRP-Portland, Rogue Climate and Families for Climate, wrote to Senator Merkley, urging him to introduce the Philippines Human Rights Act (PHRA) into the US Senate.

The letter equated President Duterte's indifference to the coalition's environmental agenda to "fascism":

> As Oregonians, we call on you to stand up to global fascism and recognize this bill as a crucial step towards global climate justice, accountability, protection of lands, and human rights. There is no climate justice without human rights. There is no climate justice under state-sanctioned fascist violence. Please be a champion for human rights and environmental justice by introducing the Philippine Human Rights Act into the US Senate.[55]

This Act would suspend "security assistance to the Philippines until violence against dissidents ceases and accountability against the perpetrators commences."[56]

In other words, this is a communist protection act.

Similar slander campaigns, often coupled with the last-minute withdrawal of US military support, have been used to destroy many anti-communist governments in the past – from China and Vietnam to Cuba and Nicaragua, and many others.

Will Senator Merkley's efforts condemn the people of the Philippines to a similar fate?

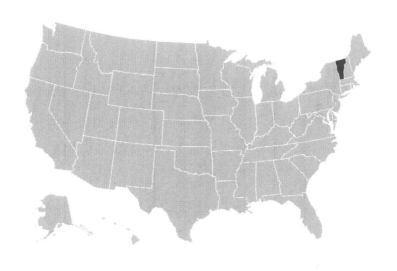

SENATORS FROM THE STATE OF
VERMONT

PATRICK LEAHY

PATRICK LEAHY IS THE SENIOR US SENATOR FROM VERMONT

BACKGROUND

PATRICK LEAHY WAS elected in 1974 at the age of 34 on the Democratic Party ticket. He graduated from Saint Michael's College in 1961 with his B.A. and earned his J.D. from Georgetown University Law Center in 1964. He is the president pro tempore of the Senate.[1]

INFLUENCE

Patrick Leahy chairs the Committee on Appropriations. He serves on the Joint Committee on the Library, as well as the Committee on Rules and Administration and the Committee on Agriculture, Nutrition, and Forestry. Leahy chairs the Subcommittee on Intellectual Property on the Committee on the Judiciary.[2] Leahy is also the co-chair of the Senate National Guard Caucus and co-founder and co-chair of the Congressional Internet Caucus.[3]

'LEAKY LEAHY': THE 'ANTI-ANTI-COMMUNIST'

Leaking intelligence to strategically selected journalists to undermine classified information is a potentially dangerous tactic. Yet, Senator

Patrick Leahy made the practice an art form during Ronald Reagan's presidency, where he revealed himself as both an "anti-anti-communist" and a security risk. He deservedly earned the nickname "Leaky Leahy".

Columnist Geoff Metcalf provided a brief overview of Senator Leaky Leahy's record of divulging secrets:

> Senator Pat Leahy was annoyed with the Reagan administration's war on terrorism in the 1980s. At the time he was vice chairman of the Senate Intelligence Committee. Therefore, 'Leaky Leahy,' threatened to sabotage classified strategies he didn't like.
>
> Leahy 'inadvertently' disclosed a top-secret communications intercept during a 1985 television interview. The intercept had made possible the capture of the Arab terrorists who had hijacked the cruise ship Achille Lauro and murdered American citizen. But Leahy's leak cost the life of at least one Egyptian 'asset' involved in the operation.
>
> In July 1987, it was reported that Leahy leaked secret information about a 1986 covert operation planned by the Reagan administration to topple Libya's Moammar Gaddhafi. US intelligence officials stated that Leahy sent a written threat to expose the operation directly to then-CIA Director William Casey. Weeks later, news of the secret plan turned up in the Washington Post, causing it to be aborted.

Los Angeles Times

Leahy Discloses He Quit Panel Over His Own Leak

L.A. TIMES ARCHIVES
JULY 29, 1987 12 AM PT

ASSOCIATED PRESS

WASHINGTON — Sen. Patrick J. Leahy (D-Vt.) disclosed Tuesday that he resigned from the Senate Intelligence Committee last January because he was responsible for the leak of a draft staff report on the panel's Iran-*contra* investigation.

A year later, as the Senate was preparing to hold hearings on the Iran-Contra scandal, Leahy had to resign his Intelligence Committee post after he was caught leaking secret information to a reporter. The Vermont Democrat's Iran-Contra leak was considered to be one of the most serious breaches of secrecy in the committee's 28-year history. After Leahy's resignation, the Senate Intelligence Committee decided to restrict access to committee documents to a security-enhanced meeting room.[4]

LEAHY SIDES WITH NICARAGUAN COMMUNISTS

In the 1980s, Leahy traveled to Nicaragua[5] and was a leading opponent of the anti-communist Nicaraguan Contra fighters. Leahy did his best to ruin the Contra's reputation and used his Senate majority to cut US military aid.

From the Washington Post:

> *Critics of US aid to anti-government rebels in Nicaragua have the votes in the Senate to halt the program, Sen. Patrick J. Leahy (D-Vt.) said yesterday.*
>
> *Emerging from an intelligence committee meeting with Secretary of State George P. Shultz, Leahy said, 'I think the administration is finally getting the picture that there will be no more covert aid.'*
>
> *Leahy, who is committee vice chairman, said many senators are concerned about atrocities allegedly committed by the rebels, known as 'contras,' against Nicaraguan civilians.*
>
> *'I'm convinced there aren't enough votes in the Senate for a further covert action program,' he continued. 'The administration is going to have to stop trying to substitute a covert action program for foreign policy.'*[6]

In 1990, Senator Leahy joined with Senator Robert Byrd (D-WV) in spearheading the fight to cut $500 million out of an emergency aid package that President George H.W. Bush had requested for anti-communist initiatives in Panama and Nicaragua.

In addition, Leahy and Senator Chris Dodd (D-CT) co-sponsored legislation to cut US aid to the government of El Salvador, which was at war against Marxist-Leninist militias backed by Cuba and the Soviet Union.[7]

Senators Leahy and Dodd also successfully blocked US military aid to the Colombian military, in their war against a major Marxist insurgency. Again, Leahy accused the Colombian military of "human rights violations."[8]

CUBA'S BEST FRIEND IN THE US SENATE

For nearly 60 years the Cuban communist regime has been heavily sanctioned by the US Government. US citizens have been deeply restricted in their ability to travel to or trade with the communist island. Cuba is deservedly on the US State Department's State

Sponsors of Terrorism list, alongside Syria, Iran, and North Korea.[9]

These restrictions have hampered the Cuban Communist Party's ability to foment trouble in the United States and to spread communist revolution in the Southern Hemisphere. Consequently, the Cuban regime and its American allies have long fought to end US restrictions on the island.

Senator Leahy and Cuban President Fidel Castro in Havana in 1999.

Generally speaking, Republican - and one or two moderate Democrat - legislators have opposed lifting the sanctions, while the majority of Democrats and a handful of left-leaning Republicans plus President Obama, fought to lift sanctions.

After helping several countries in Latin America down the socialist road, Senator Leahy turned his attention to aiding communist Cuba. Senator Leahy has been one of the true champions in the subversive effort to make life easier for Cuba's communist leaders.

Senator Leahy's first known visit to Cuba was in 1999. During that trip, he and his wife dined with Cuban leader Fidel Castro for five hours, according to Jasper Craven of the "VT Digger," a Vermont news organization.[10]

The Elian Gonzalez Affair

In 2000, Patrick Leahy, along with Senator Chris Dodd, fought to return six-year-old Elian Gonzalez to his Cuban father, Juan Miguel. Gonzalez was a Cuban boy found off the coast of Florida after his mother Elizabeth Brotons Rodríguez attempted to flee the communist country with the child and 14 refugees in a small boat November

1999. Tragically, Elian's mother drowned, the child was found, treated in America, and released to his great-uncle Lázaro González in Miami. Ultimately, Elian was forcibly removed by the Justice Department during a predawn raid from his family in Miami and returned to his father in Cuba. Patrick Leahy's friend and attorney Greg Craig represented Juan Miguel.

Patrick Leahy took aim at the family in Miami. "All of this could have been avoided if the family had thought first and foremost about what was best for the child and not what was worst for Castro," Leahy was quoted as saying.[11] During a press conference[12] defending the decision to forcibly remove Elian Gonzalez from his family in Miami, Leahy said in part:

> ...on the question of family reunion, family — family values are the most important values in our country. We lost sight — or many lost sight of the fact that one of those family values was to have a child back with his father, and that family value has been carried out.

Travels to Cuba

Patrick Leahy had proven himself to be a "trusted source for President Barack Obama in the early stages of negotiations with Castro's brother, Raul," Craven of VT Digger wrote. And in 2012, Senator Leahy was back in Cuba, where he attended a two-hour meeting with President Raul Castro. Leahy also visited USAID worker Alan Gross, who was jailed in 2009 for illegally distributing communications equipment on the island while on a US-funded "democracy-building program." Leahy offered to take Gross back to the US with him, but Castro refused.[13]

Senator Leahy arrived back in Cuba on February 18, 2013, in order "to gauge the island's economic changes and to lobby on behalf of Alan Gross."

The trip was described in the Cuban press as "laying the groundwork that could lead to reestablishing diplomatic relations and bilateral trade is the far greater challenge to the Obama and Castro administrations".

"Every one of us has an interest in Cuba," Leahy told the foreign press upon his arrival to Havana. "We all want to see relations improve and both sides take steps in that direction."

The delegation also included left-leaning Republican Senator Jeff Flake, and Democrat senators Sherrod Brown, Debbie Stabenow and Sheldon Whitehouse and Democrat members of Congress James McGovern (Massachusetts) and Chris Van Hollen from Maryland, Alan Gross's home state.[14]

Senator Patrick Leahy, President Raul Castro

In June 2015, Reuters reported on yet another Cuba visit:

> *Senators Patrick Leahy of Vermont and Ben Cardin (D-MD) joined Republican Dean Heller of Nevada on a trip to Havana where they met First Vice-President Miguel Diaz-Canel, Foreign Minister Bruno Rodriguez and ordinary Cubans, as reported at Reuters.*
>
> *'We think that can be achieved this year and we can make additional progress next year,' Cardin told a news conference. 'We're optimistic this path that President Obama and President Castro started will be continued.'*
>
> *Heller, one of a few Republican senators to side with Obama on Cuba, encouraged members of Congress to visit Cuba and engage with ordinary Cubans. 'I think the Senate can move the House, but the Senate's going to have to act first,' Heller told Reuters after the news conference.[15]*

Two months after Leahy's June visit to Cuba, Obama ordered the re-opening of the US Embassy in Havana. "Finally, after 55 years a failed, punitive and ineffective policy of isolation is ending," Leahy declared in a statement. "I commend President Obama and President Castro for this historic step which signifies the formal beginning of a new and more constructive chapter in US–Cuban relations," he said in part.[16]

Joining Senator Patrick Leahy at the Embassy opening were Barbara Boxer (D-CA), Amy Klobuchar (D-MN), and Jeff Flake (R-AZ), and far-left Reps Barbara Lee (D-CA), Steve Cohen (D-TN), Jim McGovern (D-MA) and Karen Bass (D-CA).[17]

Senator Leahy was also at the July 2015 celebrations for the newly re-established Cuban embassy in Washington, DC.

Phyllis Bennis

Phyllis Bennis is a former member of the Maoist revolutionary group "Line of March".

"It's an amazing moment," gushed Bennis to the Washington Post at the time:

> In the decades-long effort to normalise relations with Cuba, to stop the US attacks and hostility toward Cuba, we have not had so many victories. Suddenly we have a victory. The flag going up - that's huge.[18]

Bennis is now with the Cuba-friendly Institute for Policy Studies.

The Cuban Five

Senator Patrick Leahy played a pivotal role in the freeing of the "Cuban Five" - a group of Cuban intelligence officers jailed for spying on Cuban exiles in Florida.

According to far-left news organization Democracy Now:

> Leahy... played a pivotal role in the secret negotiations between the United States and Cuba and helped with the release of the Cuban Five. Leahy made headlines in 2014 when it was revealed that Leahy helped the wife of one of the members of the Cuban Five become pregnant. Gerardo Hernández, the baby's father, is one of

the three former Cuban intelligence agents released in December as part of a prisoner swap amidst thawing ties with Cuba.

While he was not allowed conjugal visits, Hernández was able to impregnate his wife by having his frozen sperm transferred to her in Panama, a process authorized by US officials, funded by the Cuban government, and facilitated by a staffer for Leahy.[19]

Thwarting Cuban Sanctions

Senator Leahy was very frank with Amy Goodman of Democracy Now about the incredible secrecy and subterfuge involved in subverting the long-standing US sanctions against Cuba:

> *The [Cuban] foreign minister could come to the Cuban U.N. Mission without getting permission, in New York. So. I'd meet him there… But then we had others who would go to Canada. And the Canadians deserve a great deal of credit because they set a venue where Cubans and US negotiators could meet secretly in Canada and negotiate.*
>
> *Then, I sent a letter to the pope before he met with the president. The president thought he heard some of my talking points. The pope sends a letter back to Cardinal Ortega in Havana, who brings it to the president in the White House, tells a great story of walking in a room. A man walks up to him and says, 'Hello, Cardinal, I'm Barack Obama.' He said, 'I knew who he was.' But these are all step-by-steps.*
>
> *One of the most important, the so-called accidental handshake between President Obama and President Castro at Nelson Mandela's funeral. There was no accident. President was criticized for it. I said, "Nelson Mandela, if he had been at a world leader's funeral, he would have shook hands even with enemies." And then the meeting they had in Panama, both got along very well.*[20]

Does Senator Patrick Leahy qualify as a Cuban agent?

Ongoing Visits to Cuba

In March 2016 President Obama and Secretary of State John Kerry led a triumphant delegation to Havana to symbolize "improving" US-Cuba relations.

President Obama poses with Che Guevara mural

The President was accompanied by the House Leader Nancy Pelosi and 15 other mainly far-left House Democrats. Senator Leahy, of course led the Senate delegate, all Democrats except for the lone Republican Jeff Flake of Arizona.[21]

In February 2017, one month after anti-communist President Donald Trump was inaugurated, Senator Patrick Leahy led a delegation to Havana. The program for their visit was not disclosed.[22] Perhaps there was a little panic after the unexpected election of President Trump?

Exactly a year later, Senator Leahy was back in Havana leading yet another delegation of far-left Democratic legislators. This time, Leahy's delegation met with Carlos Fernandez de Cossio, the newly appointed director for United States in the Cuban Foreign Ministry. The lawmakers were reportedly on a "fact-finding trip" concerning "changes in the Cuba policy introduced by the Trump administration".[23]

The Trump years were hard for America's Cuban Communist Party enablers. The new Administration reversed many of Obama's Cuba policies.

Senator Leahy, center meets Cuban Foreign Ministry officials

On February 4, 2021, two weeks after President Trump had left office, Senate Finance Committee Chair Ron Wyden (D-OR) introduced the US-Cuba Trade Act of 2021 to repeal sanctions on Cuba and establish normal trade relations with the communist dictatorship. Senators Patrick Leahy, Dick Durbin (D-IL), and Jeff Merkley (D-OR) cosponsored the bill.[24]

The revolution must be delayed no longer.

THE VIETNAM SCAM

Senator Patrick Leahy has also assisted, whether consciously or not, with a major deception operation perpetrated by the Communist Party of Vietnam and their American allies.

Since 2005, the Vietnam Agent Orange Relief & Responsibility Campaign (VAORRC) has been lobbying US legislators to pay major "reparations" to the communist government of Vietnam.

From the VAORRC website:

> *The US government used Agent Orange, from 1962 to 1971, as part of their war in Vietnam...Now even more than thirty years after the war, Agent Orange remains in the land and water of Vietnam, causing horrific birth defects to several generation of children.*

- *We support the Vietnamese Agent Orange survivors and their representative, the Vietnam Association for Victims of Agent Orange/Dioxin in their lawsuit against the US chemical companies. Their lawsuit is a historic first effort by Vietnamese victims of Agent Orange to achieve compensation from the manufacturers who profited from this chemical warfare.*

- *We call upon our government to meet its responsibility to compensate the more than three million Vietnamese people suffering from the effects of Agent Orange. The US government has a moral and legal obligation to heal the wounds of war.*

  Our Campaign will continue until justice for Vietnamese Agent Orange victims is achieved by winning significant US government compensation.[25]

VAORRC are masters at playing on human emotions. Their website and materials are plastered with images of heartbreaking photos of severely disabled children.

Their arguments sound almost reasonable until one considers a few important points.

Firstly, the North Vietnamese communists started the war by invading America's ally South Vietnam. 58,000 Americans died attempting to defend South Vietnam from brutal communist aggression.

Secondly, the Vietnam Association for Victims of Agent Orange/ Dioxin (VAVA) which runs this campaign from the Vietnamese end, is controlled by that country's communist party.

Thirdly, the VAORRC is led and run by strongly anti-American Marxist activists.

The VAORRC board is a radical as you can get. It is led by Marxists from Committees of Correspondence for Democracy and Socialism, the Institute for Policy Studies, Liberation Road, LeftRoots, National Lawyers Guild and the old CIA-identified Soviet front International Association for Democratic Lawyers.[26]

Listed VAORRC board members include:[27]

+ Phyllis Bennis (mentioned above) - Institute for Policy Studies[28]
+ Marjorie Cohn – National Lawyers Guild, International Association for Democratic Lawyers[29]
+ Bill Fletcher, Jr. - Institute for Policy Studies, Liberation Road[30]
+ Jeanne Mirer – National Lawyers Guild, International Association for Democratic Lawyers[31]
+ Walter Teague - Committees of Correspondence for Democracy and Socialism[32]
+ Claire Tran - Liberation Road,[33] LeftRoots[34]
+ Merle Ratner - Committees of Correspondence for Democracy and Socialism,[35] LeftRoots[36]

VAORRC works by bringing disabled Vietnamese children, alleged Agent Orange victims, for sympathy visits with US legislators and civic groups.

VAORRC and VAVA delegation on Capitol Hill

November 14, 2019 | Legislation

Congresswoman Rashida Tlaib (MI-13) met with VAVA member Tran Thi Hoan, and VAORRC delegation, Jeanne Mirer, Merle Ratner, and Paul Cox (featured image, top).

In return, US legislators are sent on tours to Vietnam courtesy of the Vietnam Association for Victims of Agent Orange/Dioxin, where they are introduced to more deformed and disabled alleged Agent Orange victims and shown through treatment facilities.

Senator Leahy has a decades-long history of aiding Vietnamese communism. He was at least partially responsible for the defeat of South Vietnam in 1975.

From the Vermont Digger:

> Within weeks of his swearing in, on April 17, 1975, Leahy, then the most junior member of Senate Armed Services Committee, cast the deciding vote in the panel to cut off funding for the Vietnam War.
>
> The vote took place 13 days before the fall of Saigon, and President Gerald Ford asked Congress for $722 million to help support the South Vietnamese army in its battle against the North Vietnam army and the Viet Cong.
>
> "I personally, and I realize this is not necessarily the feelings of the majority of the committee, I personally would then not give any further money to South Vietnam for military purposes," he added. Congress then took no action despite Ford's request, and American soldiers were evacuated from the country shortly thereafter.[37]

Leahy's vote killed the last hope for a free Vietnam.

Leahy and VAORRC

Senator Leahy has a long and deep connection to VAORRC. From the VAORRC blog November 30, 2021:

> *November 15, 2021: Sen. Patrick Leahy (Vermont) the president pro tempore of the Senate, longest-serving member in the chamber, third in the Line of Succession and five-time cameo in Batman films announced he will not seek reelection in 2022, concluding his final term in the Senate after nearly five decades. We have worked with Senator Leahy and his staff since the beginning of the Agent Orange campaign and thank him for his hard work and dedication to realizing US responsibility to those affected by Agent Orange.*

Senator Patrick Leahy at a ceremony marking U.S. humanitarian aid to victims of Agent Orange in Bien Hoa last month. NGUYEN THAC PHUONG/USAID

From the VAORRC website

> *This is also the time to acknowledge the contributions of Tim Rieser, the Democratic Clerk for the Senate Appropriations Subcommittee on State and Foreign Operations. He has worked for Senator Leahy since 1985 and can be credited with drafting many of the Senate's best laws during that time, including the 1992 law that banned the use of land mines.*
>
> *He helped secure funds to mitigate Agent Orange's human and environmental damage and to eliminate the dangers of unexploded ordnance in Vietnam, Laos, and Cambodia.*[38]

In April 2019, Senator Leahy wrote a column about reconciliation with Vietnam that included "taking responsibility" for the devastation caused by Agent Orange and other herbicides.

Republished on the VARRC blog:

> **Introduction** *Senator Leahy this week is heading an official bipartisan US Senate delegation of nine senators to Vietnam and to the Korea DMZ, during the current Senate recess. On Wednesday Leahy and the delegation will take part in the official inauguration of a second Agent Orange remediation project in Vietnam.*
>
> *Leahy has led the congressional work in launching and funding the two remediation projects, which address one of the most difficult legacies of the Vietnam War. These Leahy-led projects have been key elements in helping to forge the strong new relationship between the United States and Vietnam.*
>
> **Senator Leahy** *My involvement with post-war Vietnam began in 1989, when former President George H. W. Bush and I talked about the need for reconciliation with Vietnam – something that many Americans, including veterans, were calling for. President Bush agreed to use what was later named the Leahy War Victims Fund to provide prosthetics and wheelchairs to Vietnamese who were disabled from landmines and other unexploded bombs...*
>
> *Over the years I had many conversations with Vietnamese officials, before and after diplomatic relations were reestablished in 1995. No matter what the subject of those conversations was, the Vietnamese always brought up Agent Orange, and its effects on their people...*

Senator Leahy with Vietnamese President Nguyen Phu Trong

We started at the Da Nang Airport, a former US military base where Agent Orange, contaminated with dioxin, had been stockpiled. The US Agency for International Development (USAID) deserves great credit for undertaking and completing such a complex, difficult, and ultimately successful project to decontaminate 100,000 cubic meters of soil and sediment. The Vietnamese Ministry of Defense worked closely with USAID to overcome many obstacles to complete the project...

On April 17th I will arrive in Vietnam for the third time, accompanied by 8 senators of both political parties. This time we will travel to the Bien Hoa Air Base near Ho Chi Minh City, which was the largest US military base in Vietnam during the war. Along with US Embassy and Vietnamese officials, we will inaugurate the remediation project at Bien Hoa, the largest remaining hotspot of dioxin contamination. This will be one of the largest environmental remediation projects in the world.

At the same time, we will witness the signing of an agreement between the United States and Vietnam, spelling out a new 5-year commitment to support health and disabilities programs for persons with disabilities in provinces that were heavily sprayed with Agent Orange.[39]

During the visit to Bien Hoa, Senator Leahy and Senators Stabenow (D-MI), Lisa Murkowski (R-AK), Rob Portman (R-OH), Sheldon Whitehouse (D-RI), Mazie Hirono (D-HI), Tammy Baldwin (D-WI), Tim Kaine (D-VA, and Tom Udall (D-NM) pledged $50 million taxpayer dollars "to assist children and young Vietnamese born with disabilities linked to exposure of a parent, grandparent or great grandparent to Agent Orange/dioxin".

In addition, the senators promised $300 million to "clean up dioxin residues left by Agent Orange at the Bien Hoa Airbase."[40]

Senator Leahy helped bring communism to Vietnam in 1975 with his vote to abandon America's South Vietnamese allies to the mercies of the northern communist aggressors.

That vote annulled the sacrifice of 58,000 American lives.

Now while American Vietnam veterans struggle to get treatment for their Agent Orange induced diseases, Senator Leahy is using their family's tax-dollars to subsidize the economic recovery of the communist aggressor nation.

All the while working directly with American communists to arrange it. Does that qualify as a scam for the ages?

Senator Leahy retires from the US Senate in January 2023.

His work here is done.

BERNIE SANDERS

BACKGROUND

BERNIE SANDERS (BORN September 8, 1941) has served as the junior United States Senator from Vermont since 2007. He attended Brooklyn College before graduating from the University of Chicago in 1964. As an independent, Sanders was elected mayor of Burlington, Vermont in 1981 and reelected three times. He won election to the US House of Representatives in 1990 and to the US Senate in 2006.

He is married to Jane O'Meara Sanders.[1]

INFLUENCE

Bernie Sanders is the Chair of the Committee on the Budget. Sanders chairs the subcommittee on Primary Health and Retirement Security for the Committee on Health, Education, Labor and Pensions, where he also sits on the subcommittee on Children and Families.

He is a member of the Committee on Energy and Natural Resources, where he sits on subcommittees on Energy; Natural Parks; and Water and Power. Further, Sanders sits on the Committee on Veterans' Affairs, and the Committee on Environment and Public Works, where he sits on the subcommittees on Chemical Safety, Waste Management, Environmental Justice, and Regulatory Oversight; Clean Air, Climate, and Nuclear Safety; and Transportation and Infrastructure.[2]

A SOCIALIST LIFE

Was there ever a time in Bernie Sanders' life when he was not a Marxist revolutionary?

Early radicalism

After a year at Brooklyn College, Bernie Sanders spent four years at the University of Chicago, where he joined the Young Peoples Socialist League – (the youth wing of the Socialist Party USA), the far-left dominated Congress of Racial Equality and the Student Peace Union.[3] He also worked briefly for the communist-led United Packinghouse Workers Union.[4]

Bernie Sanders protesting segregation, Chicago, circa 1964

Sanders went on to spend several months in 1963 working on Kibbutz Sha'ar Ha'amakim near Haifa in northern Israel, as a guest of the Hashomer Hatzair youth movement. Other socialist groups described Hashomer Hatzair as Leninist or Stalinist – the group openly pledged allegiance not to Israel but to the Soviet Union.[5]

The commune's founder, Ya'akov Hazan, described the Soviet Union as a second homeland and eulogized Stalin.[6]

Kibbutz co-founder Aharon Cohen, who was a regular critic of Israel and opponent of its policy, was jailed for five years after illegally meeting a Soviet "diplomat".[7]

VERMONT ACTIVISM

Like thousands of other anti-Vietnam War activists and hippies, Bernie Sanders moved to Vermont in the mid-1960s. He worked as an occasional carpenter and journalist and became active in the far-left Liberty Union Party.

Liberty Union's program included nationalizing all US banks, public ownership of all utilities, ending compulsory education and establishing a worker-controlled government.[8]

Sanders ran for public office on the Liberty Union ticket four times, topping out at 6% of the vote before finally quitting the party in 1977. Sanders began casting around for better options including with his old comrades in the Socialist Party USA.

Bernie Sanders, Socialist Party USA, date unknown

Peter Diamondstone, a co-founder of the Liberty Union Party claims that "[I]n 1980 Sanders wanted to be connected to a socialist name. He asked me to talk to the Socialist Party about getting him the vice-presidential nomination and I did but it was too late, they already nominated someone else".[9]

That year Sanders endorsed a bona fide communist for president: Andrew Pulley of the pro-Cuba Socialist Workers Party.[10]

MARXIST MAYOR

In 1980, Sanders ran for mayor of Burlington, Vermont (population 38,000) winning by only 10 votes. He was mayor for eight years, leaving office in April 1989 to run for Congress.

According to the Socialist Workers Party newspaper "The Militant", less than 24 hours after Sanders was sworn into office, the FBI was in the Vermont Secretary of State's office looking for information on his radical political affiliations.[11]

While Sanders governed Burlington comparatively moderately, his foreign connections more than justified the FBI's concerns.

In his 1997 memoir, "Outsider in the House", Sanders asked, "how many cities of 40,000 have a foreign policy? Well, we did."[12]

Mayor Sanders commented on international issues, supported foreign radical causes, and travelled to communist countries. He made no secret of where his sympathies lay.

In May 1981, Mayor Sanders wrote a letter to British Prime Minister Margaret Thatcher complaining about treatment of Irish Republican Army terrorist prisoners.[13]

Sandernista

Civil war raged in Nicaragua through Sanders entire mayoral tenure. The pro-Soviet Sandinista government was fighting a bitter guerrilla war against US Contra freedom fighters. Bernie Sanders squarely backed the Marxist Sandinistas. He boasted of it in his 1997 biography "Outsider in the House":

> *Many Burlingtonians, including myself, supported the Sandinista government in Nicaragua. President Reagan did not. We disagreed with him. We expressed our displeasure.*

> *Somewhere in the Reagan archives, or wherever these things are kept, is a letter from the mayor of Burlington on this subject. There are also official proclamations from the Burlington Board of Alderman, made after long and emotional public hearings. 'Stop the war against the people of Nicaragua! Use our tax dollars to feed the hungry and house the homeless. Stop killing the innocent people of Nicaragua.'*
>
> *This was an issue that many of us in the progressive movement felt very strongly about. Not only was the war against Nicaragua illegal and immoral, it was an outrageous waste of taxpayer money. As a mayor, I wanted more federal funds for affordable housing and economic development. I did not want to see taxpayer dollars going to the CIA for an appalling war.[14]*

Mayor Sanders did way more to support his Marxist-Leninist heroes than write letters and complain.

In 1985, Sanders travelled to New York City to meet with Nicaragua's pro-Soviet leader Daniel Ortega – shortly after his regime had imposed a "state of emergency" that included mass arrests of regime critics and the closing down of opposition newspapers.

Sanders later said that the Sandinistas' crackdown "makes sense to me."[15]

Sanders also traveled to Nicaragua's capital Managua to give his full moral support to the embattled dictatorship.

According to White House correspondent Hunter Walker:

> *In July 1985, Bernie Sanders traveled to Nicaragua, where he attended an event that one wire report dubbed an 'anti-US rally.'*
>
> *The leftist Sandinista government was celebrating the sixth anniversary of the revolution that saw it take power from an American-backed dictator, Anastasio Somoza. Sanders was in a crowd estimated at a half million people, many of whom were clad in the Sandinistas' trademark red-and-black colors and chanting 'Here, there, everywhere/the Yankee will die.'*
>
> *Onstage, Nicaraguan President Daniel Ortega accused the US government of 'state terrorism' for supporting the rebels who were seeking to overthrow him. The Sandinistas and the CIA-backed Contras would fight into the next decade, with allegations of human rights abuses on both sides. At the 1985 rally Sanders*

attended, Ortega vowed the Sandinistas would 'defend the revolution with guns in hand.'

Sanders was being hosted by the Sandinistas as part of a delegation of American 'solidarity groups.' He told reporters their decision to show 'support' for the Nicaraguan government was 'patriotic.'

'We want to show support for a small country trying to be independent, and we want to tell the truth to the American people when we return,' Sanders said.[16]

Sanders met with President Ortega. He later called the trip "profoundly emotional" and praised the Nicaraguan president. Burlington and Managua became sister cities.

In 1987, Sanders hosted Sandinista politician Nora Astorga in Burlington. Reportedly Astorga had seduced Nicaraguan General Reynaldo Perez-Vega in her apartment. Perez-Vega's body was later found wrapped in a Sandinista flag - his throat cut by his kidnappers. When Astorga died in 1988, Mayor Sanders publicly praised her as a "very vital and beautiful woman..."[17]

Cuba/Soviet Union

Mayor Sanders also visited Cuba in 1989, on a trip organized by the New York-based Center for Cuban Studies – once described by former communist Ronald Radosh as "the semi-official propaganda agency for Castro in the United States".[18]

Sanders tried but failed to meet with Fidel Castro, so he settled for the Mayor of Havana and other officials instead.

When he returned to Burlington, Sanders excitedly reported that Cuba had "solved some very important problems" like hunger and homelessness. "I did not see a hungry child. I did not see any homeless people...Cuba today not only has free healthcare but very high-quality healthcare."[19]

In Bernie Sanders' world, Cubans liked living in a communist dictatorship:

The people we met had an almost religious affection for [Fidel Castro]. The revolution there is far deep and more profound than I understood it to be. It really is a revolution in terms of values.[20]

Sanders would later recall "being very excited when Fidel Castro made a revolution in Cuba…It just seemed right and appropriate that poor people were rising up against a lot of ugly rich people."[21]

Mayor Sanders married his current wife, Jane, in May of 1988 and the following day they left for Yaroslavl, near Moscow in the former Soviet Union. The newlyweds were part of an official delegation from Burlington to cement a Yaroslavl-Burlington sister-city relationship. "Trust me. It was a very strange honeymoon," says Sanders.[22]

Sanders hung a Soviet flag in his mayoral office in Burlington to mark the trip.[23]

RUNNING FOR CONGRESS

In 1988, Sanders ran as an Independent for Vermont's sole congressional seat. He narrowly lost despite a notable endorsement.

In October 1988, iconic journalist I.F. Stone, a former fully recruited Soviet agent,[24] wrote a letter in support of Bernie Sanders' congressional run.

Stone wrote:

> I've been politically active all my life. I was a member of the Executive Committee of the Socialist Party in New Jersey, before I was old enough to vote.
>
> Now I'd like to ask you to join me in a historic step forward in American politics. My favorite Mayor -- Bernie Sanders of Burlington, Vermont -- is running for Congress, and with our help he can win an unprecedented victory for us all.
>
> Bernie is a unique figure in our political system. He's an unapologetic socialist who has been elected Mayor of Vermont's largest city four times. He has proved that a socialist, running as an Independent against the combined opposition of Republicans and Democrats, can be successful by speaking out for working people, the elderly and the poor…
>
> Bernie has been a leader in the struggle for peace and justice. His activism was instrumental in Vermont's strong support of the Nuclear Freeze in its town meetings in 1982. He has traveled to Nicaragua to speak out against the Reagan Administration's war, and to establish a Sister City relation between Burlington and

Puerto Cabezas. More recently, he went to the Soviet Union to set up a Sister City program with Yaroslavl...

Having Bernie in Washington will widen out the limits of political discussion. He'll speak up loudly, as he has in Vermont, for real alternatives. He'll show that we need a pragmatic socialism to deal with the grave problems of our economic system.[25]

I.F. STONE

Dear Friend,

I've been politically active all my life. I was a member of the Executive Committee of the Socialist Party in New Jersey, before I was old enough to vote.

Now I'd like to ask you to join me in a historic step forward in American politics. My favorite Mayor -- Bernie Sanders of Burlington, Vermont -- is running for Congress, and with our help he can win an unprecedented victory for us all.

Bernie is a unique figure in our political system. He's an **unapologetic socialist** who has been elected Mayor of Vermont's largest city <u>four times</u>. He has proved that a socialist, running as an <u>Independent</u> against the combined opposition of Republicans and Democrats, can be successful by speaking out for working people, the elderly and the poor.

Under Bernie's leadership, Burlington has become a vibrant, innovative city, nationally recognized for its accomplishments. The U.S. Conference of Mayors recently gave it the "Most Liveable City" award, and even the conservative <u>U.S. News and World Report</u> has spotlighted Bernie as one of the country's Top Twenty Mayors (December 21, 1987).

Bernie has been a leader in the struggle for peace and justice. His activism was instrumental in Vermont's strong support of the Nuclear Freeze in its town meetings in 1982. He has traveled to Nicaragua to speak out against the Reagan administration's immoral war, and to establish a Sister City relation between Burlington and Puerto Cabezas. More recently, he went to the Soviet Union to set up a Sister City program with Yaroslavl.

While socialism has a long and proud history in America, extending back to the utopian experiments of the early 1800s, it's been a long time since we've had a socialist voice in Congress. Not since Victor Berger of Milwaukee in the twenties, has the debate gone beyond the limits set by the conventional two-party system.

Having Bernie in Washington will widen out the limits of political discussion. He'll speak up loudly, as he has in Vermont, for real alternatives. He'll show that we need a pragmatic socialism to deal with the grave problems of our economic system.

I.F. Stone October 1988

Two years later Sanders ran for the seat again and defeated his Republican opponent by a margin of 56% to 39%.

Sanders was the first independent elected to the US House of Representatives in 40 years. The Washington Post noted that it was the first election of a socialist to the US House of Representatives in decades.[26]

"Open" socialist would have been a more accurate term – there were many covert socialists in the House at the time. And Bernie Sanders was ready to organize them.

THE CONGRESSIONAL PROGRESSIVE CAUCUS

One of Congressman Sanders first projects was to gather far-left Congressmembers into a new grouping, the House Progressive Caucus – now known as the Congressional Progressive Caucus.

The Progressive Caucus was established in 1991 by Sanders and five others - Representatives Ron Dellums (D-CA), Lane Evans (D-IL), Thomas Andrews (D-ME), Peter DeFazio (D-OR) and Maxine Waters (D-CA). Sanders was the convener and first Progressive Caucus Chairman.

One of the original founders, Ron Dellums, was a member of Democratic Socialists of America (DSA).[27] Lane Evans was very close to the organization.[28]

Maxine Waters employed former DSA organizational director Patrick Lacefield[29] as her press secretary and speechwriter.[30]

Additional House members joined soon thereafter, including DSA members Major Owens (D-NY)[31] and future DSA member David Bonior (D-MI).[32]

Representative Sanders clearly already had a relationship with DSA by 1991 because that organization took credit for helping him to initiate the new caucus.

According to Ron Baiman of Chicago DSA:

> [Congressman] Sanders and Representative Barney Frank, both leaders of the Progressive Caucus in Congress which DSA has helped to organize.[33]

Young Democratic Socialists of James Madison University were even more explicit on the "About" page of their late 1990s website:

> DSA is not a political party, but rather works within the left wing of the Democratic Party and other third parties. DSA is a driving

force for the Progressive Caucus in the US House of Representatives
(led by Rep. Bernie Sanders, Socialist Congressman of Vermont).[34]

Influencing Policy

Representative Sanders and DSA worked together through the Progressive Caucus to move socialist policies into the Democratic Party through a series of forums, conferences and policy papers.

For example, on January 9, 1997, over 600 people attended "The Progressive Challenge: Capitol Hill Forum" sponsored by the House Progressive Caucus and DSA.

According to DSA's Democratic Left:

> *The primary goal of this day-long 'kick-off' forum was to 'identify the unifying values shared by progressives at this point in US history, to help define core elements of a forward-looking progressive agenda, and to pinpoint ways to connect that agenda with the concerns of millions of disillusioned people who lack voices in present politics and policy-making.'*[35]

After a welcome by Representative Bernie Sanders, "an impressive array of legislators, activists, and thinkers offered their insights" – most of them affiliated in some way to DSA.

Senator Paul Wellstone (DFL-MN), Reverend Jesse Jackson, Patricia Ireland of NOW, Richard Trumka of the AFL-CIO, Noam Chomsky (DSA), William Greider of Rolling Stone, and DSA Honorary Chair Barbara Ehrenreich were among the many who spoke.[36]

From a DSA membership letter:

> *What virtually all participants acknowledged (thanks in no small part to DSA's role in helping to organize this event and in focusing the activities of the Working Group on Economic Insecurity) was that the centerpiece of a progressive agenda involves addressing the question of the economy and the disruptions, suffering, powerlessness and fear created by the mobility and power of corporations-without glossing over the racism, sexism, xenophobia, homophobia, and other injustices exacerbated by economic uncertainty.*[37]

Next comes a direct admission that DSA and its allies were involved in drafting Democratic Party legislation:

> *The next step at the policy level is a series of briefings for Congressional staff and members on specific issues related to economic justice (global economy, corporate responsibility, and welfare reform are among the topics to be covered). These briefings are planned for January and February, and out of the briefing sessions working groups on the issues will be formed. The working groups will include Congressional staff and progressive organizations who will help draft legislation.*[38]

Then DSA committed to working with "grassroots" activists to sell these socialist policy proposals to the public:

> *The coalition of activist groups is working on plans to bring the issues to the grassroots through a round of town meetings this spring and through the development of a network of progressive elected officials. The town meetings will be modeled on DSA's Public Hearings on Economic Insecurity and the AFL-CIO town meetings of 1996 and will bring Progressive Caucus members together with local activists.*[39]

DSA's influence on the Progressive Caucus was not confined to domestic policy.

According to Democratic Left, Winter 1996:

> *DSA tries to link the US Congressional Progressive Caucus to Parliamentary parties of the left in other countries.*[40]

Today, dozens of Progressive Caucus members have close relationships with DSA, Liberation Road, the Communist Party USA or similar organizations. These groups view the Caucus as a transmission belt for their socialist policies into the Democratic Party.

Consider a 2002 report by Joelle Fishman, Chair, Political Action Committee, Communist Party USA to the Party's National Board, who evaluated the Congressional Progressive Caucus when it was just over half the strength it is today:

> *Although this Caucus is not large enough to control the Congressional agenda or even to break into the media, the existence of this group of 57 members of Congress, which includes 20 members of the Congressional Black Caucus and six members of the Congressional Hispanic Caucus, provides an important lever that can be used to advance workers' issues and move the debate to the left in every Congressional District in the country.*[41]

In a report delivered at the 14th International Meeting of Communist and Workers Parties, held in Beirut, Lebanon, November 22-25, 2012, Erwin Marquit, a member of the International Department of the Communist Party USA explained the role of the steadily growing Progressive Caucus in influencing US Government policy:

> *In our electoral policy, we seek to cooperate and strengthen our relationship with the more progressive elements in Democratic Party, such as the Progressive Caucus in the US Congress, a group of seventy-six members of the Congress co-chaired by Raúl Grijalva, a Latino from Arizona, and Keith Ellison, an African American Muslim from Minnesota...*
>
> *In its domestic policy, for example, the Progressive Caucus has put forth a program for using the public sector to deal with unemployment. It has opposed the use of the so called 'war on terror' to incarcerate US citizens indefinitely without criminal charges. In its foreign policy, the Progressive Caucus and the Black Caucus are outspoken in their opposition to US imperialist policies abroad.*
>
> *The Progressive Caucus, now that Obama has been reelected, will be playing an important role in contributing to the mobilization of mass activity on critical issues to bring pressure on the Congress and administration to act on them...*[42]

Today the Congressional Progressive Caucus is now almost 100 members strong or 40% of the Democratic caucus.

They are responsible for promoting socialist policies such as the Green New Deal [i.e., Inflation Reduction Act], socialized healthcare or "Medicare for All", higher taxes, Greater union power, illegal immigrant amnesty and almost everything else on the DSA/Communist Party USA wish list.

All thanks to Bernie Sanders, who is today the Congressional Progressive Caucus' single Senate member.

THE DSA CONNECTION

Senator Sanders' connections to DSA go well beyond their mutual interest in the Progressive Caucus. DSA has backed Bernie Sanders' political career from his earliest days in Congress through three US Senate campaigns and both presidential runs. It is fair to say that Bernie Sanders would not have acheived any signification polictical influence without DSA.

As early as July 1986, Sanders addressed a DSA-sponsored event in Los Angeles on the situation in Nicaragua.[43]

J. Charles Gardner Reading Times
Robert J. Miller, left, chairman of the Reading-Berks Democratic Socialists, presents the Maurer-Stump Award to Bernard Sanders, independent socialist mayor of Burlington, Vt.

Mayor Bernie Sanders of Burlington Vermont received the third annual Maurer-Stump Award from the Reading-Berks Democratic Socialists, an affiliate of DSA, at a meeting in Pennsylvania, January 1988. Sanders told the Reading Times: "Revolution can be done through the government, if you raise the right issues."[44]

Through the '90s, Sanders addressed multiple DSA events and conferences.

DSA member Stephen Soifer even wrote a book eulogizing Sanders: "The Socialist Mayor: Bernard Sanders in Burlington, Vermont" (Bergin and Garvey).[45]

In July 1996, the DSA Political Action Committee endorsed "Bernard Sanders, Vermont At Large", in that year's Congressional elections.[46]

In an editorial published at the Spring 2000 edition of Democratic Left, DSA confessed:

> *Electoral tactics are only a means for DSA; the building of a powerful anti-corporate and ultimately socialist movement is the end. Where third party or non-partisan candidates represent significant social movements DSA locals have and will continue to build such organizations and support such candidates.*
>
> *DSA honored independent socialist Congressperson Bernie Sanders of Vermont at our last convention banquet, and we have always raised significant funds nationally for his electoral campaigns.*[47]

Bernie Sanders addresses Detroit DSA conference June 2006

DSA Supports Bernie's Senate Run

DSA and Sanders worked closely together through the early 2000s – but everything went up a notch when Sanders committed to running for US Senate in 2006.

DSA's 2005 National Conference in Los Angeles committed the organization to supporting Sanders' 2006 US Senate race-while using the campaign to recruit some new comrades along the way:

> From now through November 2006, the Sanders for Senate campaign in Vermont will focus national media attention on the most serious socialist electoral effort in the United States since the Debsian period. Bernie Sanders has been an articulate voice for democratic socialist politics among the 435 members of the House of Representatives and has spoken at DSA events on many occasions.
>
> Sanders would become a much more visible national spokesperson for socialist politics if and when he serves as one of 100 members of the more powerful United States Senate.
>
> His election is by no means assured and he will need the financial and organizational help of the broad democratic left around the country. In addition, Sanders support work provides a natural vehicle in any locality for DSA to reach out to—and potentially recruit—unaffiliated socialists and independent radicals.
>
> Thus, this convention commits itself to:
>
> a. The national staff and NPC developing feasible, legal, ways that DSA locals, networks, individuals, and campus groups can aid the Sanders for Senate campaign.
>
> b. The national leadership providing guidance as to how local groups engaged in aiding the Sanders campaign can utilize such efforts to recruit for and build DSA.[48]

In the most expensive political campaign in Vermont's history, Sanders defeated his Republican opponent by a 2-to-1 margin.

DSA was ecstatic and Senator Sanders sent a thank you note – which was proudly published on the cover of DSA's Democratic Left Winter 2006 issue.

Mid-Term Elections:
A Time for Hope?

Latin America:
Challenges to Neo-Liberalism

BERNIE AND THE COMMUNISTS

While DSA is Bernie Sanders' greatest love - he has also occasionally flirted with DSA's main "frenemy": the Communist Party USA (CPUSA). Aside from a little jealousy, there was no great conflict here. DSA is a small "c" communist organization. The Communist Party is big "C". The two organizations have collaborated for decades and share some cross-membership. Their policy positions are almost identical. DSA's more innocuous name does however make it a little easier to work inside churches, the Democratic Party and other organizations.

Peace Council

A notice was placed in the Maoist-leaning newspaper, the Guardian (NY) on November 8, 1989, concerning an upcoming US Peace Council 10th anniversary national conference.

The US Peace Council was a CPUSA front[49] and an affiliate of the Soviet-controlled World Peace Council.[50]

Mayor Sanders addressed the event[51] as did DSA and Communist Party friendly Representative John Conyers (D-MI), former Communist Party leader Jack O'Dell of the Rainbow Coalition,[52] Zehdi Terzi of the terrorist Palestine Liberation Organization and Gunther Drefahl of the communist East German Peace Council[53]

CoC connection

In 1991, the CPUSA split, with a third of members forming Committees of Correspondence (CoC).

When CoC held a convention in July 1996, Representative Sanders sent a congratulatory note:

> Thanks to members of the Committees of Correspondence for keeping up the fight during these reactionary times…Best wishes for a successful Convention.[54]

The Case connection

In 2010, John Case wrote about his personal experiences with Bernie Sanders while serving as Communist Party District Organizer in New England. The article in the Communist Party's Political Affairs was entitled "Sanders for President?":

> There are few, if any, politicians on the left, shrewder than Bernie Sanders… I got to know him somewhat in my years as a UE rep in Vt, and later as DO for the Communist Party in N. New England. With a few arguable exceptions, he has always -- both ideologically and politically -- pursued a working-class line.
>
> As important, he become a demonstrated master of very concrete tactics directed at isolating the right, without appearing irresponsible or reckless to center forces. He kept focused on the concretes -- especially economics, and non-corrupt governance -- that blunted repeated attempts by the right to isolate him.[55]

Chicago communists

In April 2015, just a weekend away from Election Day in Chicago's Mayoral and City Council races, Senator Sanders came to Chicago to speak in support of Jesus "Chuy" Garcia the far-left's candidate against incumbent mayor Rahm Emmanuel.

In front of a crowd of 700 gathered on Chicago's far southeast side, Senator Bernie Sanders and district Steelworker retiree leader Scott Marshall fired up the voters for their friend Chuy Garcia.

Scott Marshall with Bernie Sanders

Garcia had 40-year history with the Chicago Communist Party.[56] Scott Marshall was head of the Communist Party Labor Commission.[57]

According to a report of the event in the Communist Party's People's World:

> US Senator Bernie Sanders elaborated on the theme of building a people's movement. 'What we are doing is not just to make the 10th ward better,' he said, 'but demonstrating when people stand together there's nothing we can't accomplish.'
>
> Then he laid out what looked to the enthusiastic crowd a lot like a platform for the 2016 presidential race.

'We're gonna ask the richest people - billionaires and corpora-
tions - to start paying their fair share,' he said right off the bat.
Next, he spoke of putting millions to work at green and living
wage jobs by 'investing in the crumbling infrastructure' and cre-
ating energy systems that cut carbons. He advocated free tuition
in public colleges and universities, Medicare for All, raising Social
Security benefits, overturning Citizens United and public funding
for elections.

Change is in the air, observed steelworker retiree Marshall. 'A
powerful movement, led by labor, is being born.'[58]

Chuy Garcia lost the mayoralty race but was later elected to
Congress in 2018 where he proudly serves in Bernie Sanders'
Congressional Progressive Caucus.[59]

SOCIALISTS BACK BERNIE FOR PRESIDENT

DSA, and to a degree CPUSA, served as the backbone of both of
Bernie Sanders' presidential campaigns.

In 2015, DSA boasted around 6,000 members nationwide. After
the 2016 campaign and the leftist backlash against President Trump,
the organization expanded to more than 50,000 comrades.[60]

In the beginning, DSA's leading role in the Bernie movement was
kept very low key – partially to keep on the right side of election law
but likely also to avoid exposure of the heavy Marxist influence in the
campaign.

On May 20, 2016, Metro DC DSA members "enthused by the
presidential candidacy of Senator Bernie Sanders" gathered to iron
out the "details and constraints involved in individual and group support for the effort".

Members at the gathering agreed that "activities both promoting
the Sanders campaign (and emphasizing his leftmost policy proposals) and simultaneously raising the visibility of DSA as an organization were optimal".

The comrades went on to discuss the DC political terrain and
which long-standing local groups might be allies. One leading DSA
comrade, Kurt Stand - released from prison after 17 years for spying

for communist East Germany-urged that the spirit of this should be "to win", not just "pull a major candidate leftward".[61]

Socialists operated at every level of both of Sanders' presidential campaigns. Some held senior positions in the campaign itself. Others worked at lower levels as paid field directors and organizers.

People for Bernie was led by DSA comrade Charlies Lenchner.[62] Labor for Bernie was led by long time DSAers Rand Wilson and Steve Early.[63] Atlanta DSA activist Anoa Changa was a leader of Women for Bernie.[64]

Our Revolution

But the mass base of the Sanders movement runs through "Our Revolution".

This organization was set up specifically to help grow and support the Sanders movement. Our Revolution claims more than 200,000 members and about 600 locals nationwide. It is almost an entirely DSA-controlled entity - with a little help here and there from Liberation Road and Communist Party US[65]

Our Revolution won over 70 races in the 2018 general election cycle, including electing DSA Congresswomen Alexandria Ocasio-Cortez and Rashida Tlaib and far-leftists Ilhan Omar, and Deb Haaland to the US House of Representatives.[66]

DSA has infiltrated the Democratic Party in almost every state. In some areas DSA *IS* the Democratic Party.

Danny Fetonte, formerly a leader of Austin DSA boasted when standing for DSA National Political Committee in 2017:

> *I was active in building the Bernie Campaign across Texas. In Texas we put Bernie on the ballot by gathering over 12,000 petition signatures. 37 out of the 75 Bernie delegates to the Democratic National Convention from Texas were DSA members.*[67]

These organizations all tend to exaggerate their active membership. However, between DSA, CPUSA, Working Families Party, Progressive Democrats of America and Our Revolution, the Sanders support network was able to activate an army of donors, doorknockers and phone-bankers, campaign officials and field staff.

This was the largest Marxist movement the United States has seen since the heyday of the Communist Party USA during WW2 – and it was all working for Bernie.

THE 'PROGRESSIVE INTERNATIONAL'

Bernie Sanders' wife Jane O'Meara Sanders founded the Vermont-based Sanders Institute in June 2017. The organization's aim was to "revitalize democracy by actively engaging individuals, organizations and the media in the pursuit of progressive solutions to economic, environmental, racial and social justice issues".[68]

Several Fellows joined the organization including Congresswoman and Congressional Progressive Caucus member Tulsi Gabbard,[69] DSA member and radical Theologian Cornel West,[70] Medicare for All activist and DSA member Michael Lighty, Canadian member of parliament for the socialist New Democratic Party Niki Ashton, radical activist/actors Sidney Poitier and Danny Glover, environmentalist Bill McKibben, Black Lives Matter activist Shaun King, globalist economist/activist Jeffrey Sachs, left-leaning former US Secretary of Labor Robert Reich,[71] and Nina Turner and Ben Jealous from Our Revolution.[72]

Bernie Sanders has for some time been advocating an alliance of left-wing forces to stand up to "international capital".

The Progressive International was launched on November 30, 2018, at a Sanders Institute event attended by many progressive politicians, economists and activists including Naomi Klein, Cornel West,[73] Jeffrey Sachs, Niki Ashton, and Fernando Haddad, a socialist who ran for president of Brazil with a communist running mate, and Ada Colau the radical mayor of Barcelona, Spain.[74]

The new organization was aimed at "uniting progressive left-wing activists and organizations" and was led by Bernie Sanders and Yanis Varoufakis, a former Cabinet Minister from the far-left Greek party Syriza.[75]

Some of the Progressive International promotional videos were produced by Means of Production, the DSA-run Detroit studio[76] behind a viral campaign ad for Congresswoman Alexandria Ocasio-Cortez.[77]

At that point, Sanders may have been unsure whether he would run for president again in 2020. Perhaps mindful of Hillary Clinton's problems with the Clinton Foundation, Sanders' wife closed the Sanders Institute in March 2019 to avoid "an appearance of impropriety".[78]

Party of the European Left

The Progressive International project appears to be ongoing however as the Sanders movement has formed close ties to the Party of the European Left.

In April 2019, the European Parliament issued an announcement on an upcoming visit by Bernie Sanders supporters Maria Svart (DSA), David Duhalde (DSA and Our Revolution), Alan Minsky DSA and Progressive Democrats of America), Alexandra Rojas (Justice Democrats), and Sanders foreign policy adviser Matt Duss (invited):

> *On the eve of the elections to the European Parliament, and at the beginning of the race to the US Presidential elections in November 2020, Western Democracy is at a crossroads…there is a need to unite in our defence, and to win this struggle together in order to be in the position to prevent climate change, build prosperous post-growth economies, and organise inclusive and rights-based societies in a new technological environment.*
>
> *This event will provide information about the progressive candidates, including Bernie Sanders, who will successfully challenge Donald Trump, and the campaign techniques applied. The discussion will analyse the state of play of new political camps*

being constructed in Europe in the context of the elections for the European Parliament, and the diversity of the struggle inside and outside of Parliaments on both sides of the Atlantic.[79]

Today, our member party @strankalevica met the delegation from US leftist and progressive forces in #Brussels to build bridges on the 2 sides of the Atlantic.
@LukaMesec @OurRevolution @DemSocialists @pdamerica

From left: Alan Minsky (DSA), Maria Svart (DSA) Luka Mesec,
Slovenian Left Party, Ethan Earle (DSA), David Duhalde (DSA)

The visit was sponsored by the Party of the European Left, and the Confederal Group of the European United Left/Nordic Green Left (GUE/NGL) which hosted several meetings for the visiting American socialists.

On April 5, 2019, the Party of the European Left issued a statement, "To Bernie Sanders we say yes":

In the spirit of Bernie Sanders' recent call to begin building an 'international progressive front', the European Left invited leaders from the US Left to Brussels to develop concrete working relationships.

Over two productive days, Maria Svart, National Director of the Democratic Socialists of America, David Duhalde, Political Director of Our Revolution and Alan Minsky, Executive Director of Progressive Democrats of America, met with leaders of the European Left and GUE/NGL, as well as with representatives from civil society, ETUC, and national parties across Europe.

We look forward to working together to combat the domination of the 1% and the rise of what Sanders calls the 'new authoritarian axis', and to developing positive alternatives together.

—Maite Mola & Paolo Ferrero
Vice-Presidents of the Party of the European Left.[80]

Maite Mola is Vice-President of the Communist Party of Spain. Paolo Ferrero is the Vice-President of the Italian Party of Communist Refoundation.[81]

The Party of the European Left is an alliance of over 30 European communist and "democratic socialist" parties including the Communist Party of France, Communist Party of Austria, Communist Party of Finland, the Party of Communists of the Republic of Moldova, the communist Swiss Labor Party, and the descendants of the "former" communist parties of Czechoslovakia, Romania, Hungary, Belarus, Bulgaria, and East Germany.[82]

The GUE/NGL is an overlapping federation of Scandinavian and Sothern European communist, socialist and Green parties. It includes the Maoist leaning Workers party of Belgium, the Cypriot communist party AKEL, Sinn Fein – the "legal" of the terrorist Irish republican Army, the Communist party of Portugal and the heir to the notoriously Stalinist former East German Communist Party Die Linke.[83]

Bernie Sanders' new "Progressive International" is not "democratic socialist"; it is completely communist. DSA is a small "c" communist organization that is becoming increasingly integrated into the international communist movement.

It is impossible to believe that with nearly 60 years on the Left, Bernie Sanders does not understand that the people he is working with both "foreign and domestic" are totalitarian communists – even if sometimes hiding behind a "democratic socialist" banner.

The probability is that Sanders is aware of this fact and is perfectly fine with it.

He might not want the voting public to know about that quite yet. Thanks to the legacy media and clueless republicans, Bernie Sanders' deep ties to international communists stay hidden from the American people.

BERNIE SANDERS AND THE COUNCIL FOR A LIVABLE WORLD

Bernie Sanders has been very close to the far-left Council for a Livable World (CLW) for many years. For decades the CLW has been working to elect US Senators and Congressmembers who will vote against cut US defense spending (which Moscow and Beijing loves) in favor of higher "social" spending. They have a solid ally in Bernie Sanders.

Pentagon Budget

On February 3, 1999, CLW convened a seminar in Rayburn House titled "Is the Pentagon Budget Increase Needed?"

Participants included Robert Borosage of the far-left Institute for Policy Studies,[84] card-carrying DSA members of congress Major Owens and Jan Schakowsky,[85] DSA-friendly Congressmembers John Conyers and Barney Frank,[86] DSA-friendly Rolling Stone Editor Bill Greider plus Nancy Pelosi and Bernie Sanders.[87]

The consensus was strongly against any Pentagon budget increases.

At the annual Father Robert F. Drinan National Peace and Human Rights Award ceremony in 2008, CLW honored Senator Dianne Feinstein (D-CA), a "leader and expert on nuclear weapons issues who is also dedicated to bringing our troops home from Iraq".

Following Feinstein's speech, Senator Sanders addressed the crowd and "shifted the discussion from nuclear weapons to the US military budget".

Sanders noted that "with the money America spends on one week of the war in Iraq, the United States could ensure that every man, woman and child in the United States has primary health care."[88]

When endorsing Sanders' 2012 US Senate race, the CLW website noted:

Bernie, as he is universally known, has a perfect record on Council for a Livable World's voting scorecard on key national security issues...He opposed the authorization for war in Iraq when in the House and supported measures in both the Senate and House to withdraw troops...

He also opposed additional funding for national missile defense and efforts to cut U.N. peacekeeping funds. He enthusiastically endorsed the New START treaty and opposed all Republican attempts to cripple the agreement.

Council for a Livable World endorses Bernie Sanders for US Senate with the greatest enthusiasm... He is committed to the elimination of weapons of mass destruction, opposes preemptive wars and works hard on these issues.[89]

More butter, less guns

CLW and their sister organization Center for Arms Control and Non-Proliferation hosted an event on January 21, 2013, near the US capitol celebrating the second inauguration of President Barack Obama, Vice President Joe Biden and their endorsed candidates in the 113th Congress.

According to a CLW report:

> A number of prestigious guests attended the event, including Senators Tammy Baldwin, Martin Heinrich, Angus King and Bernie Sanders...
>
> Senator Bernie Sanders (I-VT), electrified the room as usual, and used his time in front of the audience to discuss economic inequalities in the United States and what is necessary to address this pressing issue.[90]

The CLW has always gotten its money's worth out of Senator Sanders.

SENATORS FROM THE STATE OF
VIRGINIA

TIM KAINE

TIM KAINE IS THE JUNIOR US SENATOR FROM VIRGINIA

BACKGROUND

TIM KAINE HAS been junior senator of Virginia since 2013 on the Democratic Party ticket. He graduated from the University of Missouri and went to Harvard Law School after a time working at a school founded by Jesuit missionaries in Honduras. Kaine worked as an attorney for 17 years and taught law part time at the University of Richmond in 1987. Tim Kaine started his political career as a city council member, and later as mayor of Richmond. Kaine became Lieutenant Governor of Virginia in 2002 and then served as Governor in 2006.

Tim Kaine was chairman of the Democratic National Committee from 2009-2011 and was elected as senator in 2012. He was chosen by Hillary Clinton to be her running mate in the 2016 presidential race.[1]

INFLUENCE

Tim Kaine chairs the Subcommittee on Readiness and Management Support for the Committee on Armed Services. He also chairs the Subcommittee on Western Hemisphere, Transnational Crime,

Civilian Security, Democracy, Human Rights, and Global Women's Issues in the Committee on Foreign Relations. Tim Kaine also sits on the Committee on the Budget and the Committee on Health, Education, Labor, and Pensions.[2]

HONDURAS AND LIBERATION THEOLOGY

There is no doubt that Senator Kaine's leftist ideology is influenced by his experiences as a young man in Honduras, and his exposure to "Liberation Theology" – essentially Marxism with a Catholic veneer.

Honduras

From a Catholic background, Tim Kaine attended a Jesuit-run high school. After graduating from Harvard Law School, he spent 9 months, in 1980, doing voluntary missionary work with the Jesuits in Honduras.

Tim Kaine taught carpentry and welding to 70 vocational students in El Progreso, a mid-size municipality located in the Honduran department of Yoro.

Kaine had first travelled to Honduras during Holy Week of 1974 while a sophomore at Rockhurst High School, a Jesuit academy in Kansas City, Missouri. He delivered donations to a Jesuit mission in El Progreso.[3]

Tim Kaine ✔ @timkaine · Jul 27, 2016

"I took a year off law school to volunteer with Jesuit missionaries in Honduras. I taught kids welding & carpentry."

From the New York Times:

> Mr. Kaine was a young Catholic at a crossroads, undergoing a
> spiritual shift as he awakened to the plight of the deeply poor in
> Honduras. In its far-flung pueblos, banana plantation company
> towns and dusty cities, Mr. Kaine embraced an interpretation of
> the gospel, known as liberation theology, that championed social
> change to improve the lives of the downtrodden.[4]

Kaine later told his pastor in Richmond, Virginia, "that his exposure to liberation theology had 'changed him, it deepened him.'"[5] The
pastor, Monsignor Michael Schmied, said Kaine inspired him to
travel to civil war-torn El Salvador in 1987.[6]

Honduras soon politicized the young man.

According to the New York Times:

> In Honduras, his recitation of the traditional Catholic mealtime
> blessing changed to "Lord, give bread to those who hunger, and
> hunger for justice to those who have bread."[7]

 Tim Kaine ✔ @timkaine · Sep 3, 2016   ···
Before meals in **Honduras**, we asked, "Give bread to those who hunger and
hunger for justice to those who have bread." nyti.ms/2ciOsmX

  ♡ 52   ⟲ 596   ♡ 1,280   ⬆

> Honduran military leaders, American officials and even Pope
> John Paul II viewed liberation theology suspiciously, as dangerously
> injecting Marxist beliefs into religious teaching. But the strong
> social-justice message of liberation theology helped set Mr. Kaine
> on a left-veering career path in which he fought as a lawyer against
> housing discrimination, became a liberal mayor, and rose as a
> Spanish-speaking governor and senator with an enduring focus on
> Latin America.
>
>   It also gave Mr. Kaine a new, darker view of his own country's
> behavior. 'It was a very politicizing experience for me because the
> US was doing a lot of bad stuff,' he said. 'It made me very angry. I
> mean I still feel it.'[8]

At least some of the Jesuit priests at El Progreso were Marxists.

Reverend Jack Warner, who knew Tim Kaine well says: "the gospel is an extremely communist document."[9]

During a short stay in Nicaragua, Tim Kaine looked up Father

Father James Carney

James Carney, an American who "embraced liberation theology and revolution in the 1970s and was exiled from Honduras in 1979 for his increasingly radical activities and promotion of Marxist ideology."[10]

According to the New York Times:

> Mr. Kaine hopped off a bus in northern Nicaragua, walked miles to Father Carney's remote parish and spent a memorable evening listening to the priest describe 'both getting pushed around by the military and getting pushed around by the church.'[11]

Father Carney was stripped of his Honduran citizenship and deported as a result of his political activities. After traveling to both Nicaragua and Cuba, he became associated with the Revolutionary Workers Party of Central America (PRTC)–a multi-country insurgent communist organization.

Carney resigned from the Jesuit order and accompanying a group of armed PRTC insurgents across the Nicaragua-Honduras border in July 1983.[12] He was "disappeared", probably, by the Honduran military, later that year.[13]

According to Catholic News Agency:

> Sympathy for Father Carney's radicalized vision of liberation theology continues today through the work of Father Ismael Moreno Coto, S.J., director of Radio Progreso, who also worked with Kaine during his time in Honduras.[14]

Senator Kaine has remained supportive of the El Progreso mission and has visited the graves of his mentors there.

Tim Kaine ✓ @timkaine · Feb 26, 2015   ···

Many thanks to my staff for terrific bday gift - framed photo of my reunion
w/dear Jesuit friends in **Honduras** last wk

He is also inspired by Pope Francis, who is himself heavily influenced by Liberation Theology.

Senator Kaine told the New York Times:

> *I really feel I know him...The age he was in 1980 and '81 was about the same age as a lot of my friends were. The Jesuits.*[15]

Archbishop Romero

The young Tim Kaine was deeply inspired by the life of the late El Salvadorean Archbishop, Oscar Romero.

As the Archbishop of San Salvador, Romero practiced a civil war was raging in the country between Cuban backed Marxist guerillas and the anti-communist government.

Archbishop Romero

Romero criticized violence from both sides, but he was definitely seen as siding with the "poor".

From the National Catholic Register:

> *Archbishop Romero's...third pastoral letter, issued in 1978, con-*
> *demned the Salvadoran government's repressions. However, it also*
> *criticized liberation theology-inspired guerrilla violence...*
>
> *His fourth and final letter on the 'national crises of El Salvador,'*
> *condemned Marxism's materialism: 'Naturally, if one understands*
> *by Marxism a materialistic, atheistic ideology that is taken to*
> *explain the whole of human existence and gives a false interpreta-*
> *tion of religion, then it is completely untenable by a Christian....*
> *Marxist political praxis can give rise to conflicts of conscience*
> *about the use of means and of methods not always in conformity*
> *with what the Gospel lays down as ethical for Christians.'[16]*

On March 24, 1980, Archbishop Romero delivered a sermon in which he called on Salvadoran soldiers, as Christians, to obey God's higher order and to stop carrying out the government's "repression."

Just as Romero finished celebrating mass, a lone gunman, firing a rifle from a nearby car, shot the Archbishop through the heart.[17]

Archbishop Romero instantly became an internationally known martyr. While never a Marxist, the revolutionaries made him an "unofficial patron saint of liberation theology".

The Left made Archbishop Romero their icon.

Soon revolutionary murals and posters bearing Romero's imagine began to appear all over Central America.

Tim Kaine arrived in neighboring Honduras months after Romero's murder.

He met Jon Sobrino, a Spanish theologian and former adviser to Archbishop Romero.

Sobrino was the author of "Jesus the Liberator," which was criticized in 2006 by the Vatican's Congregation for the Doctrine of the Faith on the grounds that it might "cause harm to the faithful."[18]

On February 3, 2015, Senator Tim Kaine released the following statement on Pope Francis's approval of a martyrdom declaration for Archbishop Oscar Romero:

> I am thrilled by the Vatican's announcement today of a martyrdom declaration for Salvadoran Archbishop Oscar Romero, who was murdered in 1980. I worked in neighboring Honduras in late 1980-81 and came to know of Archbishop Romero's powerful Christian advocacy for the poor and his courageous witness against violence. He is a saintly figure for the ages and his life and words continue to offer us guidance today.[19]

Did Tim Kaine accept the leftist version of the Oscar Romero story?

TIM KAINE AND THE MUSLIM LEFT

Senator Kaine has had extensive ties, spanning many years, to the Muslim Left.

National Muslim Democratic Council

Founded at an event on May 16, 2012, the National Muslim Democratic Council was essentially an alliance between senior leaders of Hamas front Council on American-Islamic Relations (CAIR), such as Nihad Awad, and prominent leaders of the Democratic Party including Nancy Pelosi.

NANCY PELOSI WITH CAIR LEADER, NIHAD AWAD
DCCC FUNDRAISER
W HOTEL, WASHINGTON, D.C.
MAY 16, 2012

Also in attendance was Jamal

Barzinji, a co-founder of the Muslim Students Association (MSA), an incubator for Islamic radicalism in the US and Canada.

In 2012, a memo detailing the creation and agenda of the National Muslim Democratic Council marked "CONFIDENTIAL; NOT FOR PUBLIC DISTRIBUTION" was leaked.

In the section marked "2012 election strategy", the group specifically spelled out detailed plans to support the Democrats and target Republicans in "key races where American Muslims can make a difference."[20]

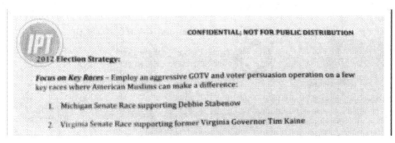

National Muslim Democratic Council memo

These races included:

> Supporting Sen. Debbie Stabenow, D-Mich., in her bid for re-election against former House Intelligence Committee Chairman Pete Hoekstra, R-Mich
>
> Supporting former Gov. Tim Kaine, D-Va., in his race against former Sen. George Allen, R-Va., in the race for Virginia's vacant Senate seat[21]

Contact people for the memo included Sacramento CAIR leader Basim Elkarra, Jihad Williams of Islamic Relief USA and formerly of the MSA and Linda Sarsour of the Arab American Association of New York.

Saleh Williams' organization Islamic Relief USA is an offshoot of Islamic Relief Worldwide (IRW), found to be providing financial and other assistance to the terrorist group Hamas.[22]

Linda Sarsour later trained at the Liberation Road-affiliated Rockwood Leadership Institute[23] and went on to formally join Democratic Socialists of America.[24]

The National Muslim Democratic Council later endorsed Tim Kaine outright in his 2012 US Senate race.

Several Virginia Muslim groups helped Senator Kaine get elected that year.

Muslim American Society

Senator Kaine has been particularly close to the Muslim American Society (MAS), which is both a front group for the Muslim Brotherhood and a strong supporter of the US State Department designated terrorist organization Hamas.

MAS has helped Senator Kaine and other Virginia Democrats electorally.

From the Washington Times, October 2007:

> How much political power does the Muslim American Society wield? Depends on whom you ask — and when.
>
> 'Ask Jim Webb what kind of impact we have. Ask the governor of Virginia what kind of impact we have,' Mahdi Bray, the Muslim American Society's executive director told The Washington Times last week.
>
> The Muslim American Society (MAS) claims credit for helping Jim Webb, Virginia Democrat, defeat incumbent Republican Sen. George Allen in 2006, and Democrat Tim Kaine defeat Republican Jerry W. Kilgore in 2005. MAS said it has registered 65,000 voters in Virginia since the 2005 gubernatorial race, and most of them backed Mr. Webb in a race decided by fewer than 8,000 votes.
>
> 'The Democrat's win hinged on the Muslim vote,' Mr. Bray

said during interviews Tuesday and Wednesday about the orga-
nization's political activities planned for upcoming elections in
November and the 2008 presidential race.

Governor Tim Kaine of Virginia gave the keynote address for
the 5th Annual Muslim American Society Freedom Foundation
'Standing for Justice Dinner' in 2007.[25]

During the event, Tim Kaine appeared alongside Mahdi Bray.

Mahdi Bray, bottom left

Mahdi Bray works very closely with Brian Becker, long time
national director of the national "peace" organization ANSWER
Coalition.

Brian Becker left, Mahdi Bray, right

Becker is also a founder and central organizer of the Party for Socialism and Liberation,[26] a militant communist group which supports North Korea, China, the "Palestinian" cause and even the Putin regime in Russia.

Brian Becker
@BrianBeckerDC

Russia is saying clearly that it will not let Ukraine be used as a staging ground for advanced US/NATO missiles that target Russia with a flight time of five minutes to their targets. NATO will not be allowed to make Crimea into a NATO base. These are Red Lines! Time to listen! twitter.com/sahouraxo/stat...

This Tweet was deleted by the Tweet author. Learn more

10:50 PM · Feb 9, 2022 · Twitter for iPhone

Becker is a regular on the Kremlin-funded Russian propaganda channel RT.

Imam Mahdi Bray @MahdiBray · Jan 2, 2015
Great job Brian **Becker** on your RT TV interview on Palestine
@answercoalition

Esam Omeish

Mahdi Bray is also very close to former MAS president, Virginia-based Muslim and Democratic Party activist Dr. Esam Omeish.

At Georgetown University, Omeish helped start the first chapter of the MSA and later became president of MSA for the US and Canada.[27]

He is also a former national board member of the Council on American-Islamic Relations (CAIR).[28]

Omeish also served for two years on the national board of the Islamic Society of North America (ISNA), which the Justice Department also labeled as a US Muslim Brotherhood entity and

Mahdi Bray, Dr. Esam Omeish

unindicted co-conspirator in a Hamas-financing trial.[29]

Omeish is a former vice president and current board member of the Dar al-Hijrah mosque in Falls Church, Virginia.

In 2000, Esam Omeish hired Anwar al-Awlaki as the mosque's imam. Months later al-Awlaki was helping some of the Saudi hijackers who attacked the pentagon on 9/11 2001 prepare for their "martyrdom".[30]

Dr. Omeish loves to associate with influential Democratic Party figures. His Facebook and Twitter accounts are full of photos of him with Virginia Governors, Senators and congressmembers, former Secretary of State John Kerry and former presidents Bill Clinton and Barack Obama.

President Clinton and Esam Omeish in the Oval Office, late 1990s

Esam Omeish
December 13, 2013 · Twitter · 👥

Meeting President Obama today, spoke about Islam in America, thanked him for Libya and urged help for Syria http://t.co/Tes9XJHtL0

Dr. Omeish was also close to Governor Kaine and his family circa 2007.

Governor Kaine, left, Dr. Esam Omeish right, and their wives, circa 2007

In August 2007, Governor Kaine appointed Dr. Omeish to the Virginia Commission on Immigration.

Controversy soon erupted.

Following public revelations of controversial remarks by Omeish in

several videos, which criticized Israel and the United States government and appeared to encourage jihad.[31]

At a Jerusalem Day Rally on December 22, 2000, Omeish said:

> *You have known that the jihad way is the way to liberate your*
> *land.*[32]

At a rally protesting the then-ongoing war in Lebanon on August
12, 2006, Omeish said:

> *The invasion of Lebanon and the destruction of its infrastructure*
> *and the deliberate targeting of civilians through the barbaric, indis-*
> *criminate, disproportionate Israeli war machine is indeed criminal*
> *and must end now.*[33]

Governor Kaine asked for Omeish's resignation from the commission on September 27, 2007, and he complied. In his resignation press
conference, Omeish appeared under a MAS sign, flanked by Mahdi
Bray and Brian Becker of the Party for Socialism and Liberation.

Left to right - Mahdi Bray, Dr. Omeish, Brian Becker

In accepting the doctor's resignation, Kaine said, "Omeish is a
respected physician and community leader, yet I have been made
aware of certain statements he has made which concern me." He
added that background checks of commission nominees would be
more thorough in the future.[34]

However, when a Virginia state delegate wrote a letter to then-Governor Kaine warning him that the MAS has "questionable origins," a Kaine spokesperson said the charge was "bigotry".[35]

Omeish said calls for his resignation were unfair. "This was a smear campaign against me," he said in a press release from MAS.[36]

On March 4, 2020, a host committee of the Arab American Democratic Caucus of Virginia, which included Dr. Omeish, hosted a private dinner in honor of Senator Kaine at an Italian restaurant in Arlington.[37]

NIAC pressure

Senator Kaine has consistently followed the path of appeasement and non-confrontation when it comes to dealing with the Islamic Republic of Iran and its long-stated goal of becoming a nuclear-armed power.

While Senator Kaine is prepared to criticize Iran's human rights record and support for terrorism, he still strongly supports former President Obama's Joint Comprehensive Plan of Action (JCPOA), or "Iran Nuclear Deal".

Tim Kaine ✓ @timkaine · Jan 17, 2016
Replying to @timkaine
Iran's missile tests, human rights violations & support for terrorism & arms programs will not go unpunished, even as we implement the JCPOA

Senator Kaine's "line" on Iran has been almost identical to that of Iran's leading US lobby group National Iranian American Action Council (NIAC).

A Virginia NIAC team visited Senator Kaine in his Washington office in August 2015 to lobby for the Iran Nuclear Deal.

NIAC
August 6, 2015 · 🌐

Iranian-American Virginians met with U.S. Senator Tim Kaine recently, and he voiced his support for the #IranDeal yesterday! Tell your lawmakers to join the Senator in support of peace: niacaction.org/vote4peace

When Democratic presidential candidate Hillary Clinton picked Tim Kaine as her running mate in 2016, NIAC was more than pleased with her decision.

NIAC gave Senator Kaine huge credit for helping to pass the "Iran Nuclear Deal".

NIAC Action Executive Director Jamal Abdi issued the following statement:

> As advocates for diplomacy, we have high hopes for Hillary Clinton's decision to pick Tim Kaine as her running mate.
>
> This is not a pick that will please neocons who hoped to build influence with a Clinton administration to hedge their bets on Trump. Kaine serves on the Senate Foreign Relations Committee and was the ranking Democrat on Middle East Subcommittee, and played a leading role in shepherding the Iran deal through Congress...
>
> Kaine played a leadership role among Democrats on the substance and fraught politics surrounding the Iran deal. He was at the center of blocking the Kirk-Menendez sanctions that would have killed the nuclear talks when they first started. He helped secure Congressional authority to review and vote on the Iran deal and worked to win that vote when it came. Kaine was one of the first in the Senate to refuse to attend the Benjamin Netanyahu

speech organized by House Republicans in a brazen and unprecedented bid to defeat President Obama and block the nuclear deal.[38]

NIAC sent a delegation to Senator Kaine's office in March that year to thank him for snubbing Israeli president Netanyahu.

NIAC
March 3, 2015 · 🌐

Virginia NIAC supporters at U.S. Senator Tim Kaine's office, THANKING him for taking a courageous stand by skipping Netanyahu's speech, and urging him to continue supporting diplomacy with Iran! — with **Mastee Badii.**

In July 2019, the Trump administration imposed sanctions on Iranian Foreign Minister Mohammad Javad Zarif.

A senior administration official said Zarif had acted more as a "propaganda minister" than a diplomat. "Today, President Trump decided enough is enough," the official said.

In a statement about the sanctions on Zarif, Secretary of State Mike Pompeo said the foreign minister was "complicit" in Iran's support of terrorists, torture and other malign activity around the world.[39]

When the Trump administration barred Foreign Minister Zarif from entering the US to address the UN Security Council in January 2020, Senator Kaine was among the first to complain.

Tim Kaine ✅
@timkaine

⋯

Those who reject diplomacy make war more likely.
#NoWarWithIran

huffpost.com
Trump Admin Bars Top Iranian Diplomat From Entering U.S.
Iranian Foreign Minister Mohammad Javad Zarif had requested a visa to come to
address the United Nations Security Council.

7:56 PM · Jan 6, 2020 · Twitter for iPhone

In March 2020, in a great victory for the Iran lobby, the House of Representatives passed Senator Kaine's resolution (S.J. Res. 68) requiring the Trump administration to withdraw US forces from hostilities with Iran.

Ryan Costello, Policy Director of NIAC Action, issued the following statement:

> *Bipartisan majorities in both the House and Senate have passed legislation clarifying that President Trump does not have authorization for war with Iran. This reflects the American people's wishes, who have twice watched the President lead us to the edge of a new and disastrous war with Iran in recent months.*
>
> *Senators Kaine, Durbin, Paul and Lee, along with Speaker Pelosi and key voices like Reps. Ro Khanna and Barbara Lee, deserve tremendous credit for working across the aisle to send on legislation clarifying Congress' role in matters of war and peace after the January crisis with Iran. So too do all legislators who saw*

*through the administration's fearmongering and backed legislation
to rein in their reckless war push, and the countless Americans and
allied organizations who told President Trump loud and clear: no
war with Iran.*[40]

In his 2018 US Senate race, Senator Kaine was endorsed and
funded by the NIAC-allied Iranian American Political Action
Committee (IAPAC).[41]

COUNCIL FOR A LIVABLE WORLD

Senator Kaine is fully on board with the Council for a Livable World
(CLW)'s key goal – weakening US nuclear defence capabilities.

Any arms limitation agreement with Russia will automatically
weaken the US, because Washington will stick to the agreement
while Moscow has consistently cheated both in the Soviet and post-
Soviet eras.

From CLW's endorsement of Tim Kaine's 2012 US Senate race:

*Tim Kaine, who has never turned away from taking practical
and progressive positions on tough issues, supports approval of the
Comprehensive Test Ban Treaty and new nuclear reductions negotiations with Russia building on the success of the New START
Treaty.*

*As DNC Chairman, Kaine went on the record in support of
the ratification of New START, the nuclear arms reduction treaty.*

*'This treaty fulfills one of President Obama's fundamental prom-
ises by moving the United States an important step closer to a safer,*

more peaceful, world that is working toward the elimination of nuclear weapons...I hope that we will see a strong and prompt bipartisan effort in the United States Senate to embrace this step forward and ratify the new START treaty.'

Tim Kaine will be a valuable member of United States Senate who will fight for the issues that matter to Council supporters.[42]

CLW endorsed Senator Kaine again in 2018. This time they emphasized the Senator's support for the Iran Nuclear Deal:

Senator Tim Kaine, former nominee for Vice President, former Governor and Lieutenant Governor of Virginia, former Chair of the Democratic National Committee, former Mayor and City Councilman from Richmond, Virginia, and civil rights attorney is running for re-election. Council for a Livable World enthusiastically endorsed him in his first race for Senate in 2012.

He strongly supports the Iran nuclear agreement. He tweeted on October 14, 2017: 'Decertifying the #IranDeal guts US diplomacy and, yes, raises the serious risk of the Trump administration leading us into war.'[43]

It seems fortunate that Tim Kaine did not become US vice president in 2016.

LINWOOD 'WOODY' KAINE

President Biden's son Hunter is not the only child of a prominent elected official who has raised eyebrows. Tim Kaine's youngest son Linwood "Woody" Kaine appeared masked and dressed in all black with a gang of Antifa thugs to a pro-Trump rally at the Minnesota Capitol rotunda in March 2017.

The son of then vice-presidential candidate Tim Kaine engaged in violence alongside his comrades, and aggressively battled with a police officer who attempted to subdue him.

Linwood "Woody" Kaine

From the Twin Cities Pioneer Press:

> *Woody Kaine, 24, was among five masked, black-garbed people suspected of lobbing a smoke bomb minutes earlier inside the Minnesota Capitol rotunda Saturday afternoon.*
>
> *Officers had chased him down, but Kaine wasn't about to submit, according to a more detailed account provided Wednesday by St. Paul police.*
>
> *In the end, it took three officers, a 'knee strike' and a chemical spray to subdue Kaine after he was identified as one of the counter-protesters who allegedly used fireworks or a smoke bomb to disrupt a rally in support of President Donald Trump at the Minnesota State Capitol, according to police spokesman Steve Linders.*[44]

The article continued to report that a smoke bomb "allegedly struck a 61-year-old woman..."

The Ramsey County attorney's office "declined to file criminal charges as there were insufficient facts to prove felony-level riot." However, Minnesota statute 609.71 defines "Riot second degree" as:

> *When three or more persons assembled disturb the public peace by an intentional act or threat of unlawful force or violence to person or property, each participant who is armed with a dangerous weapon or knows that any other participant is armed with a dangerous weapon is guilty of riot second degree and may be sentenced to imprisonment for not more than five years or to payment of a fine of not more than $10,000, or both.*[45]

John Krenik, then-chairman of the Republican Party in St. Paul requested that St. Paul City Attorney Samuel Clark and Ramsey County attorney John Choi recuse themselves "as their objectiveness has clearly been clouded by their political affiliation and Democrat Party loyalty".

A press conference on the matter finally took place over two months later on May 26, 2017. Choi said in part:

> *Unfortunately, some of the protesters arrived prepared to cause problems, and they were equipped with face and head coverings and goggles. This unlawful group attempted to enter the rally from the second floor staircase by pushing, shoving and eventually employing smoke bombs, Mace, fireworks, thereby creating a dangerous situation and a very chaotic environment for all of those present at the rally.*[46]

It was reported that after two months, Woody Kaine "faces fleeing and concealing identity charges, as well as a gross misdemeanor count of obstructing legal process with force, after fighting with a St. Paul police officer trying to apprehend him."[47] In late December, it was reported that the youngest son of Tim Kaine got off with a slap on the wrist. He was placed on probation and "ordered to pay $236 in fines and fees".[48] Woody Kaine is clearly a product of his upbringing.

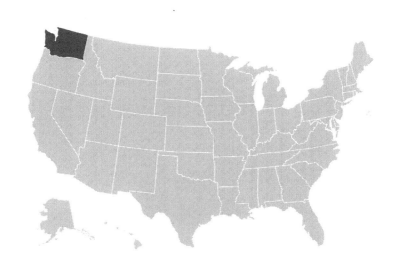

SENATORS FROM THE STATE OF

WASHINGTON

PATTY MURRAY

PATTY MURRAY IS THE SENIOR SENATOR
REPRESENTING THE STATE OF WASHINGTON.

BACKGROUND

ORN IN BOTHELL, Washington, in 1950, Patty Murray received her Bachelor of Arts Degree in Physical Education from Washington State University in 1972. She was a preschool teacher for several years and taught a parenting class at Shoreline Community College from 1984 to 1987.[1]

In 1988, was elected to the Washington State Senate.

In 1992, Murray ran for the United States Senate in a grassroots campaign to beat a 10-year veteran of the US House of Representatives. Senator Murray was re-elected in 1998, 2004, 2010 and 2016 on the Democratic Party ticket.[2]

INFLUENCE

Patty Murray is the Ranking Member on the Senate Health, Education, Labor & Pensions (HELP) Committee and also serves on the Appropriations Committee where she is the Ranking Member of the Subcommittee on Labor, Health and Human Services, and Education.

Senator Murray is the former Democratic Senatorial Campaign Committee Chair and is the current Assistant Democratic Leader.[3]

COMMUNIST PARTY ASSOCIATIONS

Patty Murray has a pattern of association with the Washington State branch of the Communist Party USA (CPUSA) – which was for many years one of the most influential in the country.

Committees of Correspondence Connection

When the CPUSA split in 1991, about a third of the membership left to join a new Marxist group: Committees of Correspondence (CoC).

One prominent CoC member was Seattle activist Sally Soriano.[4]

In January 1993, just after Patty Murray had just been elected for the first time to the US Senate, Soriano wrote an article in the CoC's newsletter "Corresponder" about her local branch's campaign against US sanctions on Cuba. Soriano describes the sanctions as a "blockade."

From Corresponder:

> We in Washington State are looking forward to working with newly elected Sen. Patty Murray who has said that she understands Cuba's Struggle against the blockade.[5]

Coalition of Labor Union Women

Speakers at the November 1997 Coalition of Labor Union Women (CLUW) conference in Seattle included Richard Trumka and Linda Chavez-Thompson of the AFL-CIO; Nancy Riche, Executive VP of the Canadian Labor Congress; Representative Jim McDermott (D-WA) and Senator Patty Murray.[6]

Washington Senator Patty Murray was one of CLUW's featured convention speakers.

CPUSA founded the CLUW as one of its key front groups in 1973.[7] In Washington well-known CPUSA such as Irene Hull[8] and Lonnie Nelson, ran the Puget Sound branch of CLUW for many years.[9]

CPUSA supporter Pat Stell,[10] Vice-President of the Washington State CLUW, welcomed the 800 delegates from local chapters and national unions to that organization's biennial convention in Seattle on October 9, 2003.

CLUW President Gloria Johnson, set a tone of defiance against the Bush administration "running roughshod over our schools and reproductive rights, invading our privacy, and other nations." Taking on the Patriot Act and its assault on civil liberties, Johnson challenged the assembly, "Do we want to go back to the days of McCarthyism?" "No!" they roared back. "Hell no!"

"In the scheme of things, there are them and us," said Democratic Socialists of America (DSA) member and Coalition of Black Trade Unionists president William Lucy, going on to describe "all-out class warfare between those who have the power to make the rich richer and the rest of us who just want a good life."

CPUSA reporter Roberta Wood recorded the event for the People's World and noted that comrade Irene Hull was among the attendees.[11]

CPUSA member and Washington CLUW activist Lonnie Nelson was also involved in the food bank movement – which was used by the communists to lobby for increased welfare spending.

Lonnie Nelson was part of a roundtable discussion held at the Seattle Labor Temple on August 18, 2008, with Senator Murray and several clients and directors of area food banks.

Senator Murray toured the Puget Sound Labor Agency food bank and then participated in the discussion on "growing needs at area food banks caused by food and fuel inflation and a slumping national economy". She stated that such events have made her "increasingly aware that as food prices increase, many more families are going hungry".

"This (forum) has been very helpful," Murray said. "At the federal level, we have got to pass a supplemental bill (on food assistance). That's the message I will take back to Congress."[12]

Communist Retiree Fronts

Senator Murray has also supported communist-led senior activism. On June 30, 2004, Senator Murray spoke to more than 150 retirees at the second annual convention of the Washington State Alliance for Retired Americans. During her speech, Murray addressed the new Medicare prescription drug law and ongoing threats to Social Security.

Senator Murray was introduced by high-ranking Washington CPUSA member Will Parry.[13, 14]

A 75th Birthday Celebration of Social Security, featuring Senator Murray and US Representative Jim McDermott, was held on August 16, 2010 at the Phinney Neighborhood Association's Greenwood Senior Center in Seattle.

The event was organized by the Puget Sound Alliance for Retired Americans and Social Security Works – Washington, which included CLUW; the Puget Sound Chapter of the far-left Asian Pacific American Labor Alliance; the Seattle Chapter of the DSA-led Physicians for a National Health Program; and the Western Washington Chapter of the Jobs with Justice, a CPUSA influenced organization.[15, 16]

At the time, Puget Sound Alliance for Retired Americans Board was led by its founder CPUSA member Will Parry and Party affiliated board members Gene Lux[17] and Rachael Levine.[18]

In September 2018, Senator Murray co-sponsored the SWIFT Act, a bill designed to expand Social Security Benefits and endorsed by a number of leftist organizations including the Alliance for Retired Americans.[19]

In August 2019, Senator Murray addressed the Washington State Alliance for Retired Americans about Social Security during their Summer Anniversary Educational Forum.

You scratch my back...

Patty Murray has also helped steer state money towards a CPUSA supported project.

Roslyn, Washington's Old City Hall building was affected by the 2001 Nisqually earthquake, revealing major structural issues with the old building. A committee appointed by the city began working on finding ways to address needed changes in the structure. Fundraising began. A major grant made possible by Senator Murray "sealed the deal" for the first phase of the improvements in September 2010.

Marc Brodine, Chairman of both the Roslyn Library Board of Directors and of the Washington State Communist Party, said many in the community were looking forward to the day the project would start.[20, 21]

Patty Murray's support for CPUSA front groups and causes was reciprocated.

In 1998, according to then Washington State Communist Party Chair B. J. Mangaoang; the "Party weighed in to re-elect Democratic Senator Patty Murray and to unseat three ultra-right GOP house members."[22]

In 2010, veteran CPUSA leaders Tim Wheeler and Joyce Wheeler worked in Senator Murray's campaign in Sequim, Washington State.

Tim Wheeler wrote about the campaign in the CPUSA newspaper People's World:

> The highest profile election victory here Nov. 2 was the reelection of Sen. Patty Murray. She defeated Republican Dino Rossi by more than 100,000 votes.
>
> I was asked to coordinate street-corner "waves" for Murray here in my hometown. We could tell Murray was doing well by the number of motorists, especially women, who honked and gave us the thumbs-up salute, far outnumbering the Republicans who gave us a sour look and the thumbs-down...
>
> Washington State voters helped put up a firewall against the ultra-right in reelecting Murray, blocking a GOP majority takeover of the Senate. Victory was won when the coalition of unions and other progressive organizations succeeded in getting out the vote."[23]

Joyce Wheeler also campaigned for Senator Murray in 2016.

MUSLIM LEFT CONNECTIONS

Senator Murray has long been sympathetic to the Muslim Left.

In 2002, Senator Murray told a group of high-school students in her state that the US should adopt Al Qaeda terrorist leader Osama bin Laden's "nation-building tactics".

"We've got to ask, why is this man so popular around the world?" said Murray, "Why are people so supportive of him in many countries that are riddled with poverty?"

Murray said that bin Laden has been "out in these countries for decades, building schools, building roads, building infrastructure, building day care facilities, building health care facilities, and the people are extremely grateful. We haven't done that."

"How would they look at us today if we had been there helping them with some of that rather than just being the people who are going to bomb in Iraq and go to Afghanistan?" Murray asked.[24]

Council on American Islamic Relations

Senator Murray also has a relationship with the Council on American Islamic Relations (CAIR) that stretches back until at least 2011.[25]

Senator Murray with CAIR and other groups, immigration reform meeting Seattle January 2013

In November 2015, the Washington chapter of CAIR organized a Spokane "breakfast, training and meetings with Senator Patty Murray's Central WA Outreach Director Raquel Crowley:"

> *If you're ready to keep working to end anti-Muslim hate and bullying by getting lawmakers to stand publicly and vocally with Muslim families and children and changing the way mainstream media editors cover our communities, this is for YOU!*[26]

In October 2017, Senator Murray said of CAIR:

> *I am proud to stand with an organization that has dedicated itself to upholding some of our country's most important values,*

including equity, justice, and civil rights protections for the most vulnerable American citizens.[27]

CAIR also loves Senator Murray. The organization has given the Senator a 100% rating for her legislative efforts.[28]

COUNCIL FOR A LIVABLE WORLD SUPPORT

The Council for a Livable World (CLW) supported Patty Murray in her long-shot successful Senate run in 1992[29] and again in 2010 and 2016.

According to the 2010 endorsement on the Coalition's website:

> *Patty Murray has made a difference, particularly on arms control, nuclear disarmament and foreign policy. In 2002, Murray was one of 23 Senators to vote against the President's request for authority to take military action in Iraq… In key Senate votes, she supported amendments to bring US troops out of Iraq, opposed funding for a new generation of nuclear weapons and voted against amendments to increase national missile defense funding.*[30]

In 2016, CLW praised Senator Murray for her belief that the "US nuclear weapons budget should be reduced because the US has more than enough nuclear weapons, and other security and foreign policy programs are of higher priority".[31]

No doubt Moscow was very pleased.

MARIA CANTWELL

BACKGROUND

MARIA CANTWELL WAS born on October 13, 1958 in Indianapolis, Indiana. She received her Bachelor of Arts Degree in Public Administration from Miami University.

She also pursued an academic course at the Miami University European Center, Luxembourg.

In 1986, Cantwell was elected to the Washington State House of Representatives before serving in the 103rd Congress (January 3, 1993-January 3, 1995). She was elected to the US Senate in 2000 on the Democratic Party ticket.[1]

Influence

Senator Cantwell serves on the Senate Committee on Commerce, Science and Transportation-Ranking Member, and the Committees on Finance, Energy and Natural Resources and Indian Affairs.[2]

CRANSTON CONNECTION

Maria Cantwell moved to Seattle, Washington in 1983 to campaign for California Senator Alan Cranston in his unsuccessful bid for the 1984 Democratic Presidential nomination. As caucus campaigns director ,Cantwell ran things in Washington, Idaho and Alaska for Cranston.[3]

Cantwell went to Washington DC as a staffer for Cranston and credits the Senator as an inspiration for her own political career.[4] Maria Cantwell could not have chosen a more subversive mentor.

Through a long career which spanned most of the "Cold War" Cranston consistently voted against almost all aid to countries fighting Communist aggression or insurgencies, including South Vietnam and El Salvador. He also refused to support anti-communist movements fighting in Communist dictatorships like Nicaragua, Angola, Mozambique etc.

His 1988 rating from the pro-defense American Security Council rating was 0%.[5] After a stint in the student left at Stanford in the 1930s, which included working with "revolutionary forces in Mexico", Cranston joined the Office of War Information when the United States entered WWII.[6] Cranston was Chief of the Foreign Language Division of the Office of War Information, the US information and propaganda organization.

In this position he made several surprisingly pro-communist moves. For example, Cranston recommended that the Office hire David Karr, as "a senior liaison officer working with other Federal agencies." Karr had been writing for the Communist Party USA newspaper, The Daily Worker, as well as for Albert Kahn, an author who was later revealed in Congressional testimony to be a Soviet agent.

Cranston recommended Karr for employment, knowing he had worked for the the Daily Worker but "did not know he was a communist".

After the War Karr launched a successful career in international finance some of which benefited the Soviet Union. In 1975, for example, he arranged a $250 million credit for the Soviet, Foreign Trade Bank.

His main contact in Moscow was reportedly Dierman Gvishiani, deputy chairman of the Soviet State Committee for Science and Technology and son-in-law of Soviet Premier Kosygin.[7]

Cranston remained a long-time friend of Karr and said later that Karr "had a strong social conscience that made him an intense promoter of Detente."[8]

World Government

Cranston, like many communist sympathizers of the time was an avid promoter of world government. From 1949 to 1952, he served as national president of the United World Federalists, which was dedicated to promoting "peace through world law."[9]

COMMUNIST CONNECTION

Maria Cantwell liked Cranston and Cranston liked communists. Communists also like Cantwell.

According to the Seattle Post Intelligencer on November 8, 2006:

> Irene Hull, a supporter of US Senate candidate Maria Cantwell, keeps her fingers crossed, one for the US Senate and one for the US House, to fall into Democratic control during an election return party on Tuesday November 7, 2006 at the Sheraton Hotel in downtown Seattle.
>
> Irene Hull was there, crossing her fingers, watching returns projected on a screen at the Sheraton and telling the story of many of her comrades within the Democratic Party.[10]

Though a Democrat, Irene Hull was also a life-long member of the Communist Party USA (CPUSA).[11]

SOCIALIST CONNECTIONS

Senator Cantwell has long been an active ally of the American socialist left.

Next Agenda Conference

Senator Cantwell was a "special guest" at the Next Agenda Conference held at the National Press Club in Washington DC on February 28, 2001. The gathering was organized by the Institute for Policy Studies/Democratic Socialists of America-initiated Campaign for America's Future. The Next Agenda project consisted of a socialist wish-list of policy proposals that the far-left sought to have introduced into Congress.

Organizers of the conference would release a new book, The Next Agenda: Blueprint for a New Progressive Movement, edited by Institute for Policy Studies (IPS) Trustee Robert Borosage:

> At Feb. 28 Conference on Next Agenda, progressive activists, [and] Congressional leaders will unite to forge strategy for working

families agenda — the day after President Bush delivers his plans to [a] joint session of Congress.

— Calling themselves the real "democratic majority," organizers and thinkers, led by the Campaign for America's Future, to release [a] new book outlining an agenda for changes they insist most voters endorsed in 2000 elections.

Sponsored by the progressive advocacy group, the Campaign for America's Future and its sister research organization, the Institute for America's Future, the Conference on the Next Progressive Agenda has been endorsed by a who's who of prominent leaders from the labor unions, women's organizations, civil rights groups, environmentalists and individual members of the House and Senate. Their goal: to forge a progressive movement to fight for the "working family" agenda they insist was endorsed by a majority of the voters in the 2000 election."[12]

Washington Public Capaigns

June 19, 2010, Senator Cantwell gave the keynote address for Washington Public Campaigns' Fourth Annual Awards Banquet, at South Seattle Community College. Cantwell had been selected by the IPS-affiliated The Nation magazine, as "Most Valuable Senator" in 2009 for "her effort challenging fellow members of Congress to get serious about financial services reform. As this year's guest speaker, Cantwell" lent her voice to the call for fair elections nationally."

The awards banquet generated financial support for Washington Public Campaigns to support their efforts to achieve voter-owned elections (public funding of election campaigns) in Washington State. Writing about the Awards Banquet, WPC Director Craig Salins, former Washington head of Democratic Socialists of America (DSA),[13] stated:

At the 4th Annual Awards Banquet June 19th - with guest speaker Senator Maria Cantwell - Washington Public Campaigns will celebrate our progress in the past year and recognize individuals and groups who have contributed mightily to our work.[14]

Apollo Alliance

Maria Cantwell was also a founder of the far-left controlled Apollo Alliance, a leftist scheme to unite labor unions, the environmental movement and some businesses behind a "green jobs" movement - essentially huge government make work programs designed to funnel taxpayer's money to socialist causes. This concept was very similar to the Green New Deal currently being promoted by DSA, CPUSA and the Democratic Party left.

From Common Dreams, here is an Apollo Alliance press release from January 14, 2004:

> An unusual alliance of labor, environmental, civil rights, business, and political leaders today laid out a vision for a New Apollo Project to create 3.3 million new jobs and achieve energy independence in ten years. Named after President Kennedy's moon program, which inspired a major national commitment to the aerospace industry, the Apollo Alliance aims to unify the country behind a ten-year program of strategic investment for clean energy technology and new infrastructure.
>
> The Alliance also announced that it has received support from 17 of America's largest labor unions, including the United Auto Workers, the Steelworkers and Machinists, as well as a broad cross section of the environmental movement, including the Sierra Club, the NRDC, the Union of Concerned Scientists, and Greenpeace.
>
> The press conference was held as President Bush is expected to make a final push for his energy agenda, which was defeated under widespread criticism last November. The press conference was attended by co-chairs of the Apollo Alliance, Senator Maria Cantwell (by phone), Leo Gerard, president of the United Steelworkers of America, Carl Pope, executive director of the Sierra Club, as well as by California State Treasurer Phil Angelides, Congressman Jay Inslee (by phone), John Podesta, president of the Center for American Progress and Bracken Hendricks, executive director of the Apollo Alliance...
>
> Sen. Maria Cantwell (D-Wash.) said, "At the time of Kennedy's moon shot, we were in space race with the Soviet Union. Now we are in an economic race with the Europeans and Japanese. Bush is focused on the past, the New Apollo Project for energy independence is focused on the future. America led the electronic and

communications revolutions. Now we must lead the clean energy revolution if we are to maintain our global economic leadership."[15]

In 2006, Senator Maria Cantwell served on the National Advisory Board of the Apollo Alliance,[16] alongside such "progressive" socialist notables as Chairman and DSA member Julian Bond,[17] Leo Gerard, United Steel Workers of America and a friend of DSA,[18] and DSA member Bill Lucy, Secretary/Treasurer of AFSCME.[19] Later Apollo Alliance board members included Robert Borosage of the IPS and Gerry Hudson, International Executive VP, SEIU, also a DSA member.[20]

COUNCIL FOR A LIVABLE WORLD

The Council for a Livable World supported Maria Cantwell in her successful 2000 and 2006 Senate races.[21]

Mariah Sixkiller previously served as "research director" for Senator Maria Cantwell. She now serves as a board member for the Council for a Livable World, a post she has held since January 2018.[22] According to her LinkedIn account,[23] Sixkiller currently serves as "Strategic Defense Affairs Officer" at the "Microsoft Defense Business Unit". She has also worked as a "Public Affairs Officer" for the National Democratic Institute for International Affairs (NDI), which is affiliated with the Socialist International.[24]

"I am a proud Board Member of the Council for a Livable World, a PAC dedicated to supporting candidates who support reduction (and ultimately elimination) of the world's nuclear weapons," Sixkiller states on LinkedIn.

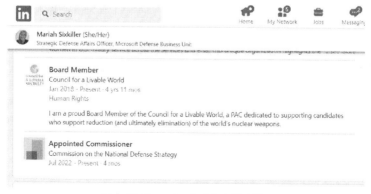

LinkedIn Screenshot for Maria Sixkiller

Further, Mariah Sixkiller was the Appointed Commissioner of the "Commission on the National Defense Strategy" by Majority Leader Nancy Pelosi.[25] The "long delayed"[26] National Security Strategy Report was finally released in October 2022.[27]

Notably, Sixkiller's husband Casey Sixkiller was appointed in May 2022 by Joe Biden to "lead EPA's [Environmental Protection Agency] Pacific Northwest regional office", one of ten regional EPA offices, all led by Biden political appointees. Casey Sixkiller has previously served as a legislative aide to extreme left Representative Jim McDermott (D-WA) and also Senator Patty Murray (D-WA).

Since being appointed, Casey Sixkiller has surely impressed Joe Biden, as well as Maria Cantwell, in his aggressive effort to scrap construction of a mine in Bristol Bay, Alaska. The area was found to have "one of the greatest stores of mineral wealth ever discovered," according to the mine developer. Senator Maria Cantwell has been a "high-profile congressional critic of the mine."[28]

CUBAN CONNECTION

Like her mentor Senator Alan Cranston, Senator Cantwell has long campaigned for increased US ties with the US's sworn enemy communist Cuba.

In mid-January 2002, Senator Cantwell visited Cuba on an agricultural mission with the University of Washington's Center for Women in Democracy. During the visit she encouraged Cuban leaders, "including President Fidel Castro and the Director of Alimport, Cuba's Import Agency, to purchase Washington state peas and apples."[29]

Seated from left: Maria Cantwell, Castro,
and Kirby Jones (Juanita Vera, translator, standing)

On February 19, 2003, Cuban President Fidel Castro met with participants of the US-Cuba Business Conference at Palacio de Convenciones in Havana. Participants included Raul de la Nuez, Cuban Minister of Trade; Ricardo Alarcon, President of Cuba's National Assembly; US Senator Maria Cantwell; translator Juanita Vera; President Fidel Castro; Kirby Jones, President of Alamar Associates, a long-time advocate of US-Cuba trade; Senator Kent Conrad (D-ND); Pedro Alvarez, Chairman of Alimport; and John Moore, Lieutenant Governor of Kansas.[30]

In 2009, Senator Mary Landrieu joined four other senators to push for more small business opportunities with Cuba.

Landrieu, chairwoman of the Senate Committee on Small Business and Entrepreneurship, wrote to Treasury Secretary Timothy Geithner requesting that changes in American telecommunications policy toward Cuba include access to new exports and opportunities for US small businesses.

In April, President Barack Obama announced of a series of changes to limits on travel and gifts from the US to Cuba, as well as the authorization of greater telecommunications links between the two countries.

The letter was also signed by leftist Senators Maria Cantwell, Byron Dorgan, (D-ND), Jeanne Shaheen, (D-NH)., and Ron Wyden, (D-OR).

> As the administration negotiates with the Cuban government and comes up with new regulations, we would respectfully request your consideration to make US small business interests a priority in these discussions, the senators wrote. Small businesses are the engine of the American economy and, now more than ever, deserve a level playing field for new opportunities in Cuba.
>
> The Senators asked about several specific administration policies relating to small business participation in telecommunications activities in Cuba. These included whether US Small Business Administration and Export-Import Bank loans would be eligible to be used for authorized small business activities with Cuba, whether there would be streamlining of rules and licensing requirements for US small business activities to Cuba and whether the administration planned to encourage the Cuban government to support

joint ventures between Cuban and US small businesses on these projects".[31]

Senator Cranston would have been be so proud.

SENATORS FROM THE STATE OF
WISCONSIN

TAMMY BALDWIN

BACKGROUND

TAMMY BALDWIN WAS born and raised in Wisconsin. Baldwin was raised by her grandparents due to her mother's mental illness and drug abuse. After graduating from Smith College, Baldwin received her law degree in 1989 from the University of Wisconsin Law School. The future senator received her first taste of public office in 1986 while she was still in law school, filling an aldermanic vacancy on the Madison Common Council. From there, Baldwin was elected to four terms on the Dane County Board of Supervisors and then onto the Wisconsin State Assembly, where she served as a State Representative for the 78th District for three terms. Tammy Baldwin continued her public service as an "openly gay" member of congress, serving seven terms. She was elected to the US Senate on November 6, 2012 on the Democratic Party ticket.[1]

INFLUENCE

Tammy Baldwin chairs the Subcommittee on Agriculture, Rural Development, Food and Drug Administration, and Related Agencies on the Committee on Appropriations. Additionally on the Committee on Appropriations, Baldwin sits on the Subcommittees on Defense; Energy and Water Development; Homeland Security; Labor, Health and Human Services, and Education, and Related Agencies; and Military Construction, Veterans Affairs, and Related Agencies. Tammy Baldwin also sits on the Committees of Commerce, Science, and Transportation and Health, Education, Labor, and Pensions.[2]

SOCIALIST ROOTS

Rainbow Coalition

Senator Tammy Baldwin began her political career in a Marxist led organization –Reverend Jesse Jackson's famous Rainbow Coalition.

The Rainbow Coalition was built by Jackson to support his two presidential campaigns of 1984 and 1988. The nationwide organization was mainly led by Maoists from League of Revolutionary Struggle, Line of March, and Communist Workers. However, in some states, particularly in 1988, Democratic Socialists of America (DSA) also got involved.[3] These were[4] Tammy Baldwin's comrades.

From The Nation:

Tammy Baldwin
Age: 30
Personal: single, lives in downtown Madison
Occupation: Attorney on leave from Madison law firm
Political experience: Dane County supervisor since 1986, serving on personnel and finance committee and Human Services board; member Dane County Task Force on AIDS; Madison alderperson, 1986
Other public service: Rainbow Coalition; National Organization for Women; National Women's Political Caucus; American Civil Liberties Union; National Gay and Lesbian Task Force
Education: J.D., UW-Madison Law School; Smith College, bachelor's degree

Tammy Baldwin, who worked for the Rainbow in Wisconsin, entered politics and fashioned a coalition of students, farmers, workers, environmentalists and progressives that would, by 1998, elect her to Congress, the first woman in the state's history and the first openly gay non-incumbent in the nation's.

> When Baldwin talks about building support both inside
> Washington and outside in the communities for universal health-
> care or daycare or civil rights, she echoes Jackson's campaigns".[5]

Socialist Leapfrog

Tammy Baldwin transitioned from the Rainbow Coalition by leap-
frogging through a series of low-level offices, all conveniently assisted
by Democratic Socialists of America members. DSA was very strong
in Madison Wisconsin at the time and had thoroughly infiltrated the
local Democratic Party at every level.

Tammy Baldwin took full advantage of these connections during
her political ascension.

In the fall of 1985, DSA member Lynn Haanen[6] decided not to run
again for the Dane County Board, so Tammy Baldwin approached
her to run for her seat. Haanen hosted Baldwin's first fundraiser
at 123 West Gilman Street, in December 1985, with the assistance
of DSA comrade Kevin Topper.[7] Baldwin was elected to the Dane
County Board of Supervisors in April 1986.

Baldwin was then drafted by Alder and DSA comrade Anne
Monks[8] to replace her on the Madison Common Council that
summer, and was appointed by the to fill the vacancy until the general election in November 1986.

From 1973-1987, 123 West Gilman was a center for Madison's gay
and socialist left.[9, 10] Alder Jim Yeadon, State Representative David
Clarenbach, County Supervisors Lynn Haanen and Earl Bricker,
Governor Tony Earl's staff for the State Council on Lesbian and Gay
Issues, and Kevin Topper, a campaign strategist for numerous progressive candidates from Lynn Haanen to Tammy Baldwin worked
out of 123 West Gilman. All of them "accomplished their ground-
breaking work, ordinances and legislation while living there".[11]

In 1985, Tammy Baldwin attended the first West Hollywood conference of openly gay and lesbian elected appointed officials. The event
was organized[12] by leading DSA comrade Christine Riddiough.[13]

At the 1987 Gay March on Washington, Madison was represented
by Dane County supervisors Dick Wagner, Tammy Baldwin, and
Kathleen Nichols, yet another DSA comrade.[14]

Tammy Baldwin, Dick Wagner, Kathleen Nicholls.

In 1992, Baldwin ran for and won David Clarenbach's former seat in the 78th State Assembly District when Clarenbach opted out of an Assembly race to run for Congress. In September Baldwin won the Democratic primary for the local State Assembly race. Her three primary opponents Billy Feitlinger, Dave Cieslewicz and Ken Strasma all endorsed her and praised her for running as an open lesbian.[15]

In a letter to the editor dated October 31, 1992, published at The Capital Times in Madison, Wisconsin Lynn Haanen and Billy Feitlinger joined progressive comrades State Senator Chuck Chvala, Mary Lou Munts, and state representative Rebecca Young in supporting Tammy Baldwin for state assembly.[16]

Feitlinger, a former Madison City Council present and an aide to US Senator Russ Feingold was also a DSA member.[17]

In 1998, Tammy Baldwin campaigned successfully for Wisconsin's 2nd Congressional District. Baldwin's financial director for the 1998 campaign, Kate Peyton, would go on to work on several future Baldwin congressional campaigns.[18]

A decade earlier, Kate Peyton had served on the Board of Directors of the Progressive Chicago Area Network (PROCAN), an organization led by several prominent Chicago Marxists including DSA comrades Roberta Lynch,[19] Nancy Shier,[20] Dr. Ron Sable[21] and future Congressman Danny K. Davis.[22]

After the 1998 Congressional elections, Bob Roman of Chicago DSA commented:

> In addition, the increase in numbers of Democrats in the House was due to the election of Progressives. These include Tammy Baldwin (WI2), the first open lesbian to be elected to Congress and a strong progressive.[23]

Ongoing DSA Support

DSA has continued to support Baldwin in a low-key manner throughout her career.

In DSA 's Democratic Left Winter 2004/2005, Theresa Alt wrote:

> We reported on the candidates that DSAers were supporting in the last issue of Democratic Left. How did they do?
>
> In Wisconsin, progressive incumbents Feingold, Baldwin and Obey won. In a race for an open state Senate seat, the favored Mark Miller won handily. However, progressive insurgent Bryan Kennedy lost badly."[24]

In May 2012, SEIU Healthcare Wisconsin vice president of politics and growth, DSA member Bruce Colburn[25] said of US Senate candidate Tammy Baldwin. "We were looking for a champion, and Tammy fit the bill."[26]

Commenting on the 2018 elections long-time DSA comrade Jack Clark, said the US Senate races were going to present DSAers with a "yes or no option" in many cases.

He acknowledged that Democrats running for reelection were not going to come right and "say they are socialists". However, if their ideals and approaches approximate the vision of DSA, Clark said "it'd be silly not to at least give them a shot". Senators like Elizabeth Warren (D-MA), Sherrod Brown (D-OH) and Tammy Baldwin

(D-WI) represented a "pretty good group of Democrats" in Clark's opinion.[27]

CONNECTION TO COMMUNIST CLARENCE KAILIN

To Tammy Baldwin's credit, she didn't just favour socialists. She was also willing to praise communists for good work, when deserved.

Clarence Kailin, was Madison, Wisconsin's most well-known communist. He had been a Communist Party USA member from 1935 to 1949 and again from 1970 to 1991. At that point he quit the party to establish a breakaway communist group, the Committees of Correspondence.

In the late 1930s, Kailin travelled to Spain to fight for two years with the communist-led Abraham Lincoln Brigade on the pro-Stalin side of the Spanish Civil War. In 1999, Kailin was pivotal in an effort supported by Tammy Baldwin to erect a memorial to the Wisconsin leftists who fought in Spain.[28]

In 2009, Kailin died, aged 95.

Representative Tammy Baldwin honored Clarence Kailin by reading a tribute into the Congressional Record:

IN HONOR OF CLARENCE KAILIN AND THE WISCONSIN VOLUNTEERS OF THE ABRAHAM
LINCOLN BRIGADE ON THE DEDICATION OF THEIR MEMORIAL IN JAMES MADISON
PARK, MADISON, WISCONSIN

———

HON. TAMMY BALDWIN

of wisconsin

in the house of representatives

Thursday, October 28, 1999

Ms. BALDWIN. Mr. Speaker, I rise to honor Mr. Clarence Kailin of
Madison, and the brave men and women who volunteered to serve in the
Abraham Lincoln Brigade during the Spanish Civil War, especially those
courageous volunteers from my home state of Wisconsin.

Mr. Speaker, I rise to honor Mr. Clarence Kailin of Madison, and the brave men and women who volunteered to serve in the Abraham Lincoln Brigade during the Spanish Civil War, especially those courageous volunteers from my home state of Wisconsin.

They, along with 45,000 volunteers from over 50 different countries, fought side by side during the early struggle against fascism.

Their foresight in recognizing the rising tyranny of fascism was a call to arms that went unheeded by the free world and resulted in the long and bloody conflict that became World War II.

Mr. Speaker, I want to express my gratitude to these men and women who helped to defend the democratic Spanish Republic from fascist aggression, at a time when the fate of democracy in Europe was being threatened by all sides of the political spectrum.

Mr. Speaker, I ask you and my colleagues to honor these dedicated men and women in the same rightful fashion as my state. The strength of character of Clarence Kailin and others from Wisconsin who volunteered in the Abraham Lincoln Brigade are the qualities which we all can take pride in and celebrate in this Congress."[29]

Tammy Baldwin failed to mention that Clarence Kailin was a lifelong communist. She also forgot to say that he and his comrades were serving Stalin, a mass butcher who killed millions of his own people through deliberate starvation, slave labour, torture execution and simple neglect.

IPS AND PDA

Tammy Baldwin is very close to the far-left Washington DC-based Institute for Policy Studies (IPS), and Progressive Democrats of America (PDA), which is a joint project of IPS and Democratic Socialists of America.

The goal of IPS is to turn socialist policy ideas into Democratic Party programs and legislation.

The goal of PDA is to elect as many far-left legislators as possible to the US Senate and the House of Representatives to implement those policies.

In 1998, fourteen new Members of Congress were elected on "progressive" platforms.

The 14 were judged "progressive" by the IPS after comparing their campaign literature and past activities with the IPS's "Fairness Agenda for America:"

On issues ranging from shifting budgetary priorities from military spending and corporate giveaways to health care and education, to promoting worker and environmental rights, fair trade, and equality, these 14 candidates stood for the liberal values that recent polls show most Americans embrace.

The 14 new "progressive" members included:

Tammy Baldwin, won in Wisconsin's 2nd district after a tough grassroots campaign. She has led the fight on progressive issues throughout her career in the Wisconsin state legislature, proposing bills on a range of issues from living wage and worker's rights, to support for public education and strong environmental protection. She has advocated a progressive tax system, universal health care and women's rights. She is also the first openly gay, nonincumbent elected to Congress.

"This vote represents a vital shift in the US Congress towards progressive Democrats," said Karen Dolan of the IPS. "It is important to point out that Tammy Baldwin and the other new progressives in Congress won by impressive mobilization at the grassroots," concluded Shelley Moskowitz, Political Director of Neighbor to Neighbor." Baldwin, for example, had 1,500 volunteers in the field on primary day."[30]

Progressive Majority Advisory Committee

Through the early 2000s Tammy Baldwin served on the Progressive Majority Advisory Committee[31] alongside several DSA Congressmembers members including John Conyers, (D-MI),[32] Jerry Nadler (D-NY),[33] Major Owens (D-NY),[34] and Jan Schakowsky (D-IL).[35]

According to Progressive Majority's website:

Progressive Majority has a clear and bold purpose: To elect progressive champions who will help change the direction of this country. We will do this by building a nationwide member network that will provide much-needed early support to progressive candidates - helping them to win elections and bring our values back into the halls of government.[36]

Progressive Majority's Board Chair was Robert Borosage,[37] a long time IPS Trustee and like Tammy Baldwin, a veteran of the Rainbow Coalition.[38]

Other Board members[39] included Karen Ackerman, political director of the AFL-CIO and a former member of the Young Workers Liberation League[40] – youth wing of the Communist Party USA.

Also, on the letterhead were Steve Phillips the former Stanford University Maoist, Rainbow Coalition veteran,[41] Democratic Party influencer and PowerPAC+ founder.[42] Phillips' old Stanford fellow radical and PowerPAC+ board member[43] Julie Martinez Ortega also served on the Progressive Majority board.

Letelier-Moffitt Award

Every year Institute for Policy Studies gives two awards — one domestic and one international — to what are described as "heroes of the progressive movement."

In 2011, representatives from Madison Teachers Inc. (MTI) accepted the national Letelier-Moffitt Human Rights Award on behalf of Wisconsin progressives involved in massive Marxist led demonstrations and civil disobedience directed at Republican Governor Scott Walker.

In a release from the IPS, executive director John Cavanagh wrote, "MTI, along with a rainbow of other groups, were leaders in the demonstrations against Walker's proposed legislation in February and March."

They were described as "gallantly fighting to preserve workers' rights and dignity in Wisconsin."

John Matthews, executive director of MTI for 43 years and Peggy Coyne, a middle school teacher and MTI president, accepted the award in Washington, DC on October 12. Representative Tammy Baldwin presented the award.[44]

Electoral Help

IPS/PDA worked hard to put Tammy Baldwin in the US Senate in 2012.

On November 2, 2012, PDA hosted a guided discussion at the Wisconsin Federation of Nurses & Health Professionals offices in Milwaukee, moderated by John Nichols (The Nation, MSNBC Contributor). Guest speakers included PDA's National Director Tim Carpenter, DSA dominated National Nurses United's Director of Public Policy Michael Lighty and Judith LeBlanc from Peace Action.[45]

John Nichols keynotes Detroit DSA dinner, November 2013

John Nichols is a DSA supporter, Tim Carpenter[46] and Michael Lighty[47] were DSA comrades and Judith LeBlanc is a leader of the Communist Party USA.[48]

Lighty and Carpenter joined with author/commentator and DSA supporter Jim Hightower[49] at the UAW Local 95 Hall in Janesville Saturday November 3, 2012:

*Rob Zerban—who was challenging Paul Ryan in Wisconsin's
1st District—and John Nichols also appeared. Then, Carpenter
and Lighty appeared in Madison, WI, with Mark Pocan,
Congressional Candidate in Wisconsin's 2nd District, one of the
leaders of the Wisconsin walkout. All three Wisconsin events
sought to help Congresswoman Tammy Baldwin, win her close
race for the US Senate.*[50]

Jim Hightower said, "PDA, NNU, and I are joining together to
make sure Tammy Baldwin carries Wisconsin. She is now under a
slanderous last-minute attack from Karl Rove! I once wrote a book
called 'If the Gods Had Meant Us to Vote They Would Have Given
Us Candidates.' Well, the Gods mean for us to vote—and donate—
and make phone calls—this year, because you don't find great progressive candidates like Tammy Baldwin and Mark Pocan and Rob
Zerban every day."[51]

Every step of Tammy Baldwin's political career has been guided
and abetted by Marxists from DSA, PDA and IPS.

COUNCIL FOR A LIVABLE WORLD

Senator Baldwin is a big favorite of the anti-US military Political
Action Committee Council for a Livable World (CLW). The Council
supported Tammy Baldwin in at least one Congressional run and for
both US Senate races.

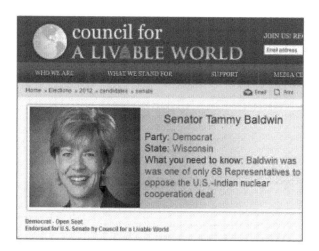

In 2012 CLW gave Baldwin a ringing endorsement:

> *In her first race for Congress, Baldwin was supported by Council for a Livable World's PeacePAC. She has proved worthy of the endorsement by scoring a perfect 100% on Council for a Livable World's PeacePAC voting scorecard over the past six years...*
>
> *She has opposed deployment of National Missile Defense and attempts to build new generations of nuclear weapons.... She advocates negotiations with Iran to eliminate its nuclear weapons program while some of her colleagues have advocated launching a military attack.*[52]

CLW and the Center for Arms Control and Non-Proliferation hosted an event on Monday, January 21, 2013 celebrating the second inauguration of President Barack Obama and Vice President Joe Biden and their endorsed candidates in the 113th Congress. The event was held at the Phoenix Park Hotel ballroom across from Union Station and just two blocks from the US Capitol:

> *Chairman of the board, Ira Lechner, introduced one of the most inspiring leaders in the country today, Senator Tammy Baldwin (D-WI). Senator Baldwin, who made history in November as the first openly gay member of the United States Senate, received a warm round of applause from the Council enthusiastic supporters who filled the ballroom. She expressed her gratitude for the early grassroots support and encouragement in what was a hard-fought victory.* [53]

The Council's 2018 US Senate endorsement was as effusive as the first:

> *Tammy Baldwin has been a progressive star in Congress since 1998 when she was first elected to the US House of Representatives...*
>
> *In the Senate, Baldwin has voted terrifically on national security issues. On the Iran nuclear agreement, she said: "I'm proud that America led six countries toward an historic international agreement with Iran. I believe we are right to choose a path of international diplomacy to achieve our goal of verifiably preventing Iran from acquiring a nuclear weapon."*

> On North Korea, she has urged the crisis be de-escalated and
> that the United States exhaust every diplomatic option. On the
> Council scorecard, she has scored a perfect 100% on key votes in
> the Senate."[54]

The Council for a Livable World's praise for Baldwin should hor-
rify every Wisconsin voter. The organization has consistently worked
to weaken America and strengthen her enemies since 1962.

TAMMY BALDWIN AND COLOMBIAN COMMUNISM

Tammy Baldwin has worked for decades with the Madison Wisconsin-
based Colombia Support Network (CSN).

Colombia, an American ally, has been fighting a war against
Cuban-backed Marxist guerrillas of the Revolutionary Armed Forces
of Colombia (FARC) and other groups for more than half a century.
With the recent election of Colombia's first leftist President, former
Marxist guerilla Gustavo Petro, the revolution may be entering its
final stages.

According to its website, CSN "seeks to influence US Government
policy towards Colombia so that the US Government will adopt policies which support local initiatives to achieve peace with justice".[55]

"Peace" in this context, means communist victory.

CSN does not explicitly support FARC or other terror groups.
Until 2021 the FARC was designated by the US State Department as
a "Foreign Terrorist Organization".[56] Open support for FARC, until
recently, could have landed American citizens in jail.

What CSN has done instead is to support leftist communities in
Colombia, attack the Colombian military with a steady stream of
negative propaganda and lobby the US Government to reduce financial and military support for the Colombian government. It is almost
the same strategy used by US activists to support the communist
takeover of Vietnam.

CSN forged sister city ties between Dane County Wisconsin
(Madison area) and the Colombian village of San Jose de Apartado.

According to CSN's Facebook page Tammy Baldwin, with the
assistance of future Wisconsin Congressman Mark Pocan drafted
the sister community resolution for Dane County and Apartadó:

> *Tammy Baldwin and Mark Pocan went to Colombia on a CSN*
> *delegation in 1993 and visited San José de Apartadó, 4 years*
> *before San José declared itself a 'Peace Community'.*
>
> *Mark has returned since, meeting with Senator Manuel Cepeda*
> *- Vargas and 3 other leaders of the Patriotic Union movement days*
> *before Senator Cepeda was murdered.*[57]

Who were the Patriotic Union?

According to Communist Party USA member W. T. Whitney, writing in Marxism-Leninism Today:

> *In 1985, Colombia's Communist Party, elements of the*
> *Revolutionary Armed Forces of Colombia (FARC), and other left-*
> *ists formed the Patriotic Union, an electoral coalition competing*
> *for local, regional, and national political offices. Under the peace*
> *initiative launched by the Belisario Betancur government and the*
> *FARC, armed insurgents joined regular political processes.* [58]

Baldwin and Pocan are both active in lobbying US Government officials on behalf of the Colombian Left.

Circa 1993, not long after Russ Feingold was elected to the US Senate for his first term, several members of the CSN Board went to meet him at his office accompanied by Tammy Baldwin and Mark Pocan, at the time both members of the Dane County Board.

> *Senator Feingold listened carefully to our concerns about the dra-*
> *matic situation in our sister community of Apartado, even though*
> *he had no particular reason to be interested in Colombia, South*
> *America.*[59]

CSN's Action on Colombia newsletter of Summer 1994 included a letter sent to President Bill Clinton and Colombian President Samper.

The letter called on the US to "cut off all aid to Colombia until the violence has ended" and called for the appointment of a UN Rapporteur on human rights in Colombia.

Signatories included several well-known CSN leaders, as well as Dane County Supervisor Mark Pocan, and Wisconsin State representative Tammy Baldwin.[60]

By 1996, Tammy Baldwin and Mark Pocan were both serving on the CSN Advisory Board, alongside well-known commentator Noam Chomsky – a member of the Communist Party USA splinter group Committees of Correspondence for Democracy and Socialism.[61]

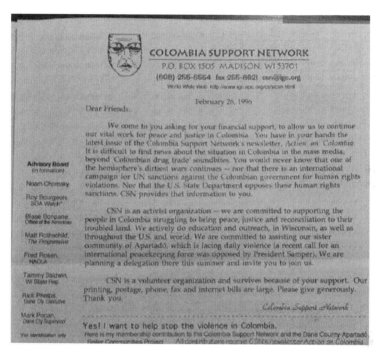

Pressuring the Colombian Government

In 2002, CSN organized a "dear colleague" letter to President Andres Pastrana Arango, of Colombia, through Ned Steiner, a staffer in Representative Sam Farr's office.

The letter called on President Pastrana to end a military blockade on the CSN's favorite Colombian town of San Jose de Apartado. Tammy Baldwin, of course, signed the letter.[62]

In September 2009, Representative Baldwin, Jim McGovern (D-MA) and Jan Schakowsky (D-IL), circulated a letter urging members of Congress to question US military access to Colombian army bases.

In their letter, the congressmen also express concern regarding the allegedly "high number of human rights violations attributed to the Colombian military":

Human rights organizations have documented the involvement of military and paramilitary groups in Colombia, in many cases been carried out extrajudicial killings, disappearances and displacement of peasants, Afro-Colombians and indigenous peoples.[63]

In 2011, Tammy Baldwin campaigned actively against a proposed US Colombia Free Trade Deal.[64]

Tammy Baldwin maintained some connections to CSN until recent times.

In November 2012, CSN issued a public statement congratulating Mark Pocan and Tammy Baldwin on their elections to the House and the Senate respectively.

From the CSN's Facebook page pictured:

Colombia Support Network (CSN) celebrates the election last night of two great friends: Tammy Baldwin, elected to the United States Senate, and Mark Pocan, elected to the United States House of Representatives.

Tammy and Mark have provided great support to our human rights and sister community work on Colombia. We look forward to their solidarity from their new positions as Senator and Representative in Washington DC We congratulate them on their election and on their commitment to good government and support for a sensible U. S. foreign policy toward Colombia.

Colombia Support Network
November 7, 2012 · 🌐   ...

CSN CELEBRATES THE ELECTION OF TAMMY BALDWIN AND MARK POCAN!

Colombia Support Network (CSN) celebrates the election last night of two great friends: Tammy Baldwin, elected to the United States Senate, and Mark Pocan, elected to the United States House of Representatives. Tammy, with the assistance of Mark, drafted our sister community resolution for Dane County and Apartadó. Both Tammy and Mark went to Colombia on a CSN delegation in 1993 and visited San José de Apartadó, 4 years before San José declared itself a Peace Community. Mark has returned since, meeting with Senator Manuel Cepeda - Vargas and 3 other leaders of the Patriotic Union movement days before Senator Cepeda was murdered. He is a former CSN Board Member and is currently on our Advisory Board.

Tammy and Mark have provided great support to our human rights and sister community work on Colombia. We look forward to their solidarity from their new positions as Senator and Representative in Washington D.C. We congratulate them on their election and on their commitment to good government and support for a sensible U. S. foreign policy toward Colombia.

Madison, November 7, 2012

COLOMBIA SUPPORT NETWORK

👍 5   1 Share

In 2015 Senator Baldwin's Finance Assistant Mai Tyler[65] was listed as an official translator for CSN.[66]

Senator Baldwin sent a message to CSN's National Conference in June 2017 through Flora Csontos, her Southcentral Regional Representative.[67]

Tammy Baldwin has for more than 30 years worked to undermine the anti-communist governments of Colombia, reduce support for the Colombian military and ease the path of the Colombian Left in its decades long bid for complete power.

She even has a connection to Colombia's recently elected Marxist President.

In 2007, Jack Laun of CSN took Senator Gustavo Petro of the Polo Democratico Colombia to the US Congress. They met, with Senator Russ Feingold and a representative of Senator Ted Kennedy, and with Representative Tammy Baldwin.

CSN's *Colombia Action newsletter*, Summer 2007 issue

Senator Pero is now President Pero. Once a member of the militant guerrilla group 19th of April Movement, Senator Pero was now able to meet senior members of the US Congress – all long-time supporters of the Colombian Left.

Thanks in part to Senator Tammy Baldwin, the once pro-America Columbia is now travelling down the communist road.

EPILOGUE

HOW TRUTH AND 'AMNESTY' CAN SAVE AMERICA

U PON TAKING OFFICE, US Senators state the following:

> I do solemnly swear that I will support and defend the
> Constitution of the United States against all enemies, foreign
> and domestic; that I will bear true faith and allegiance to the same;
> that I take this obligation freely, without any mental reservation or
> purpose of evasion; and that I will well and faithfully discharge the
> duties of the office on which I am about to enter: So help me God.

Do you now believe that the senators profiled in "Security Risk
Senators" are sincerely upholding their oath?

I hope I have made a convincing case in these two volumes of
"Security Risk Senators" that the US government is deeply penetrated
by its enemies – both foreign and domestic.

The question then becomes: "What do we do to correct this situation - while we still have a country?"

There are the obvious answers of voting, increased citizen political
involvement at every level, "raising awareness" and prayer.

These should all be a given. Anybody who takes the time to read
"Security Risk Senators" should already be making plans to step up
all the above.

And please remember – prayer is supposed to be a guide for action,
not a substitute for it.

So, you say "Loudon, what concrete actions can we take to solve
this problem?"

BASIC MUST DOS

There are a few basic steps we must take, and one radical program
that would be a "game-changer".

Firstly:

- All Senators and Congressmembers who wish to serve on committees must be subject to security assessments. Political candidates should not be vetted by a government entity. That's the people's job. However, any elected politician who wishes to serve on a House or Senate Committee – Armed Services, Intelligence, Homeland Security, Natural Resources, Labor etc., should be willing to have their connections to foreign and domestic enemies thoroughly examined. If they are not willing to do this, they should not put their name forward.

- We must build pressure among our representatives to reinstate security clearances and loyalty oaths – with perjury charges for false affirmations for congressional staff and all government employees and contractors.

- We must begin strict enforcement of the Foreign Agents Registration Act (FARA) and the Logan Act – which forbids private citizens from engaging in unauthorized correspondence with foreign governments. Influence peddling and bribery on behalf of foreign powers need to be treated seriously again.

- We must establish a public register of subversive organizations allied to or working on behalf of foreign governments, or problematic international institutions and organizations.

- We must apply the various federal and state laws limiting foreign ownership of land, businesses, and strategic assets.

- We must institute an immigration moratorium (excepting for nuclear family re-unification) until this country has its internal security and loyalty issues under control.

- We must seal all borders and points of entry to illegal aliens and unvetted foreign nationals. We must implement E-Verify on a national basis, federally defund all "sanctuary" cities and districts, and begin the methodical repatriation of all illegal aliens and subversive non-citizens.

+ We must shut down hostile foreign propaganda operations in this country, including RT and Al Jazeera and any entities connected in any way to the Chinese Communist Party. The First Amendment does not apply to foreign governments and their US agents.

+ We must deny all student and residency visas to citizens of China, Russia, and other belligerent nations.

All these steps won't save America. They will only stem the bleeding. All of them are essential but even if fully implemented, will only buy some time - maybe enough time to avert civil war or mass social breakdown, or foreign invasion.

Now comes the big one. This one will actually take back territory. This step, if implemented, could actually save the country.

DROPPING THE AMNESTY BOMB

What we need more than anything is an amnesty for all foreign agents and allies of foreign powers operating in this country.

NEW SECURITY AGENCY

The FBI, CIA, Justice Department and most other federal intelligence and law enforcement agencies are deeply compromised.

The next "America First" president must quickly establish a new agency, specifically focused on identifying and shutting down foreign intelligence operations and their domestic collaborators.

Let's call it the Foreign Agents Investigation Taskforce (FAIT) for now.

FAIT must be led by former officers from CIA, FBI, DEA, NSA, IRS etc. who left service at the beginning of the Obama era or before the contamination really set in.

These must be joined by new recruits of unquestionable patriotism, drawn from the military, police forces and technical institutions.

FAIT must be an elite unit, with all staff and leadership vetted to the nth degree. The organization must be highly compartmentalized to minimize foreign and "deep state" penetration.

In the 1930s, New York special prosecutor Thomas Dewey was assigned the task of taking down a network of assassins, criminals and extortionists popularly known as "Murder, Inc." Many police forces were penetrated by Murder Inc. informants or were on the mob payroll. Witnesses were too terrified to testify against the gang.

Consequently, Murder Inc. was able to operate with near impunity.

Thomas Dewy personally interviewed 1200 people, until he found enough honest and courageous men willing to take on the gang. By offering protection to witnesses and turncoat mobsters, he began to build cases against Murder Inc. leaders. Dewey eventually won 72 out of 73 prosecutions, sending several murderers to the electric chair and destroying the organization.

Elliot Ness' "Untouchables", who battled the Chicago mob, are another example of an elite law enforcement unit, established to deal with a specific group of "bad actors".

Elite units, coupled with very heavy penalties for lawbreakers, coupled with protection for informants, are a time-tested way to break secretive criminal organizations.

This is how New York prosecutor Rudi Giuliani and others heavily damaged the New York mafia families.

Before New York decided to get serious about the mob, a low level mafiosi would get prosecuted for a crime and would serve a few years in prison. The "family" would look after the man's dependents. He would do his time, shut his mouth, then return to "work" upon release.

In more recent times, authorities began handing out 30-year sentences for heroin offences. They also started offering "witness protection" if the low-level mobsters would agree to testify against their bosses.

Soon the "code of silence" began to crumble. Low level mobsters would turn in their bosses, who would then turn in those above them, who would then turn in those even higher on the "food chain". Eventually even the highest-level mafia bosses were going to prison for decades long terms.

Foreign penetration of the US government is a way more serious problem, than even the worst organized criminal gangs. But it can be tackled using similar tactics to those used against organized crime.

Law enforcement agencies around the world often form small, elite, highly trustworthy taskforces to deal with specific criminal threats.

Something similar must be done at federal, and later state level to deal with foreign influence in the United States – while there is still a country left to be saved.

TIME FOR AMNESTY

Once FAIT is up and running, the President must offer a 90-day amnesty from prosecution to all foreign agents, and their domestic enablers currently operating in the US.

If the guilty parties come forward to FAIT, within the allotted time limit, and are willing to fully confess to all their crimes, and expose all of their networks, contacts and fellow traitors - they will escape prosecution for their crimes.

If they are foreign nationals they may be deported, or if they are valuable enough, offered refuge in this country. They may also be required to testify in court, so the American public can see just how deep the foreign penetration of this country is.

If they are US nationals, they must be willing to publicly acknowledge their crimes, and in some instances to appear in court as witnesses against their former co-conspirators. Some confessors may be offered "witness protection". They will never be allowed to hold or run for public office. Some may be subject to long term probation requirements. However, they will not go to prison, unless they are later found to have made less than full disclosures. Any further punishment will come from God, not the United States government.

If, however, the guilty parties try to evade exposure, or do not come forward to FAIT, then all bets are off.

After the 90-day amnesty is over, FAIT and other cooperating agencies would begin arresting and prosecuting every illicit foreign agent they could find.

Faced with the choice of amnesty and some public humiliation, or 30 years in Leavenworth – maybe even the death penalty in some cases, what do you think many foreign agents and domestic traitors would choose?

Such an approach would see thousands of Iranian, Chinese, Russian, North Korean, Cuban, Turkish, Syrian, Venezuelan and Vietnamese agents quietly leave the country.

Tens of thousands of Chinese "students", academics, and businesspeople would suddenly be recalled to China. Russian mobsters and Hezbollah "sleepers" would quickly sell their homes and businesses and skulk out of the country. Many more would be constantly looking over their shoulders.

Dozens of senators and congressman would retire for "family reasons".

Hundreds of Wall Street "titans", crooked businessmen, and big tech "moguls" would be forced to "lawyer up" or make a deal with FAIT.

Every foreign network in the country would fall into complete chaos.

Every covert Chinese spymaster would worry if the Senator he was dining with might be wearing a "wire". Every Iranian "lobbyist" would be terrified that the crooked defence contractor he was buying blueprints from had sold him out to FAIT.

Paranoia would paralyze every foreign network in the country. Foreign agents and domestic traitors could no longer trust each other. Nobody would know who has made a deal with FAIT and who hadn't.

Most foreign networks in the country would evaporate or implode in a few weeks – without a shot being fired, even before the prosecutions began.

When Senators and congressmembers, government officials, and even presidential candidates are compromised by foreign enemies, the very survival of this nation is at stake.

Such people are the reason our Southern border is wide open. They are the reason that Iran is on the verge of obtaining nuclear weapons, triggering a war in the Middle East. They are the reason why Afghanistan was handed to China with thousands of tons of US weaponry. They are the reason why Russia was emboldened to attack Ukraine and why China may soon launch a major Pacific War.

They are also the reason why, since WW2, US troops have been involved in near continuous wars – that they are only occasionally allowed to fight to win. They are the reason the US militarily is being degraded and destroyed before our very eyes

Foreign compromised politicians are the reason that Big Tech is allowed to censor Americans, why China can tell Hollywood which movies it can or cannot make.

Our compromised leaders are the reason China is allowed to steal our technology and buy our farmland, factories, newspapers, studios, businesses and real estate. They are the reason we are losing tens of thousands of young Americans every year Chinese Fentanyl. They are why our children are being taught in the schools we paid for, to hate this great nation.

If the foreign networks, operating with near impunity in this country, are not shut down, America is doomed.

MORALITY

Some readers may recoil at the thought of granting amnesty to those who have betrayed this country.

I fully understand this, but I ask you to consider a few points.

Some of our traitors are motivated by pure greed - or by some hateful, anti-American ideology. Most, however, are slowly seduced or compromised into working for our enemies. Some are lured into the trap through slightly shady business deals. Some may be blackmailed or sexually compromised while visiting a foreign country. Others may be coerced, or their families may be threatened. Others may be fooled by political or religious belief into thinking it is morally right to bring this country to its knees.

This country is founded on Christian principles. Forgiveness is an essential element of Christianity.

If those who have betrayed this country, are willing to confess their crimes in full and publicly repent, should not they be given another chance to make something of their lives?

Should we not be willing to leave it to God, to collect any debt left unpaid?

The overriding priority is not to punish every evildoer, but to alert Americans to how deeply their government is penetrated.

Once this is realized, and influence peddling, espionage, and the bribery of public officials by foreign agents becomes treated as a serious matter again, this nation will be transformed.

If enough of us get involved in pressuring the few good leaders we have left, to implement the steps outlined above, I think, with God's help we have a fighting chance to hand this great nation on to our children and grandchildren

—Trevor Loudon
in gratitude to America and all for which she stands.

INDEX

ENDNOTES

1	Melinn, Kyle. Lansing City Pulse: "The race that launched Stabenow's political career", 9/20/2018. Link: https://lansingcitypulse.com/stories/the-race-that-launched-stabenowrsquos-political-career,603

2	Stabenow, Debbie. Official Government Biography: https://www.stabenow.Senate.gov/about/biography

3	Stabenow, Debbie. https://www.Senate.gov/general/committee_assignments/assignments.htm Archive Link: https://web.archive.org/web/20220413210220/https://www.Senate.gov/general/committee_assignments/assignments.htm

4	Jeffrey, Mildred. New York Times: "In Michigan School-Tax Shift, the Poor Lose; Give Her the Credit," March 23, 1994. Link: https://www.nytimes.com/1994/04/01/opinion/l-in-michigan-school-tax-shift-the-poor-lose-give-her-the-credit-643602.html

5	Toledo Blade, "Washington finally catches up to Millie Jeffrey," September 17, 2000. Archive Link: https://web.archive.org/web/20220515034845/https://www.toledoblade.com/JackLessenberry/2000/09/17/Washington-finally-catches-up-to-Millie-Jeffrey/stories/200009170009

6	Fitrakis, Bob. Free Press "Mildred Jeffrey, 1910-2004", July 10, 2004. Archive Link: https://web.archive.org/web/20040918144917/https://freepress.org/journal.php?strFunc=display&strID=254&strJournal=28

7	Meyerson, Harold. Democratic Left: "Unsung Heroine: Millie Jeffrey," Spring 2004. Archive Link: https://web.archive.org/web/20040603220813/https://www.dsausa.org/dl/Spring_2004.pdf

8	Neuhauser, Alan. Dnainfo: "Success Academy Aims to Open First High School in Murray Hill," May 21, 2013. Archive Link: https://web.archive.org/web/20220515025959/https://www.dnainfo.com/new-york/20130521/midtown-south/success-academy-aims-open-first-high-school-murray-hill/

9	Democratic Left, Nov./Dec. 1984, page 12

10	Democratic Left, Sep./Oct. 1984, page 24

11	Democratic Left, Mar./Apr. 1990, page 12

12	Roberts, Joel. CBS News, "Thoroughly Marvelous Millie," March 29, 2004. Archive Link: https://web.archive.org/web/20220515033956/https://www.cbsnews.com/news/thoroughly-marvelous-millie/

13	Grele, Ronald J, Columbia Center for Oral History, Columbia University. CORA WEISS ORAL HISTORY PROJECT, 2014. Page 55 Archive Link: https://web.archive.org/web/20160620192454/https://static1.squarespace.com/static/575a10ba27d4bd5d7300a207/t/57601b8d9f7266ebae932dbc/1465916301804/Weiss_Cora_2014.pdf

14	Weiss, Cora. "Cascading Movements for Peace: From Women Strike for Peace to UNSCR 1325." Social Justice, vol. 46, no. 1 (155), 2019, pp. 13–22. JSTOR, https://www.jstor.org/stable/26873833. Accessed 28 Jun. 2022.

15	United States-Soviet relations: hearings before the Committee on Foreign Relations, United States Senate, Ninety-eighth Congress, first session. United States, US Government Printing Office, 1983. Page 254.

16   The War Called Peace: The Soviet Peace Offensive. United States, Western Goals, 1982. Archive Link: https://web.archive.org/web/20020502142615/http://www.knology.net/~bilrum/PeaceGrpGloss.htm

17   Loudon, Trevor, Keywiki. "Edith Villastrigo" Link: https://keywiki.org/Edith_Villastrigo

18   Loudon, Trevor, Keywiki. "Eleanor LeCain" Link: https://keywiki.org/Eleanor_LeCain

19   Dem. Left, Jan./Feb. 1993. page 8

20   Loudon, Trevor, Keywiki. "Diane Balser" Link: https://keywiki.org/Diane_Balser

21   Democratic left, Jan./Feb. 1990, page 12

22   Loudon, Trevor, Keywiki. "Anne Zill" Link: https://keywiki.org/Anne_Zill

23   Council for a Livable World "Our Legacy in Congress: Who We've Helped Elect" Link: https://livableworld.org/meet-the-candidates/our-legacy-in-congress-who-weve-helped-elect/

24   Council for a Livable World, "Senator Debbie Stabenow". Archive Link: https://web.archive.org/web/20120509133949/http://livableworld.org/elections/2012/candidates/Senate/dstabenow/

25   Stabenow, Debbie. Congressional Record: "Mildred McWilliams 'Millie' Jeffrey". https://www.govinfo.gov/content/pkg/CREC-2004-05-20/pdf/CREC-2004-05-20-pt1-PgS6045-2.pdf#page=1 and https://justfacts.votesmart.org/public-statement/32463/mildred-mcwilliams-millie-jeffrey

26   Bernstein, Adam. Washington Post: "Activist and Democrat Mildred Jeffrey Dies", March 26, 2004. Link: https://www.washington-post.com/archive/local/2004/03/26/activist-and-democrat-mildred-jeffrey-dies/782294df-f5ea-4ba6-873f-dd00a503a03d/

27   Democratic Left, Spring 2004, Page 10

28   Justice Caucus event August 28, 2010. from left: Gov. Jennifer Granholm, Sen. Debbie Stabenow, Paul Stevenson, Justice Diane Hathaway, Justice Alton Thomas Davis, Judge Denise Langford Morris

29   Michel, Amanda. Huffington Post, "DNC Michigan Superdelegates," February 28, 2008. Archive Link: https://web.archive.org/web/20220515040627/https://www.huffpost.com/entry/dnc-michigan-superdelegat_b_89004

30   Democratic Left, Convention Issue 1999, Page 9

31   Special Collection. Walter P. Reuther Library - Wayne State University, "The Ganley-Wellman Collection Papers," 1969. Archive Link: https://web.archive.org/web/20220515174643/https://reuther.wayne.edu/files/LP000308.pdf

32   Democratic Left, Convention Issue 1999, Page 8

33   Democratic Left, Millennium Issue 2000, Page 5

34   Democratic Left, Fall/Winter 2001, Page 11

35   Maynard, Micheline. New York Times, "Nate Gooden, 68, a U.A.W. Vice President, Dies," November 13, 2006. Link: https://www.nytimes.com/2006/11/13/business/nate-gooden-68-a-uaw-vice-president-dies.html

36   Roman, Bob. ChicagoDSA.org, "Other News", November – December 1999. Archive Link: https://web.archive.org/web/20090107025508/https://chicagodsa.org/ngarchive/ng67.html

37   Michel, Amanda. Huffington Post, "DNC Michigan Superdelegates," February 28, 2008. Archive Link: https://web.archive.org/web/20220515040627/https://www.huffpost.com/entry/dnc-michigan-superdelegat_b_89004

38   Legistorm, "Amanda A Renteria trip to Havana, Cuba on Jul. 17, 2009" Archive Link: https://web.archive.org/web/20091011050546/http://www.legistorm.com/trip/31426.html

39   Code for America, "Code for America Receives Landmark Investment Through the Audacious Project to Transform America's Social Safety Net," April 22, 2022. Link: https://codeforamerica.org/news/audacious-project-investment-to-launch-safety-net-innovation-lab/

40   Code for America, "We're supported by generous donors and organizations committed to making government work in the digital age." Link: https://codeforamerica.org/about-us/our-supporters/

41   Associated Press, The Guardian. "Senator Patrick Leahy leads US group to Cuba to seek release of Alan Gross", 18 Feb 2013 Link: https://www.theguardian.com/world/2013/feb/18/patrick-leahy-cuba-alan-gross

42   Prensa Latina, "Cuban Minister Receives United States Senators," January 20, 2015. Archive Link: https://web.archive.org/web/20220710185652/http://www.fidelcastro.cu/ru/noticia/kubinskiy-ministr-prinyal-senatorov-soedinennyh-shtatov

43   Green, David. Greater Detroit Democratic Socialists of America Newsletter, "Call to Action," March 2010. Archive Link: https://web.archive.org/web/20220515164255/https://d3n8a8pro7vhmx.cloudfront.net/detroitdsa/pages/49/attachments/original/1434223021/March_2010_DSA_Newsletter.pdf?1434223021

44   Ibid.

45   Ibid.

46   2004 Speakers, Campaign for America's Future Website. Take Back America Conference. Archive Link: https://web.archive.org/web/20080906124121/https://ourfuture.org/node/13146

47   Image: Cover Borosage, Robert L, and Roger Hickey. The Next Agenda: Blueprint for a New Progressive Movement. Boulder, Colo: Westview Press, 2001. Print.

48   Spindler, Tasha, Common Dreams News Center. "Morning After Bush's Speech, Progressive Activists to Unite," September 18, 2001. Archive Link: https://web.archive.org/web/20010918084605/https://www.commondreams.org/news2001/0226-05.htm

49   Borosage, Robert L, and Roger Hickey. The Next Agenda: Blueprint for a New Progressive Movement. Boulder, Colo: Westview Press, 2001. Print.

50   Hickey, Roger, Democratic Left. "Fighting Inflation: Strategy for a New Majority" December 1978 edition, Pages 8-9

51   Collection: Office of Staff Secretary; Series: Presidential Files; Folder: 12/19/78; Container 100 Link: https://www.jimmycarterlibrary.gov/digital_library/sso/148878/100/SSO_148878_100_12.pdf

52   Carter, Jimmy. Official Government Statement. "Consumers Opposed to Inflation in the Necessities Statement Following a Meeting with the Organization," December 20, 1978. Link: https://www.presidency.ucsb.edu/

documents/consumers-opposed-inflation-the-necessities-statement-following-meeting-with-the

53   Hickey, Roger & Jeff Cruz (April 2007), Waste and Inefficiency in the Bush Medicare Prescription Drug Plan: Allowing Medicare to Negotiate Lower Prices Could Save $30 Billion a Year, Institute for America's Future

54   Lubell, Jennifer, Modern Healthcare, "Report sees savings in drug negotiations," April 04, 2007. Link: https://www.modernhealthcare.com/article/20070404/NEWS/304040011/report-sees-savingsin-drug-negotiations

55   Obama, Barack and Joe Biden, Campaign Fact Sheet.: "Barack Obama and Joe Biden's Plan to Lower Health Care Costs and Ensure Affordable, Accessible Health Coverage for All." Link: https://drum.lib.umd.edu/bitstream/handle/1903/23076/HealthCareFullPlan.pdf?sequence=1&isAllowed=y

56   Wallance, Gregory J. The Hill. "Racial Reparations at the USDA", June 22, 2021. Link: https://thehill.com/opinion/civil-rights/559586-racial-reparations-at-the-usda/

57   Warnock, Raphael, Official Government Website. "Senator Reverend Warnock: Over 600 Food and Farm Leaders Support the Emergency Relief for Farmers of Color Act in the Next COVID-19 Assistance Package," March 4, 2001. Link: https://www.warnock.Senate.gov/newsroom/press-releases/senator-reverend-warnock-over-600-food-and-farm-leaders-support-the-emergency-relief-for-farmers-of-color-act-in-the-next-covid-19-assistance-package/

58   National Farmers Union's 119th Anniversary Convention. "Remarks from the Chair of the Senate Agriculture Committee Debbie Stabenow (D-MI)," Mar 2, 2021. Link: https://www.youtube.com/watch?v=QGpZskZ-VeI

59   Wheeler, Tim, Communist Party USA. "60 million rural Americans: Brothers and sisters in the struggle," June 21, 2021. Archive Link: https://web.archive.org/web/20220112173447/https://www.cpusa.org/article/60-million-rural-americans-brothers-and-sisters-in-the-struggle/

60   Pratt, William C. "The Farmers Union, McCarthyism, & the Demise of the Agrarian Left." The Historian, vol. 58, no. 2, 1996, pp. 329–42. JSTOR, http://www.jstor.org/stable/24452279.

61   Screenshot: The Wetumpka Herald, Wetumpka, Alabama, 11 Jan 1945, Page 8. Link: https://www.newspapers.com/clip/104900530/communist-beachhead-in-agriculture/

62   Communist Party USA, "If You Eat, You're Involved in Agriculture: Report from the Rural and Farm Comm," September 22, 2001. Archive Link: https://web.archive.org/web/20220703210501/https://www.cpusa.org/party_info/if-you-eat-you-re-involved-in-agriculture-report-from-the-rural-and-farm-comm/

63   Communist Party USA, "Tim Wheeler". Archive Link: https://web.archive.org/web/20220703234250/https://www.cpusa.org/authors/tim-wheeler/

64   Casey-Sawicki, Katherine, Encyclopedia Britannica. "Seattle WTO protests of 1999," November 28, 1999 - December 3, 1999 Link: https://www.britannica.com/event/Seattle-WTO-protests-of-1999

65   Associated Press, "Farmers Rally In Washington For Increased Crop Supports," Screenshot from The News-Messenger Fremont, Ohio 21 Mar 2000, Page 6 Link: https://www.newspapers.com/clip/104911286/communist-backed-rally-for-rural-america/

66   Blakely, Briar, Federation of Southern Cooperatives. "The Emergency Relief for Farmers of Color Act: A Collaborative Call to Action for the US Senate," March 4, 2021. Archive Link: https://web.archive.org/web/20220703205341/http://www.pvamu.edu/cahs/wp-content/uploads/sites/27/1The-Federation-of-Southern-Cooperatives-1.pdf

67   Detroit Free Press, "Extremism: Look Who's Talking," October 27, 1996 Link: https://www.newspapers.com/clip/104917280/

68   Albee, Amanda, Dallas News. "Black Texas farmers push on as USDA loan relief efforts remain stalled in the courts," June 21, 2022. Archive Link: https://web.archive.org/web/20220621122718/https://www.dallasnews.com/food/2022/06/21/black-texas-farmers-push-on-as-usda-loan-relief-efforts-remain-stalled-in-the-courts/

GARY PETERS

1   Gary Peters. Official Government Biography: https://www.peters.Senate.gov/about/meet-gary

2   Peters, Gary. https://www.Senate.gov/general/committee_assignments/assignments.htm Archive Link: https://web.archive.org/web/20220413210220/https://www.Senate.gov/general/committee_assignments/assignments.htm

3   Democratic Socialists of America-Greater Detroit Local newsletter January 2009, page 1. Link: https://d3n8a8pro7vhmx.cloudfront.net/detroitdsa/pages/21/attachments/original/1412450232/january2009newsletter.pdf?1412450232

4   Maxon, Seth A. In These Times "Mobilized in Motor City: How Detroit DSA works in the Democratic Party to effect change" December 25 2009 Link: https://inthesetimes.com/article/mobilized-in-motor-city "Gary Peters" Link: https://inthesetimes.com/article/mobilized-in-motor-city

5   Ibid.

6   Ibid.

7   Democratic Socialists of America-Greater Detroit Local newsletter May 2009, page 19. Link: https://d3n8a8pro7vhmx.cloudfront.net/detroitdsa/pages/44/attachments/original/1434147468/May2009.pdf?1434147468

8   Democratic Socialists of America-Greater Detroit Local newsletter March 2014, page 3. Link: https://d3n8a8pro7vhmx.cloudfront.net/detroitdsa/pages/69/attachments/original/1441478386/March_2014.pdf?1441478386

9   AFT Michigan press release. "AFT MICHIGAN ENDORSES MARK SCHAUER FOR GOVERNOR AND GARY PETERS FOR US SENATE" January 27, 2014. Link: https://aftmichigan.org/aft-michigan-endorses-mark-schauer-for-governor-and-gary-peters-for-u-s-Senate/

10   Michigan Democratic Party, "Officers-at-large" Link: https://michigan-dems.com/elected-officials/

11   Hecker, David Detroit Democratic Socialists of America newsletter, "Protect our Jobs" May 2012 Link: https://d3n8a8pro7vhmx.cloudfront.net/detroitdsa/pages/63/attachments/original/1436482319/May2012Newsletter.pdf?1436482319

12   Senator Gary Peters, press release. "Peters Announces Support for Heroes Fund to Reward Frontline Workers, Calls on Senate to Pass Proposal" June 19 2020. Link: https://www.peters.Senate.gov/newsroom/press-releases/

peters-announces-support-for-heroes-fund-to-reward-frontline-workers-calls-on-Senate-to-pass-proposal

13   Meyerson, Harold Democratic Left "Unsung Heroine: Millie Jeffrey" Spring 2004 ♦ page 10 Link: https://democraticleft.dsausa.org/files/sites/6/2018/12/DL_2004_V031_04.pdf

14   FLICKR "2009 Millie Jeffrey Dinner" Link: https://inthesetimes.com/article/mobilized-in-motor-city "Gary Peters" Link: https://www.flickr.com/photos/40034830@N07/sets/72157620725211785/detail/

15   Szumilo, Dan, Black Swamp Gazette, "The Democratic Socialist Alternative DSA", January 17, 1983

16   Democratic Socialists of America-Greater Detroit Local newsletter March, 2010. page 1 Link: https://d3n8a8pro7vhmx.cloudfront.net/detroitdsa/pages/49/attachments/original/1434223021/March_2010_DSA_Newsletter.pdf?1434223021

17   Green, David, Democratic Socialists of America-Greater Detroit Local newsletter. "John Nichols Delights the Audience at Thirteenth Annual Douglass-Debs Dinner" January 2013 page 3 Link: https://d3n8a8pro7vhmx.cloudfront.net/detroitdsa/pages/67/attachments/original/1441477885/January2013Newsletter.pdf?1441477885

18   Pecinovsky, David, People's World. "Activists, union leaders attend Peace & Justice Awards Breakfast", May 9, 2013. Link: https://peoplesworld.org/article/activists-union-leaders-attend-peace-justice-awards-breakfast/

19   Hubred-Golden, Joni Patch. "Residents Question Costs During Health Care Town Hall in Farmington Hills" May 21, 2012 Link: https://patch.com/michigan/farmington-mi/residents-raise-cost-concerns-during-health-care-townedcb264150

20   Capcon, "Are Socialists Deciding Close State House Races?" May 28, 2009 Link: https://www.michigancapitolconfidential.com/10581

21   Detroit DSA newsletter, "Agenda for March 7th General membership meeting" March 2009, page 7. Link: https://d3n8a8pro7vhmx.cloudfront.net/detroitdsa/pages/43/attachments/original/1434147077/March2009newsletter.pdf?1434147077

22   Democratic Socialists of America-Greater Detroit Local newsletter March 2014 page 3 Link: https://d3n8a8pro7vhmx.cloudfront.net/detroitdsa/pages/69/attachments/original/1441478386/March_2014.pdf?1441478386

23   MichUCAN, "BOARD OF DIRECTORS-Officers" May 28, 2009 Link: https://michuhcan.org/about/board/

24   Detroit DSA newsletter "BOARD OF DIRECTORS-Officers" January 2012 Link: https://d3n8a8pro7vhmx.cloudfront.net/detroitdsa/pages/61/attachments/original/1436481993/January2012newsletter.pdf?1436481993

25   PDA May 2013 Educate Congress Digest Letter drops

26   Democratic Left "DSA PAC ESTABLISHED" Spring 2006, page 3. Link: https://democraticleft.dsausa.org/files/sites/6/2018/12/DL_2006_V033_04.pdf

27   CampaignMoney.com "David Bonior Political Campaign Contributions 2006 Election Cycle Link: https://www.campaignmoney.com/political/contributions/david-bonior.asp?cycle=06

28   Council for a Livable World "Gary Peters" Link: http://livableworld.org/elections/2014/candidates/Senate/peters/

29   Senator Carl Levin press release: "Statement of Senator Carl Levin on the Passing of Millie Jeffrey" March 24, 2004 Link: https://web.archive.org/web/20090326072104/http://levin.Senate.gov/newsroom/release.cfm?id=219575

30   World Peace Council Tour USA. 1975, wpc information centre, Lonnrotinkatu 25 A 5 krs 00180 Helsinki 18 Finland

31   World Peace Council. "Romesh Chandra is no more – The World Peace Movement in grief!". 4 July 2016. Retrieved 7 July 2016.

32   Ibid.

33   Klehr, Harvey, et al, The Weekly Standard, Volume 16, NO. 47 "Childs at Play The FBI's Cold War triumph". September 5, 2011

34   World Peace Council Tour USA. 1975, wpc information centre, Lonnrotinkatu 25 A 5 krs 00180 Helsinki 18 Finland

35   People's World "Maryann Mahaffey, peoples champion, 81" August 11, 2006 Link: https://www.peoplesworld.org/article/maryann-mahaffey-people-s-champion-81/

36   Democratic Left, "DSA elected officials" January/February 1990, page 7

37   Testimony of Walter S. Steele regarding Communist activities in the United States. Hearings before the Committee on Un-American Activities, House of Representatives, Eightieth Congress, first session, on H. R. 1884 and H. R. 2122, bills to curb or outlaw the Communist Party in the United States. Public law 601 (section 121, subsection Q (2) July 21, 1947, pages 75.76

38   Ronald Reagan Presidential Library Digital Library Collections Collection: Blackwell, Morton: Files Folder Title: Information Digest
Box: 11 Information Digest April 16 1982 page 125. Link: https://www.reaganlibrary.gov/public/digitallibrary/smof/publicliaison/blackwell/box-011/40_047_7006969_011_011_2017.pdf

39   Council for a Livable World "On the passing of former Senator Carl Levin" July 30, 2021 Link: https://livableworld.org/on-the-passing-of-former-senator-carl-levin/

40   Spangler, Todd, Detroit Free Press. "'A champion for truth and justice': Family, friends mourn death of Carl Levin
" July 30, 2021. Link: https://www.freep.com/story/news/politics/2021/07/29/senator-carl-levin-obituary-reactions/5425624001/

41   Senator Gary Peters press release: "US Senator Peters on the Passing of Senator Levin" July 30, 2021 Link: https://www.peters.Senate.gov/news/videos/watch/us-senator-peters-on-the-passing-of-senator-levin-2021-07-30

42   Council for a Livable World: "Gary Peters for Senate (D-MI)' Link: https://livableworld.org/meet-the-candidates/Senate-candidates/gary-peters-for-Senate-d-mi/

AMY KLOBUCHAR

1   Klobuchar, Amy. Official Government Website: https://www.klobuchar.Senate.gov/public/index.cfm/about-amy

2   Amy Klobuchar. https://www.britannica.com/biography/Amy-Klobuchar

3   Klobuchar, Amy. https://www.Senate.gov/general/committee_
assignments/assignments.htm Archive Link: https://web.archive.org/
web/20220413210220/https://www.Senate.gov/general/committee_assignments/
assignments.htm

4   Klobuchar, Amy, The Senator Next Door: A Memoir from
the Heartland, page 25, Henry Holt & Company, August 2015ISBN13:
9781627794176

5   Klobuchar, Amy, The Senator Next Door: A Memoir from
the Heartland, page 88, Henry Holt & Company, August 2015ISBN13:
9781627794176

6   Klobuchar, Amy, The Senator Next Door: A Memoir from
the Heartland, page 25, Henry Holt & Company, August 2015ISBN13:
9781627794176

7   Fellner, Kim and Lighty, Michael, Democratic Left, "Ed Asner:
Socialist To the Core" September 8, 2021, Link: https://www.dsausa.org/
democratic-left/ed-asner-socialist-to-the-core/

8   Klobuchar, Amy, The Senator Next Door: A Memoir from
the Heartland, page 64, Henry Holt & Company, August 2015ISBN13:
9781627794176

9   Democratic Left, January/February 1990, "Recent books by DSA members" page 13.

10   Isaac, Jeffrey, Democratic Left, "Robert Dahl, Scholar of Democracy
and Democratic Socialist" Link: https://www.dsausa.org/democratic-left/
robert_dahl_scholar_of_democracy_and_democratic_socialist/

11   Dickinson, Matthew, Presidential Power, "AMY FOR
AMERICA! (BUT MAYBE NOT FOR DEMOCRATS)" July 29,
2019, Link: https://sites.middlebury.edu/presidentialpower/2019/07/29/
amy-for-america-but-maybe-not-for-democrats/

12   The American Prospect website: Masthead (accessed on November 15,
2009)

13   Libcom.org "Yugoslav self-management: Capitalism under the red
banner - Juraj Katalenac" October 9, 2013, Link: https://libcom.org/article/
yugoslav-self-management-capitalism-under-red-banner-juraj-katalenac

14   Klobuchar, Amy, The Senator Next Door: A Memoir from
the Heartland, page 65, Henry Holt & Company, August 2015ISBN13:
9781627794176

15   Democratic Socialists of America "Cool Periodicals for the Literate
Leftist - DSA-ish Publications" February 26, 2001, Link: https://web.archive.org/
web/19980626083306/http:/www.dsausa.org/rl/Links/Mags.html#DSAish

16   Common Dreams, Progressive Newswire "Morning After Bush's
Speech, Progressive Activists to Unite" February 26, 2001, Link: https://www.
commondreams.org/news2001/0226-05.htm

17   Interlocking subversion in government departments" July 30, 1953, page
36, Senate, Eighty-Third Congress

18   Fleischman, Harry, Democratic Left, "On the Left" May/June 1991,
page 15

19   Left Forum 2009 "Program" Link: https://www.leftforum.org/sites/
default/files/left-forum-2009-program-guide_0.pdf

20   Klobuchar, Amy, The Senator Next Door: A Memoir from the Heartland, page 86, Henry Holt & Company, August 2015ISBN13: 9781627794176

21   Congressional Record - Senate " 3248, June 5, 2019, Link: chrome-extension://efaidnbmnnnibpcajpcglclefindmkaj/https://www.govinfo.gov/content/pkg/CREC-2019-06-05/pdf/CREC-2019-06-05-pt1-PgS3248-4.pdf

22   Human Events, April 29, 1972, page 3

23   Clark, Jack, Newsletter of the Democratic Left, "In the International Arena" pages 8 and 9

24   Newsletter of the Democratic Left, October 1973, "Protest the Chilean junta" page 3

25   Minnesota Historical Society "DONALD MACKAY FRASER:" Link: http://www2.mnhs.org/library/findaids/00290.xml

26   Klehr, Harvey, Far Left of Center: The American Radical Left Today, page 182, Transaction Publishers; 1st edition – January 1, 1988, ISBN-10 : 0887382177

27   Doder, Dusko, Washington Post, "Soviets Said to Consider Faster Nuclear Missile Launch in Crisis", April 11, 198,2 Link: https://www.washingtonpost.com/archive/politics/1982/04/11/soviets-said-to-consider-faster-nuclear-missile-launch-in-crisis/10b7d6b6-f7d3-4ff3-817f-77823bb5f8ff/

28   Klehr, Harvey, Far Left of Center: The American Radical Left Today, page 182, Transaction Publishers; 1st edition – January 1, 1988, ISBN-10 : 0887382177

29   Amy Klobuchar press release, "Klobuchar Statement on the Death of Don Fraser", June 2, 2019, Link: https://www.klobuchar.Senate.gov/public/index.cfm/2019/6/klobuchar-statement-on-the-death-of-don-fraser

30   Peter, Stephan, Democratic Left "Building a Multilateral Future" Winter 2004/2005, pages 14 and 15, Link: https://www.dsausa.org/dl/Winter_2005.pdf

31   Democracy Now, "FBI Documents on Senator Paul Wellstone Raise Questions about His Death 8 Years Ago", Youtube Link: https://www.youtube.com/watch?v=6mUzofHUEX8

32   Wypijewski, JoAnn Link https://www.thenation.com/article/rainbows-gravity/ The Nation The Rainbow's Gravity July 15, 2004

33   NAM Socialist working papers on energy, NAM revised edition 1979, contents page

34   Roman, Bob New Ground November - December 2002, Link: https://web.archive.org/web/20021128205240/https://chicagodsa.org/ngarchive/ng85.html 85 Elections!

35   Democratic Left, "ON THE LEFT" November/December 1990 issue, page 5

36   DEMOCRATIC LEFT 14 MARCH-APRIL 1991, page 14

37   Schwartz, Joseph, Democratic Left, "Morning Afterthoughts" November/December 1996, "Election Dispatches, Continued" page 11

38   Democratic Left, November/December 1996, "Election Dispatches, Continued" page 18

39   Democratic Left "Send a student to Minnesota" Fall 2002, page 5

40   Democratic Left "Right Wing Attack on DSA Refuted, IRS Ends Investigation" Spring 2006, page 9

41   Dreier, Peter In These Times, Paul Wellstone's Legacy, October 12, 2012

42   Youtube Link: https://www.youtube.com/watch?v=R8aF4KEYuOU Wellstone: DC Memorial Event, Published on Oct 31, 2013

43   Klobuchar, Amy and Franken, Al Star Tribune "Paul Wellstone's legacy". October 24, 2012, Link: https://www.startribune.com/sens-klobuchar-franken-paul-wellstone-s-legacy/175687551/

44   Klobuchar, Amy, Facebook Post, October 25, 2017. Link: https://www.facebook.com/amyklobuchar/posts/pfbid0YZaqcBzr4FmqxVKaVcg6HndtpqSZUGsdPSHTpbzpHhoU4MKx56Ay8mVrz6xCpE77l Archive Link:

45   Hightower, Jim Link: https://www.austinchronicle.com/news/2006-12-22/431147/The/ Hightower Report The Nobel Prize for Greed; and Camp Wellstone Winners, FRI., DEC. 22, 2006

46   Wellstone Action advisory board, Way back machine Link: https://web.archive.org/web/20100613062146/https://www.wellstone.org/about-us/board-directors, Accessed December 2 2019

47   Democratic Left, March/April 1986, p 12

48   DSA website Link: https://www.dsausa.org/democratic-left/steinem-sanders/ NPC Statement on Gloria Steinem FEBRUARY 10, 2016

49   Rachel, SB Star-Tribune, Wellstone Action, "Klobuchar vet to advise Alliance for a Better Minnesota", August 28, 2014. Link: http://www.startribune.com/wellstone-action-klobuchar-vet-to-advise-alliance-for-a-better-minnesota/273083101/

50   Rockwood website Link: https://rockwoodleadership.org/fellowships/yearlong/yearlong-alums/ NATIONAL LEADING FROM THE INSIDE OUT ALUMS, accessed Dec. 2, 2019.

51   Keen, Judy Star Tribune Link: http://www.startribune.com/late-sen-paul-wellstone-is-a-force-in-2020-presidential-race/506606822/ Late Sen. Paul Wellstone is a force in 2020 presidential race March 2 2019

52   Keen, Judy Star Tribune Link: http://www.startribune.com/late-sen-paul-wellstone-is-a-force-in-2020-presidential-race/506606822/ Late Sen. Paul Wellstone is a force in 2020 presidential race March 2 2019

53   21st Century Democrats website Link: http://www.21stcenturydems.org/candidates/2018-candidates/ 2018 candidates

54   21st Century Democrats website Link: http://www.21stcenturydems.org/21st-century-democrats/ About Us

55   Democratic Left, Jan./Feb. 1990, page 7

56   The Business Journal staff Link: https://www.bizjournals.com/twincities/stories/2002/10/21/daily48.html Oct 25, 2002,

57   Solidarity is not a Crime: Statement from the Minnesota Committee in Solidarity with the People of Syria (Minnesota CISPOS) Link: https://pulsemedia.org/2015/01/29/solidarity-is-not-a-crime-statement-from-the-minnesota-committee-in-solidarity-with-the-people-of-syria-minnesota-cispos/

58   America's Survival, Link: http://www.usasurvival.org/docs/CCDSbckgrnd.pdf CoC conference brochure

59   WAMM Newsletter, 03 2009, Minnesota Peace Project, by Roxanne Abbas

60   WAMM website Link: http://minnesotapeaceproject.org/about/ Recent Accomplishments

61   WAMM website Linkhttps://web.archive.org/web/20150818105920/ http://minnesotapeaceproject.org/about/ 2014 highlights

62   MPP website Link: http://minnesotapeaceproject.org/klobuchar-team-meeting-may-22-2009/ Klobuchar Team Meeting – May 22, 2009

63   Jensen, Austin Fightback News Link: https://www.fightbacknews. org/2019/9/24/minnesota-protesters-demand-end-human-rights-violations-kashmir Minnesota: Protesters demand end to human rights violations in Kashmir September 24, 2019

64   Aby-Keirstead, Aby Fightback News Link:https://www.fightbacknews. org/2019/5/31/minnesotans-say-no-coup-no-war-hands-venezuela Minnesotans say "No coup! No war! Hands off Venezuela!" May 31, 2019

65   Youtube MAS MN Link: https://www.youtube.com/watch?v=VvPrLr wPoVQ&feature=youtu.be&a= MAS 2017 Convention: Message of Senator Amy Klobuchar Nov 30, 2017

66   YouTube "Senator Amy Klobuchar's Video Message to MAS MN Convention 2008" December 24, 2014Link: https://www.youtube.com/ watch?v=wJF6RvUy0VI

67   Investigative Project on Terrorism News Link: https://www.investigativeproject.org/2719/durbin-flawed-hearing Durbin's Flawed Hearing March 28, 2011

68   CAIR MN website https://web.archive.org/web/20151012035049/ http://mn.cair.com/media/press-releases/157-sold-out-cair-mn-annual-banquet-a-success.html, Sold-Out CAIR-MN Annual Banquet a Success

69   Ellison, Keith My Country Tis of Thee, page 125

70   CAIR website Link: http://islamophobia.org/about-us/184-what-they-say-about-cair.html What they say about CAIR

71   Augsburg University Link: https://www.augsburg.edu/ global/2015/02/19/cge-director-panelist-us-cuba-relations-summit/ CGE DIRECTOR TO BE PANELIST ON US – CUBA RELATIONS SUMMIT Posted on February 19, 2015

72   MPP website Link: http://minnesotapeaceproject.org/sen-klobuchar-introduces-freedom-to-export-to-cuba-act/ Sen. Klobuchar introduces "Freedom to Export to Cuba Act" March 27, 2015

73   Hall, Emily, Washington Post, "At re-opened Cuban embassy's first soiree, the crowd is eclectic, but the drink of choice is clear", July 20, 2015.

74   Yahoo News, "In Cuba, US senators urge bipartisan end to embargo", AFP, February 17, 2015. Link: https://www.yahoo.com/news/cuba-us-senators-urge-bipartisan-end-embargo-175753021.html

75   CDA website Link https://web.archive.org/web/20090301041950/ http://democracyinamericas.org/board-directors CDA board members

76   Fontova, Humberto https://cubaconfidential.wordpress. com/2013/09/02/a-castro-groupies-strategy-to-reduce-violence/ Cuba Confidential A Castro Groupie's Strategy to Reduce Violence September 2, 2013

77   French, Lauren Politico Link: https://www.politico.com/story/2016/03/

nancy-pelosi-cuba-trip-obama-220731 Pelosi, 15 House Democrats to join Obama trip to Cuba 03/14/2016

CORY BOOKER

1   Booker, Cory. Official government website: https://www.booker.Senate.gov/about-cory

2   Booker, Cory. https://www.Senate.gov/general/committee_assignments/assignments.htm Archive Link: https://web.archive.org/web/20220413210220/https://www.Senate.gov/general/committee_assignments/assignments.htm

3   Fried, Michael The Stanford Daily Link: https://archives.stanforddaily.com/1990/05/23?page=1&section=MODSMD_ARTICLE2#article League has played little-known role in campus politicsMay 23, 1990

4   Ibid.

5   Ibid.

6   Ibid.

7   Ibid.

8   Tsutaoka, Elsa, Unity "Chale con Hoover!" May 4, 1987

9   Unity, May 1985, "supplement on the Stanford University South African divestment movement"

10   Phillips, Steve "Brown is the New White" page 16, The New Press; Revised, Updated ed. edition (February 2, 2016), ISBN-10: 1620971151

11   Smart Voter, Link: http://www.smartvoter.org/2004/11/02/ca/cc/vote/brown_d/bio.html Full Biography for Dave Brown

12   Chan, Wilma (Fall–Winter 1982). "Chinese Immigrants". East Wind Magazine. Archived from the original on 2012-01-20. Retrieved 2013-07-02 – via Azine September 26, 2009.

13   LinkedIn Link https://www.linkedin.com/in/ingrid-nava-6193a932/ Ingrid Nava

14   Altshuler Berzon LLP Link: http://altshulerberzon.com/attorneys/stacey-leyton/ Stacey Leyton bio JANUARY 17, 2016

15   Center for American Progress https://www.americanprogress.org/about/staff/phillips-steve/bio/ Steve Phillips bio

16   Arnold, Laurence, Los Angeles Times, "Herbert Sandler, half of couple who built a home-lending giant, dies at 87", June 6, 2019, Link: https://www.latimes.com/business/la-fi-herbert-sandler-dies-20190606-story.html

17   Influence Watch Link: https://www.influencewatch.org/person/susan-sandler/ Susan Sandler

18   Prokop, Andrew Vox vox.com/2014/11/24/7274819/democracy-alliance The Democracy Alliance: How a secretive group of donors helps set the progressive agenda By Andrew Prokopandrew@vox.com, November 24, 2014

19   Jesse Jackson, Keep Hope Alive, pages 234-235.

20   Bioneers Link: https://bioneers.org/steve-phillips-says-brown-new-white-ze0z1709/Steve Phillips Says Brown Is the New White

21   Phillips Steve Huffington Post, Links: https://web.archive.org/web/20191219034625/https://www.huffpost.com/entry/seizing-the-time-the-role_b_107490?guccounter=2 Seizing the Time: The Role of Independent Groups in 2008 06/17/2008

22   LeftRoots, Out to Win Link: https://web.archive.org/

web/20191219200650/https://journal.leftroots.net/?fbclid=IwAR2jXHJlU25px
yhknIkvN0ODfkPlqNtFW2mHCejwLHtJOKFMYIqZ3QsKv94 VOLUME 1,
FEBRUARY 2019

23   Shouten, Fredreka USA Today Links: https://www.usatoday.com/
story/news/politics/elections/2018/08/30/andrew-gillum-meet-upstarts-political-
groups-behind-his-race-become-florida-first-black-governor/1132010002/ How
upstart groups helped Andrew Gillum's quest to become Florida's first black governor August 30 2018

24   Phillips, Steve PowerPAC+ Link: https://web.archive.org/save/http://
www.powerpacplus.org/brown_is_the_new_white Brown is the New White
Address to the City Club of Cleveland January 10, 2014

25   Forward, Volume 9, number 1, Spring 1989, pages 4 and 5.

26   Booker, Kafka receive Sterling Awards for service". Stanford University.
June 6, 1991. Retrieved November 12, 2012

27   Allison, Aimee Democracy in Color podcast Link: https://soundcloud.
com/democracyincolor/season-finale-with-senator-cory-booker-and-steve-phillips
Senator Cory Booker: Making Our Future This Election

28   Schleifer, Theodore Vox: Link: https://web.archive.org/
web/20191219144634/https://www.vox.com/2019/2/22/18233733/cory-booker-
presidential-campaign-tech-fundraising-silicon-valley-donors-super-pac Silicon
Valley loves Cory Booker. That could be a problem for him Feb 22, 2019

29   Phillips, Steve PowerPAC+ Link: https://web.archive.org/
web/20191219150845/http://www.powerpacplus.org/the_progressive_case_for_
cory_booker The Progressive Case for Cory Booker December 20, 2012

30   Cramer, Ruby Buzzfeed Link: https://web.archive.org/
web/20191219160613/https://www.buzzfeednews.com/article/rubycramer/
progressive-super-pac-will-back-booker Progressive Super PAC Will Back Cory
Booker June 6, 2013

31   Phillips, Steve, Political Intelligence, "An Open Letter About Cory
Booker October" 18, 2013 Link: https://web.archive.org/web/20191219152341/
http://www.powerpacplus.org/an_open_letter_about_cory_booker

32   Ibid.

33   PowerPAC.org Link: https://web.archive.org/web/20160322211425/
http://www.powerpac.org/staff, accessed December 18, 2019

34   Phillips, Steve "Brown is the New White" page 16, The New Press;
Revised, Updated ed. edition (February 2, 2016), ISBN-10: 1620971151

35   PowerPAC+ "The Demographic Revolution: The Path to a Permanent
Progressive Majority in America", Link: http://d3n8a8pro7vhmx.cloudfront.net/
pacplus/pages/244/attachments/original/1396464136/2013_plans_booklet.
pdf?1396464136

36   Cole, Devan Link: https://www.cnn.com/2019/07/21/politics/cory-
booker-donald-trump-worse-than-a-racist-tweet-cnntv/index.html Cory Booker:
Donald Trump is 'worse than a racist' July 21, 2019

37   MarketWatch Link: https://www.marketwatch.com/story/cory-booker-
backing-super-pac-shuts-down-2019-11-29 Cory Booker–backing super PAC shuts
down Nov 29, 2019

38   Strickland, Eliza, The East Bay Express, "The New Face of

Environmentalism" November 2, 2005, Link: http://www.truth-out.org/article/
eliza-strickland-the-new-face-environmentalism

39   Ibid.

40   Ibid.

41   AskChamp Link: http://www.askchamp.com/pdf/abt_van.pdf http://
www.askchamp.com/pdf/abt_van.pdf

42   Ear to the Ground Project Link: https://www.racialequitytools.org/
resourcefiles/ear2groundspreads.pdf

43   Phillips, Steve, Brown Is the New White Phillips,Link: https://the-
newpress.com/books/brown-new-white

44   Youtube Link: https://www.youtube.com/watch?time_
continue=22&v=7QRSS0lx90I Brown is the New White: Changing
Demographics and a New American Majority Apr 15, 2016

MARTIN HEINRICH

1   Heinrich, Martin. Official Government Website: https://www.heinrich.
Senate.gov/biography

2   Heinrich, Martin. https://www.Senate.gov/general/committee_
assignments/assignments.htm Archive Link: https://web.archive.org/
web/20220413210220/https://www.Senate.gov/general/committee_assignments/
assignments.htm

3   Chisholm, Christie ALIBI V.14 NO.24 "EXCITED ABOUT
LOSING" June 16 2005 Link: https://alibi.com/news/11947/Excited-About-
Losing.html

4   Youtube "Martin Heinrich introducing Dolores Huerta" April 2, 2011
Link: https://www.youtube.com/watch?v=5WB0GI6i6Gc

5   American Crossroads "THE MINIMUM WAGE DECEPTIONS"
May 24, 2012 Link: https://www.americancrossroads.org/2012/05/
the-minimum-wage-deceptions/

6   New Mexico Voices for Children press release, "Albuquerque City
Council Passes Minimum Wage Ordinance" April 24, 2006, Link: https://www.
nmvoices.org/pressreleases/abq_min_wage_passes_4-24-06.pdf

7   Democratic Left July/August 1995 "DSA Locals, Youth Section
Chapters, and Organizing Committees" page 16

8   Chavez, Steve. Topix New Mexico, "Heinrich, White hope for huge
absentee turnout", October 22, 2008

9   Democracy for New Mexico "NM Alliance for Retired Americans
Hosts NM-01 Candidate Issue Forums" April 03, 2008 Link: http://www.
democracyfornewmexico.com/democracy_for_new_mexico/2008/04/nm-alliance-
for.html

10   Shaw, Emil, Peoples World "Fighting for that inch of
space" November 9, 2007 Link: https://www.peoplesworld.org/article/
fighting-for-that-inch-of-space/

11   Shaw, Emil People's World "New opportunities to defeat far-right in
New Mexico" October 19, 2007 Link: https://www.peoplesworld.org/article/
new-opportunities-to-defeat-far-right-in-new-mexico/

12   Heinrich, Martin, press release "Martin Heinrich
Recognized as Champion for New Mexico Seniors" October 112,

2002 Link: https://justfacts.votesmart.org/public-statement/751509/
martin-heinrich-recognized-as-champion-for-new-mexico-seniors#.

13   Peoples World "We salute the labor movement!" September 1, 2006
Link: https://www.peoplesworld.org/article/we-salute-the-labor-movement/

14   Martinez, Betita Monthly Review "A View from New Mexico
Recollections of the Movimiento Left" July 1 2002 Link: https://monthlyreview.
org/2002/07/01/a-view-from-new-mexico/

15   Ibid.

16   Ibid.

17   Davis, Theresa. Albuquerque Journal "Biden names 2 New Mexicans to
environmental panel" May 32, 2021 Link: https://www.abqjournal.com/2395655/
biden-names-2-new-mexicans-to-environmental-panel.html

18   Maldonado, Alicia, Atlixco Productions "About" Link: https://atlixco-
productions.com/about/

19   Maldonado, Alicia,.Building Movement Project "Building Movement
Begins Work in New Mexico!" August 14, 2013 Link: https://buildingmovement.
org/blog/building-movement-begins-work-in-new-mexico/

20   RoadMap "Our Consultants" Link: https://roadmapconsulting.org/
consulting-team/

21   RoadMap "Elsa A. Ríos": Consultant and Certified
Coach Link: https://roadmapconsulting.org/consultants/
elsa-a-rios-co-director-consultant-and-certified-coach/

22   Forward Motion Summer 1994 No. 58 "Contributing Editors" Summer
1994 No. 58

23   RoadMap "Our Consultants" Link: https://roadmapconsulting.org/
consulting-team/

24   Gallegos, Bill "THE HISTORICAL AND POLITICAL
SIGNIFICANCE OF THE US ANNEXATION OF MEXICO'S
NORTHERN TERRITORIES" September 22, 2019 Link: https://roadtolib-
eration.org/the-historical-and-political-significance-of-the-us-annexation-of-mex-
icos-northern-territories/

25   RoadMap "Our Consultants" Link: https://roadmapconsulting.org/
consulting-team/page/5/

26   Holtzman, Benjamin. In the Middle of a Whirlwind "An Interview with
Robin D.G. Kelley" Link: https://www.scribd.com/fullscreen/3108689?access_
key=key-1lm99olqw7oyfm2erchm&irclickid=VS%3A2-KWX-zE3WVvwu
V1n5XRLUkDUwhymUR0jzg0&irpid=10078&utm_source=impact&utm_
medium=cpc&utm_campaign=affiliate_pdm_acquisition_Skimbit%20
Ltd.&sharedid=wordpress.com&irgwc=1

27   RoadMap "Our Consultants" Link: https://roadmapconsulting.org/
consulting-team/page/7/

28   Shapiro, Peter Viewpoint Magazine "The Necessity of Organization:
The League of Revolutionary Struggle and the Watsonville Canning Strike"
August 30, 2018 Link: https://viewpointmag.com/2018/08/30/the-necessity-of-
organization-the-league-of-revolutionary-struggle-and-the-watsonville-canning-
strike/

29   LinkedIn "Michael Montoya " Link: https://www.linkedin.com/in/
michael-montoya-00a7a420/details/experience/

30   Abramsky, Sasha, The Nation "A New Progressive Voice From New Mexico Joins the Senate" May 13, 2013 Link: https://www.thenation.com/article/archive/new-progressive-voice-new-mexico-joins-Senate/#,

31   LinkedIn "Javier Benavidez" Link: https://www.linkedin.com/in/javier-benavidez-1b5874b2/

32   Abramsky, Sasha, The Nation "A New Progressive Voice From New Mexico Joins the Senate" May 13, 2013 Link: https://www.thenation.com/article/archive/new-progressive-voice-new-mexico-joins-Senate/#,

33   Rockwood Leadership Institute "2015-16 NATIONAL YEARLONG FELLOWS ANNOUNCED" NOVEMBER 2, 2015 Link: https://rockwood-leadership.org/2015-16-national-yearlong-fellows-announced/

34   LinkedIn "Shiree Teng Developmental Evaluation Consultant" Link: https://www.linkedin.com/in/shiree-teng-24628511/

35   People's World "Emil Shaw, lifelong fighter for justice" September 28, 2010 Link: https://www.peoplesworld.org/article/emil-shaw-lifelong-fighter-for-justice/

36   People's World "Somewhere over the rainbow: Talking socialism invitation to a discussion" August 23, 2004 Link: https://www.peoplesworld.org/article/somewhere-over-the-rainbow-talking-socialism-invitation-to-a-discussion/

37   Block, Stephanie. Bellarmine Forum "A Commentary on the US Catholic Conference" September 28, 2010. Link: https://bellarmineforum.org/a-commentary-on-the-u-s-catholic-conference/4/

38   Council for a Livable World 2012 Martin Heinrich bio. Link: http://livableworld.org/elections/2012/candidates/Senate/mheinrich/

39   The Chain Reaction, "Council for a Livable World celebrates the 57th Presidential Inauguration" January 29, 2013 Link: http://blog.livableworld.org/story/2013/1/29/94232/6754

40   Council for a Livable World Martin Heinrich bio, 2018 Link: https://livableworld.org/meet-the-candidates/Senate-candidates/martin-heinrich-d-nm-Senate/

41   Anderson, Jack and Dale Van Atta, Washington Post. "Tree Spiking An 'Eco-Terrorist' Tactic", March 5, 1990. Archive Link: https://web.archive.org/web/20180921212612/https://www.washington-post.com/archive/local/1990/03/05/tree-spiking-an-eco-terrorist-tactic/a400944c-a3a0-4c03-ab99-afada6f44e7a/?utm_term=.18417d2c17d6

42   Industrial Workers of the World, "The IWW And Earth First!: Part 1 - Establishing Roots", April 29, 2013. Link: https://archive.iww.org/content/iww-and-earth-first-part-1-establishing-roots/

43   Howley, Patrick, Daily Caller. "Democratic New Mexico senator worked closely with convicted eco-terrorist", March 25, 2013. Link: https://dailycaller.com/2013/03/25/democratic-new-mexico-senator-worked-closely-with-convicted-eco-terrorist/

44   Foreman, Dave et al., "Ecodefense: A Field Guide to Monkeywrenching", 1993. Link: https://theanarchistlibrary.org/library/various-authors-ecodefense-a-field-guide-to-monkeywrenching.pdf

45   Earth First! Journal, June 21 1991. Link: http://www.environmentand-society.org/sites/default/files/key_docs/ef_11_6_1.pdf

46   Kerr, Andrew, Daily Caller. "Biden Bureau Of Land Management

Nominee Tracy Stone-Manning Was Involved In 'Eco-Terrorism' Case, Resulted In College Roommate's Conviction, Prison Sentence, Court Records Show", June 11, 2021. Link: https://dailycaller.com/2021/06/11/tracy-stone-manning-tree-spiking-bureau-land-management/

47   Heinrich, Martin, Twitter. "Tweet in Support of Tracy Stone-Manning", June 10, 2021. Link: https://twitter.com/MartinHeinrich/status/1403121044253143044 Archive Link: https://archive.ph/XQGJJ

48   Heinrich, Martin, Press Release (official). "Heinrich Votes To Confirm Bureau Of Land Management Nominee In Senate Energy And Natural Resources Committee", July 22, 2021. Link: https://www.heinrich.Senate.gov/press-releases/heinrich-votes-to-confirm-bureau-of-land-management-nominee-in-Senate-energy-and-natural-resources-committee

49   Stone-Manning, Tracy, High Country News. "On grizzlies, babies and a shrinking land", February 1, 1991. Link: https://www.hcn.org/issues/23.2/on-grizzlies-babies-and-a-shrinking-land

50   Foreman, David, "Confessions of an Eco-Warrior", 2016.

51   Call of the Wild, The Newsletter of the New Mexico Wilderness Alliance, Vol. V No. 3 Winter 2001, Masthead. Archive Link: https://web.archive.org/web/20160103085036/http://www.nmwild.org/nmwa/wp-content/uploads/newsletters/nmwa_2001_winter.pdf

52   Campaign Money, "Todd Schulke Political Campaign Contributions 2008 Election Cycle". Link: https://www.campaignmoney.com/political/contributions/todd-schulke.asp?cycle=08

53   Campaign Money, "Todd Schulke Political Campaign Contributions 2012 Election Cycle". Link: https://www.campaignmoney.com/political/contributions/todd-schulke.asp?cycle=12

54   Campaign Money, "Todd Schulke Political Campaign Contributions 2014 Election Cycle". Link: https://www.campaignmoney.com/political/contributions/todd-schulke.asp?cycle=14

55   Campaign Money, "Todd Schulke Political Campaign Contributions 2018 Election Cycle". Link: https://www.campaignmoney.com/political/contributions/todd-schulke.asp?cycle=18

56   Neary, Ben, Albuquerque Journal (Albuquerque, New Mexico). "Earth First! Protest Ends in 5 Arrests", June 27, 1989, Page 25.

57   Neary, Ben, Albuquerque Journal (Albuquerque, New Mexico). "Environmentalists Lock Up Part of Jemez Logging Site", August 15, 1989, Page 254.

58   Koleszar, John, Western Outdoor Times. "OP/ED 1994: 'The Perfect Storm'", October 1, 2016. Link: https://www.westernoutdoortimes.com/story/2016/10/01/rving/oped-1994-the-perfect-storm/2913.html

59   IRS Form 990, 2019 (Most recent year available). Link: https://www.biologicaldiversity.org/support/pdfs/Center-for-Biological-Diversity-Form-990-2019.pdf

60   Lemann, Nicholas, The New Yorker' "No People Allowed", November 1999. Link: https://www.newyorker.com/magazine/1999/11/22/no-people-allowed

61   New York Times, "A Range War of Words On Grazing in the West",

August 5, 1991. Link: https://www.nytimes.com/1991/08/05/us/a-range-war-of-words-on-grazing-in-the-west.html

62   Ruttle, Deirdre Gillin, Holy Cross, "Crusader Chronicles: Kieran Suckling '88". Link: https://www.alumni.holycross.edu/s/1380/15/index.aspx?sid=1380&gid=1&pgid=512

63   Refuse Fascism, Revolutionary Communist Party. "Teach In: Fascism in America, Could It Happen Here? Is it Happening Here?" April 27th, 2017. Link: https://www.youtube.com/watch?v=bQIYpBrOUJQ

64   Suckling, Kieran, Twitter. "Tweet praising Martin Heinrich", April 26, 2017. Link: https://mobile.twitter.com/KieranSuckling/status/857350338541744128 Archive Link: https://archive.ph/5WMG7

65   Center for Biological Diversity, "Two Hundred and Sixty-six Center Suits Filed Against the Trump Administration". Link: https://www.biological-diversity.org/campaigns/trump_lawsuits/

CHUCK SCHUMER

1   Kornacki, Steve. "Steve Solarz (1940-2010) and the making of Senator Schumer", Politico, 11/30/2010. LINK: https://www.politico.com/states/new-york/albany/story/2010/11/steve-solarz-1940-2010-and-the-making-of-senator-schumer-067223

2   Chuck Schumer. Official Government Biography: https://www.schumer.Senate.gov/about-chuck

3   Schumer, Chuck. https://www.Senate.gov/general/committee_assignments/assignments.htm Archive Link: https://web.archive.org/web/20220413210220/https://www.Senate.gov/general/committee_assignments/assignments.htm

4   New York Democratic Socialist October 1982

5   Democratic Left, May/August 1987, page 12

6   New York Magazine 22 August 1977, page 10.

7   Concerned Voters, Inc. "Communists in the Democratic Party", page 33

8   Letterhead of the "US Free Trepper Committee", November 1, 1973, 317 West 93rd Street, Apt. 7B, NY, NY 10025 Coordinating Committee

9   Concerned Voters, Inc. "Communists in the Democratic Party", page 34

10   Ibid.

11   New Democratic Coalition Dinkins endorsement poster, 1990

12   New York Magazine 22 Aug 1977, page 10

13   Fleischman, Harry. Democratic Left "On the Left" January 1983 page 14

14   Brookhiser, Richard. City Magazine, Spring 1991, "The Resistible Rise of Margaret Chin"

15   Gottfried, Richard. Personal endorsement of the Communist Party USA's People's World of June 2, 2007, page 2

16   New World Review, "We Will Make Peace Prevail!" event brochure, Grand Ballroom, Hotel Roosevelt, New York City March 28, 1982

17   Congressional Record, "Inflation and Unemployment: The Communist Party's New Drive - Part I", April 16, 1975, Extension of Remarks, pages 10436-1-439, Rep. Larry McDonald (D-GA)

18   New York Magazine "Barbra and Jesse split an egg roll". 20 February 1995, page 13.

19   MacPherson, Myra "Long time passing: Vietnam and the haunted generation", page 467.

20   Stein, Jeannine. LA Times "THE SUNDAY PROFILE: Woman Warrior: She's known as a relentless and uncompromising activist for liberal causes--and as a workaholic. But Margery Tabankin is about to change jobs and take a vacation" July 31, 1994. Link: https://web.archive.org/web/20191227170134/https://www.latimes.com/archives/la-xpm-1994-07-31-ls-21994-story.html

21   Tarzynski, Steve "DSA major donor letter draft" July 26, 1992, Tarzynski papers, Southern California Library for Social Change

22   The Guardian of November 27, 1985, "Conference on Socialism and Activism to be held on December 6-8, 1985, at Teachers College, Columbia University in New York", Page 14.

23   Democratic Left, January/February 1990, page 13

24   Haberman, Maggie. "Wives Fear Gracie Spouse Trap – They Say Mrs. Mayor Needs Zone of Privacy", nypost.com, July 23, 2001.

25   Tarzynski, Steve "DSA major donor letter draft" July 26, 1992, Tarzynski papers, Southern California Library for Social Change

26   New York Magazine "Barbra and Jesse split an egg roll". 20 February 1995 page 13

27   Corresponder, "Articles from the Corresponder Vol. 7 No. 3, 1999, CofC Update: Metro New York: " Link: https://www.cc-ds.org/pub_arch/v7n3.htm

28   New York State Communist Party "The Job Creation and Infrastructure Restoration Act of 1997 (H.R. 950)" Link: http://www.hartford-hwp.com/archives/45b/085.html

29   Ibid.

30   Fiks, Yevgeny, "Portrait of Bill Davis, Communist Party USA", Link: http://www.hartford-hwp.com/archives/45b/085.html

31   Political Affairs, January 1997, page 8

32   Pool, Bob, Los Angeles Times, "Christmas is Party Time for Communists in L.A." December 21, 1998. Link: https://piecebypiecestrategies.org/about/

33   Baker, Russ HuffPo "Behind Arrest of Clinton Backer -- the Deeper Story" Link: https://www.huffpost.com/entry/behind-arrest-of-clinton_b_271162

34   Pachetti, Federico, The Wilson Center. "Going Global: Zbigniew Brzezinski and China's Rise", October 10, 2017. Link: https://www.wilsoncenter.org/blog-post/going-global-zbigniew-brzezinski-and-chinas-rise

35   Lake, Eli, NY Sun. "Adviser to Clinton Meets With President of Syria", February 15, 2008. Archive Link: https://web.archive.org/web/20080218070717/https://www.nysun.com/article/71359

36   Vogel, Kenneth, Politico. "Obama, DNC give up Nemazee cash", August 27, 2009. Link: https://www.politico.com/story/2009/08/obama-dnc-give-up-nemazee-cash-026510

37   Weiser, Benjamin, New York Times. "He Committed a $300 Million

Fraud, but Left Prison Under Trump's Justice Overhaul", April 13, 2019. Link:
https://www.nytimes.com/2019/04/13/nyregion/hassan-nemazee-trump.html

38   Hodges, Lee, Howard, Iran News, "Iranian American Political Action
Committee Holds Kick-Off Reception in Washington DC" July 25, 2003. Link:
https://www.huffpost.com/entry/behind-arrest-of-clinton_b_271162

39   Kohanloo, Michelle. "IABA, NIAC and IAPAC Hold Unity Campaign."
NIAC (National Iranian American Council), December 1, 2002. Accessed
November 6, 2013. http://www.niacouncil.org/site/News2?page=NewsArticle&i
d=5821&security=1&news_iv_ctrl=10 63

40   Ibid.

41   IAPAC, "IAPAC Discusses Visa Regulations with Senator Schumer"
July 3, 2003. Link: http://www.iranianamericanpac.org/iapac-discusses-visa-regu-
lations-with-senator-schumer.aspx July 3, 2003

42   IAPAC "US Senator Charles Schumer Joins IAPAC Reception in
New York City" July 27, 2007, Link: https://iranianamericanpac.org/us-senator-
charles-schumer-joins-iapac-reception-in-new-york-city.aspx

43   IAPAC "IAPAC Endorsed Candidates 2010" Link: https://iraniana-
mericanpac.org/candidates/past-endorsements/

44   IAPAC "IAPAC Endorsed Candidates 2016" Link: https://iraniana-
mericanpac.org/candidates/past-endorsements/

45   Asian Americans for Equality website "About Us" Link: https://www.
aafe.org/who-we-are/about-us

46   Schalliol, David (2016). Affordable Housing in New York: The People,
Places, and Policies That Transformed a City. Princeton University Press. pp.
276–280. doi:10.2307/j.ctvs32rwj. ISBN 978-0-691-19715-9. JSTOR j.ctvs32rwj.
S2CID 242348796

47   Brookhiser, Richard. City Magazine, Spring 1991, "The Resistible Rise
of Margaret Chin"

48   Workers Viewpoint August 25-31 1980, page 15

49   Connors, Ben The Expert Red,"Time to assume leadership over the
whole society" February 1985

50   Brookhiser, Richard. City Magazine, Spring 1991, "The Resistible Rise
of Margaret Chin"

51   Ibid.

52   Ibid.

53   WPC Call from Washington, World Peace Council Helsinki Finland,
page 4

54   Brookhiser, Richard. City Magazine, Spring 1991, "The Resistible Rise
of Margaret Chin"

55   Spokony, Sam AMNY "Powerful come out to celebrate Chin's
second term" January 16, 2014 Link:https://www.amny.com/news/
powerful-come-out-to-celebrate-chins-second-term/

56   Daniel Squadron press release "Schumer, Squadron Call for
Downtown Redevelopment Funds to Be Used to Complete East River
Waterfront and Development of Ribbon Park" November 21, 2010 Link:
https://www.nySenate.gov/newsroom/press-releases/daniel-l-squadron/
schumer-squadron-call-downtown-redevelopment-funds-be-used

57   Kirsten Gillibrand press release "Schumer, Gillibrand Announce

Over $4.5M in Neighborworks Funding to Develop and Preserve Affordable Housing, Revitalize Neighborhoods, and Create Jobs Across NY" May 18, 2017 Link: https://www.gillibrand.Senate.gov/news/press/release/schumer-gillibrand-announce-over-45m-in-neighborworks-funding-to-develop-and-preserve-affordable-housing-revitalize-neighborhoods-and-create-jobs-across-ny

58   Charles E. Schumer press release "SCHUMER, GILLIBRAND ANNOUNCE OVER $1.5 MILLION IN NEIGHBORWORKS AMERICA GRANTS FOR NEW YORK CITY AND LONG ISLAND ORGANIZATIONS WORKING TO PROVIDE AFFORDABLE HOUSING" March 22, 2019 Link: https://www.schumer.Senate.gov/newsroom/press-releases/schumer-gillibrand-announce-over-15-million-in-neighborworks-america-grants-for-new-york-city-and-long-island-organizations-working-to-provide-affordable-housing

59   Kirsten Gillibrand press release "Schumer, Gillibrand Announce Over $5 Million In NeighborWorks America Grants For 16 Organizations Across New York" February 22, 2021 Link: https://www.gillibrand.Senate.gov/news/press/release/schumer-gillibrand-announce-over-5-million-in-neighborworks-america-grants-for-16-organizations-across-new-york

60   Asian Americans for Equality "SCENES FROM AAFE'S 2017 LUNAR NEW YEAR BANQUET" Link: https://www.aafe.org/2017/03/scenes-from-aafes-2017-lunar-new-year-banquet.html

61   New York Democratic Socialist January/February 1985

62   Insurgent Notes "Notes Towards a Critique of Maoism" October 15, 2012 Link: http://insurgentnotes.com/2012/10/notes-towards-a-critique-of-maoism/

63   Antonio, Carolyn "Legacy to Liberation: Politics & Culture of Revolutionary Asian Pacific America", page 248

64   Democratic Left March 1979 "No Fat" Budget Challenges Activists" page 8 Link https://democraticleft.dsausa.org/files/sites/6/2019/01/DL_1979_V007_03_final.pdf

SHERROD BROWN

1   Krawczyk, Kathryn, The Week. "Democratic Sen. Sherrod Brown's wife won't let him speak Russian in public", February 8, 2019. Link: https://theweek.com/us/1015899/fbi-and-dhs-issue-joint-bulletin-warning-of-increase-in-threats-to-federal-law

2   Bios, CNN. "Sherrod Brown". Link: https://www.cnn.com/ALLPOLITICS/CA/bios/H/472.html

3   Brown, Sherrod. Official government website: https://www.brown.Senate.gov/biography

4   Brown, Sherrod. https://www.Senate.gov/general/committee_assignments/assignments.htm Archive Link: https://web.archive.org/web/20220413210220/https://www.Senate.gov/general/committee_assignments/assignments.htm

5   Caudill, Mark, Mansfield News Journal, "'What you see is very real': Classmates fondly remember Sherrod Brown for his activist ways" January 31, 2019, Link: https://www.mansfieldnewsjournal.com/story/news/2019/01/31/sherrod-brown-classmates-remember-activist-even-high-school/2655800002/

6   Ibid.

7   Facebook "Earth Day Town Hall Featuring Sherrod Brown" April 22, 2020, Link: https://www.facebook.com/events/the-pollinator/earth-day-town-hall-featuring-sherrod-brown/1843715725759227/

8   Cleveland.com "Ohio health care advocates want Congress to extend health insurance purchasing subsidies" July 7, 2022, Link: https://www.cleveland.com/news/2022/07/ohio-health-care-advocates-want-congress-to-extend-health-insurance-purchasing-subsidies.html

9   Cleveland Lead Advocates for Safe Housing "CLASH Members" Link: https://www.clashcle.org/learn-more-about-clash/clash-members

10   The Plain Dealer, "EMILY BROWN OBITUARY", Published by The Plain Dealer from February 2 to March 1, 2009., Link: https://obits.cleveland.com/us/obituaries/cleveland/name/emily-brown-obituary?pid=123664515

11   Ibid

12   Committee on Un-American Activities. House of Representatives. Eightieth Congress, Second Session. Public Law 601 (Section 121, Subsection Q (2) "Interim Report on hearings regarding communist espionage in the United States Government" Second Session, August 28, 1948. United States Government Printing Office, page 5, Link: https://www.google.com/books/edition/Soviet_Espionage_Within_the_United_State/PcJGAQAAMAAJ?hl=en

13   United States. Congress. Senate. Committee on the Judiciary. Subcommittee to Investigate the Administration of the Internal Security Act and Other Internal Security Laws, Testimony of Louis Budenz, 1951, page 665

14   Executive Sessions of the Senate Permanent Subcommittee on Investigations of the Committee on Government Operations Volume 2, 83rg Congress, First Session, 1953, page 1349

15   Washington Post, "Frank Coe, 73, Accused In '50s Red Probe, Dies" June 8, 1980, Link: https://www.washingtonpost.com/archive/local/1980/06/08/frank-coe-73-accused-in-50s-red-probe-dies/8cc7f46b-9e65-452e-ae22-644538100dee/

16   Caudill, Mark, Mansfield News Journal, "'What you see is very real': Classmates fondly remember Sherrod Brown for his activist ways" January 31, 2019, Link: https://www.mansfieldnewsjournal.com/story/news/2019/01/31/sherrod-brown-classmates-remember-activist-even-high-school/2655800002/

17   Nagin, Molly Communist Party USA website "Rice Butterfly Memorial opens in honor of Tamir Rice" July 21, 2022Link: https://www.cpusa.org/article/butterfly-garden-opens-in-memory-of-tamir-rice/

18   Ibid.

19   Ibid.

20   Steer, Jen WKBN27 "Lawmakers ask Justice Department to reopen Tamir Rice case" April 24, 2021Link: https://www.wkbn.com/news/lawmakers-ask-justice-department-to-reopen-tamir-rice-case/

21   Tamir Rice Foundation 990, 2018 Link: chrome-extension://efaidn-bmnnnibpcajpcglclefindmkaj/https://apps.irs.gov/pub/epostcard/cor/813500175_201812_990EZ_2021042918037218.pdf

22   Nagin, Molly Communist Party USA website "Rice Butterfly Memorial opens in honor of Tamir Rice" July 21, 2022Link: https://www.cpusa.org/article/butterfly-garden-opens-in-memory-of-tamir-rice/

23   Senator Sherrod Brown press release "BROWN, KAPTUR, BEATTY, RYAN PRESS DEPT. OF JUSTICE TO REOPEN CIVIL RIGHTS INVESTIGATION INTO SHOOTING DEATH OF TAMIR RICE" April 23, 2021, Link: https://www.brown.Senate.gov/newsroom/press/release/brown-press-dept-justice-reopen-investigation-death-tamir-rice

24   Nagin, Molly Communist Party USA website "Rice Butterfly Memorial opens in honor of Tamir Rice" July 21, 2022Link: https://www.cpusa.org/article/butterfly-garden-opens-in-memory-of-tamir-rice/

25   Nagin, Rick, Peoples World, "Judy Gallo, longtime activist, dies at 70" August 22, 2012, Link: https://peoplesworld.org/article/judy-gallo-longtime-activist-dies-at-7/

26   Nagin, Molly Communist party USA website "Rice Butterfly Memorial opens in honor of Tamir Rice" July 21, 2022Link: https://www.cpusa.org/article/butterfly-garden-opens-in-memory-of-tamir-rice/

27   Toure, Yemi Los Angeles Times "Dog Days: Texas state treasurer Ann W...." March 2, 1990, Link: https://www.latimes.com/archives/la-xpm-1990-03-02-vw-1593-story.html

28   Cleveland.com "Cleveland council candidate Rick Nagin eschews communist tag" September 28, 2009, Link: https://www.cleveland.com/metro/2009/09/cleveland_council_candidate_ri.html

29   People's World "GOP can be beat in November, CPUSA says" July 7, 2006, Link: https://peoplesworld.org/article/gop-can-be-beat-in-november-cpusa-says/

30   Bostick, Bruce, Peoples World, "Is it time to think about Unemployed Councils?" April 24, 2020, Link: https://peoplesworld.org/article/is-it-time-to-think-about-unemployed-councils/

31   Ibid.

32   Bostick, Bruce, Peoples World, "Ohio labor runs for office" May 4, 2007, Link: https://www.peoplesworld.org/article/ohio-labor-runs-for-office/

33   Ohio Alliance for Retired Americans Education Fund Facebook page May 24, 2012, Link: https://www.facebook.com/OhioARA/photos/pb.368900093145364.-2207520000.1439262694./386294528072587/?type=1&theater

34   Nagin, Rick, People's World "Wally Kaufman, 89: union and Communist Party leader" February 17, 2017, Link: https://www.peoplesworld.org/article/wally-kaufman-89-union-and-communist-party-leader/

35   People's World "Ohioans "chain" Cleveland Public Square to protest Social Security cuts" July 8, 2013, Link: https://www.peoplesworld.org/article/ohioans-chain-cleveland-public-square-to-protest-social-security-cuts/

36   Ohio Alliance for Retired Americans Education Fund Facebook page October 26, 2012, Link: https://www.facebook.com/OhioARA/photos/pb.368900093145364.-2207520000.1439262694./445950602106979/?type=1&theater

37   SOAR "DISTRICT MAP" October 24, 2017, Link: chrome-extension://efaidnbmnnnibpcajpcglclefindmkaj/https://uswlocals.org/system/files/district_soar_map.pdf

38   Bostick, Bruce "Retirees, allies rally at Cleveland

hearing" April 20, 2015, Link: https://peoplesworld.org/article/retirees-allies-rally-at-cleveland-hearing/

39   Pervo, Charles, People's World, "Cleveland Laborfest & Forum, and labor exhibition" February 25, 2013, Link: https://www.peoplesworld.org/article/cleveland-laborfest-forum-and-labor-exhibition/

40   Ibid.

41   Spector, Harlan, BELT magazine "Red States" May 13, 2014, Link: https://beltmag.com/red-states/

42   Pervo, Charles, People's World, "Cleveland Laborfest & Forum, and labor exhibition" February 25, 2013, Link: https://www.peoplesworld.org/article/cleveland-laborfest-forum-and-labor-exhibition/

43   Ibid.

44   Ibid.

45   Starks, Aleena, Communist Party USA "Introducing CPUSA's new youth-run podcast: The Specter!" April 3, 2019Link: https://www.cpusa.org/article/introducing-the-specter/

46   Democrats of Cuyahoga County Volume 2 | March 2018 "Message from the Chair" Link: https://myemail.constantcontact.com/March-2018-Newsletter.html?soid=1102295467867&aid=MRupppMMekE

47   Ohio Democrat Facebook "Phone Bank For The Ohio Democratic Party!" June 30, 2018, Link: https://www.facebook.com/events/1748532918565395/

48   Zhang, Hui China Today "People's Involvement is Valued" March 5, 2019, Link: http://www.chinatoday.com.cn/ctenglish/2018/hotspots/2019lh/oi/201903/t20190305_800159619.html

49   Starks, Aleena and Cambron, Rossana Communist Party USA, "Building a shared community of struggle" March 15, 2019, Link: https://www.cpusa.org/article/building-a-shared-community-of-struggle/

50   Ibid.

51   Democratic Left, Spring 2018, "Books by DSA Members", page 14

52   Kazin, Michael, Dissent "Working Too Hard for Too Little: An Interview with Senator Sherrod Brown" Summer 2017 Link: https://www.dissentmagazine.org/article/working-hard-little-interview-senator-sherrod-brown

53   Morgen, Simone Democratic Left, Winter 2006/2007, "Trade Issues Impact Ohio Elections" Page 6

54   Democratic Left, November/December 1992, "National Board Meets To Plan Local Electoral Activity" page 9

55   Joye, Barbara Democratic Left, Winter 2008, "What We Did in the Election" Page 10

56   Nash, James. Columbus Dispatch "Kilroy, Brown cheered for health-care changes" April 2, 2010, 10 Link: http://www.dispatchpolitics.com/live/content/local_news/stories/2010/04/02/copy/kilroy-brown-cheered-for-health-care-changes.html?adsec=politics&sid=101

57   Columbus Dispatch "Ohio delegation split on gays in military" February 3, 2010, Link: https://www.dispatch.com/story/news/politics/2010/02/04/ohio-delegation-split-on-gays/24164610007/

58   PDA History, 10 December 2011 Link: https://pdamerica.org/about-pda/history

59   Youtube "Jim Scheibel addresses 21st Century Democrats 2008 Gala"
December 19, 2010, Link: https://www.youtube.com/watch?

60   Fleischman, Harry Democratic Left "DSAers Win Elections
Nationwide" JANUARY- FEBRUARY 1990, page 7

61   21st Century Democrats, "SEN. SHERROD BROWN" Link: http://
www.21stcenturydems.org/candidates/2012-candidates/senator-sherrod-brown/

62   21st Century Democrats "2018 Candidates" Link: https://
www.21stcenturydems.org/2018-candidates/

63   21st Century Democrats, "SEN. SHERROD BROWN" Link: http://
www.21stcenturydems.org/candidates/2012-candidates/senator-sherrod-brown/

64   Midwest Academy Facebook page. December 8, 2017, Link: https://
www.facebook.com/midwestacademy/photos/midwest-academy-is-so-honored-to-
give-steve-phillips-founder-of-democracy-in-col/10155909332008491

65   Hoffman, David, Democratic Left, March 1979 "DSOC Convention:
New Goals Set, Anti-Carter Mood" page 3

66   Ovide, Shira, Wall Street Journal "Meet Obama's Car Czar Turned
Manufacturing Overlord: Ron Bloom" January 4, 2011, Link: https://www.wsj.
com/articles/BL-DLB-30485

67   Midwest Academy Facebook page. December 12, 2017, Link: https://
www.facebook.com/midwestacademy/photos/midwest-academy-is-so-honored-to-
give-steve-phillips-founder-of-democracy-in-col/10155923266968491

68   Piece by Piece Strategies "FOUNDING PARTNERS: JESSICA
PIERCE & BRYAN PERLMUTTER" Link: https://piecebypiecestrategies.org/
about/

69   LinkedIn, "Jessica Pierce", Link: https://www.linkedin.com/in/
jessicapierce/

70   Freedom Road Socialist Organization "A Letter from Our National
Organizer" July 19th, 2016, Link: https://web.archive.org/web/20160824121819/
https://freedomroad.org/2016/07/a-letter-from-our-national-organizer/

71   Democratic Left Fall 2012 "Democracy Endangered: DSA's Strategy
for the 2012 Elections and Beyond" August 1, 2012, pages 14, 15

72   New American Movement Public group Facebook page "Jay
Jurie" June 27, 2016, Link: https://www.facebook.com/groups/13120987813/
posts/10154980680287814/

73   DSA News, January 1986, page 2

74   Nagin, Rick, People's World, Health Care for America Now "Health
care reform rally: Yes we can!" April 28, 2009 Link: https://peoplesworld.org/
article/health-care-reform-rally-yes-we-can/

75   Health Care for America Now "Our Team" Link: https://www.health-
careforamericanow.org/about/staff/

76   Ohio Organizing Collaborative "History" www.ohorganizing.org.
Retrieved November 16

77   Ohio Organizing Collaborative "Senator Brown & OOC Talk Health
and Retirement Security" Link: https://web.archive.org/web/20131127022504/
https://www.ohorganizing.org/index.php/newsmedia/community-news/271-sen-
ator-sherrod-brown-and-ooc-talk-social-security-medicare-and-medicaid

78   YouTube Tribute to Sen. Sherrod Brown Midwest Academy Uploaded
on Jan 14, 2018. Link: https://www.youtube.com/watch?v=sAtyh9tRYKY

79   Foley, Joi, Rockwood Leadership Institute, "ANNOUNCING THE 2017 LEADERSHIP NOW: OHIO FELLOWS" Link: https://rockwoodleadership.org/2017-leadership-now-ohio/

80   Rogers, Avery Lea and Wicentowski, Danny, St. Louis Public Radio "St. Louis has a new basketball court. Its funders were raided by the FBI" August 26, 2022, Link: https://news.stlpublicradio.org/show/st-louis-on-the-air/2022-08-25/st-louis-has-a-new-basketball-court-its-funders-were-raided-by-the-fbi

81   Council for a Livable World 2018 Senate endorsements "Sherrod Brown (D-OH) for Senate" Link: https://livableworld.org/meet-the-candidates/Senate-candidates/sherrod-brown-d-oh-Senate/

82   Council for a Livable World 2012 Senate endorsements "Sherrod Brown (D-OH) for Senate" Link: http://livableworld.org/elections/2012/candidates/Senate/sbrown/

83   Council for a Livable World 2018 Senate endorsements "Sherrod Brown (D-OH) for Senate" Link: https://livableworld.org/meet-the-candidates/Senate-candidates/sherrod-brown-d-oh-Senate/

RON WYDEN

1   Ron Wyden. Official Government Biography: https://www.wyden.Senate.gov/meet-ron

2   Wyden, Ron. https://www.Senate.gov/general/committee_assignments/assignments.htm Archive Link: https://web.archive.org/web/20220413210220/https://www.Senate.gov/general/committee_assignments/assignments.htm

3   Obituary. The Philadelphia Inquirer. "Edith R. Wyden," June 22, 2011. Link: https://www.inquirer.com/philly/obituaries/20110622_Edith_R__Wyden___Senator_s_mother__91.html&outputType=app-web-view

4   Image retrieved from "Bay of Pigs: The Untold Story" by Peter Wyden. back cover.

5   McLellan, Joseph, Washington Post. "Diving for Pearls in the Bay of Pigs," July 25, 1979. Link: https://www.washingtonpost.com/archive/lifestyle/1979/07/25/diving-for-pearls-in-the-bay-of-pigs/d804c2f6-109f-4f9f-a4f9-02d534d1289c/

6   Jack, Old Ridgefield Blog. "Peter Wyden: 20th Century Issues" Link: http://www.naturegeezer.com/2016/11/peter-wyden-20th-century-issues-peter.html

7   Wyden, Ron, Official Government Website. "Guantanamo Bay Trip," January 01, 2006. Archive Link: https://web.archive.org/web/20220619041034/https://www.wyden.Senate.gov/news/photo-gallery/guantanamo-bay-trip

8   Bolton, Alexander, The Hill. "Baucus bill portends Dem fight over Cuba," May 4, 2009. Archive Link: https://web.archive.org/web/20090505145404/https://thehill.com/leading-the-news/baucus-bill-portends-dem-fight-over-cuba-2009-05-04.html

9   Obama, Barack, White House Archives. "Remarks by the President at the Summit of the Americas Opening Ceremony," April 17, 2009. Link: https://obamawhitehouse.archives.gov/the-press-office/remarks-president-summit-americas-opening-ceremony

10   Obama, Barack, White House Archives. "Remarks by the President

at Cairo University, 6-04-09," June 4, 2009. Link: https://obamawhitehouse. archives.gov/the-press-office/remarks-president-cairo-university-6-04-09

11   Landrieu, Mary, US Senate Committee on Small Business & Entrepreneurship. "Landrieu, Others Seek Small Business Opportunities in Cuba," May 11, 2009. Link: https://www.sbc.Senate.gov/public/index.cfm/ pressreleases?ID=D96FDAE9-50A5-4F7D-AE3E-8D0AE5FF09D5 Archive link to letter: https://web.archive.org/web/20090528002841/https://www.sbc. Senate.gov/oversight/lettersout/2009/05_11_Cuba.pdf

12   Obama, Barack, White House Archives. "Statement by the President on Cuba Policy Changes," December 17, 2014. Link: https://obamawhitehouse. archives.gov/the-press-office/2014/12/17/statement-president-cuba-policy-changes

13   Wyden, Ron, Twitter. "Opening relations with Cuba is good for the Cuban people & America's economy," Tweet dated December 17, 2014. Link: https://twitter.com/RonWyden/status/545324167932182528

14   Wyden, Ron, Official Government Website. "Wyden Statement on Policy Changes to Open Relations with Cuba," December 17, 2014. Archive Link: https://web.archive.org/ web/20220619033507/https://www.wyden.Senate.gov/news/press-releases/ wyden-statement-on-policy-changes-to-open-relations-with-cuba

15   Gamez Torres, Nora, Miami Herald. "Cuba shares plans for a single currency and more during a visit by US lawmakers," February 21, 2018. Archive Link:

16   Sanger, David E, New York Times. "Biden Administration Lifting Some Trump-Era Restrictions on Cuba," May 16, 2022. Link: https://www. nytimes.com/2022/05/16/us/politics/biden-cuba-policy.html

17   The Quint. "Democrat lawmakers slams Trump's stance toward Cuba" Link: https://www.thequint.com/news/hot-news/ democrat-lawmakers-slams-trump-s-stance-toward-cuba

18   "Cuban leader Raúl Castro talks to Sen. Patrick Leahy and other US members of Congress on Feb. 20th. Estudios Revolución Cuban Foreign Ministry" Archive Link: https://web.archive.org/web/20180222004738/ https://www.miamiherald.com/news/nation-world/world/americas/cuba/ article201418909.html

19   Leahy, Patrick, Official government website. "Leahy Joins In Introducing Bill To End Cuba Embargo And Establish Normal Trade Relations," February 5, 2021. Link: https://www.leahy.Senate.gov/press/leahy-joins-in-intro- ducing-bill-to-end-cuba-embargo-and-establish-normal-trade-relations

20   Wyden, Ron, Twitter. May 18, 2022 Link: https://twitter.com/ RonWyden/status/1526944054570803202

21   Oakland Tribune, Oakland, California, 09 Jul 1976, Page 38

22   Ron Wyden, Government website, "Issues", "Seniors". Link: https:// www.wyden.Senate.gov/issues/seniors

23   Wyden, Ron, Vox. "Medicare's system for chronic illness failed my parents. Here's how I want to fix it," Jun 14, 2016 Link: https://www.vox. com/2016/6/14/11932128/update-medicare-guarantee

24   Wyden, Ron, The Atlantic. "To Save Medicare, Think Like the Patients Who Use It," May 21, 2012 Link: https://www.theatlantic.com/health/ archive/2012/05/to-save-medicare-think-like-the-patients-who-use-it/257299/

25   Wyden, Ron. Congressional Record. "The Passing of an American Hero," June 7, 1995. Link: https://www.congress.gov/crec/1995/06/08/CREC-1995-06-08-pt1-PgE1181-3.pdf

26   Strelnick, Hal, Health/Pac Bulletin, Health Policy Advisory Center of the Institute for Policy Studies. "Maggie Kuhn: "All of us are in this together," January-February, 1983 Link: http://www.healthpacbulletin.org/wp-content/uploads/1983/01/1983-Jan-Feb_Correct.pdf

27   Connor-Rice, Maureen, Ukiah Daily Journal (Ukiah, California). "Kuhn's credits climb" 29 Mar 1992, Page 13.

28   Geriatric Nursing. "Profile of a panther," Pages 81-82. Link: https://www.sciencedirect.com/journal/geriatric-nursing/vol/1/issue/1

29   Kuhn, Maggie (1905-1995), Encyclopedia.com. Link: https://www.encyclopedia.com/women/encyclopedias-almanacs-transcripts-and-maps/kuhn-maggie-1905-1995

30   Democratic Left, Sept./Oct. 1991, page 28 (Screenshot)

31   Democratic Left, May/June 1989, Page 10

32   Democratic Left, May/June 1989, Page 10

33   Sanjek, Roger, University of Pennsylvania Press. "Gray Panthers," 2012. Page 184.

34   Strelnick, Hal, Health/Pac Bulletin, Health Policy Advisory Center of the Institute for Policy Studies. "Maggie Kuhn: "All of us are in this together," January-February, 1983 Link: http://www.healthpacbulletin.org/wp-content/uploads/1983/01/1983-Jan-Feb_Correct.pdf

35   Tait, Gordon, (From the Associated Press). York Daily Record. "Court Outlaws Witch-hunting in Tax Case," November 19, 1966, Page 19.

36   Lydgate, Chris, Williamette Week. "FAMILY FEUD Who's gonna wind up with Reuben Lenske's millions?" November 19, 2002. Link: https://www.wweek.com/portland/article-1489-family-feud.html

37   Loudon, Trevor. Keywiki.org. "Rosenberg Case." Link: https://keywiki.org/Rosenberg_Case

38   Pulliam, Mark, Law & Liberty. "Revisiting William O. Douglas," June 22, 2020. Link: https://lawliberty.org/book-review/revisiting-william-o-douglas/

39   United States. Congress. Senate. Committee on the Judiciary. Subcommittee on Administrative Practice and Procedure: Constitutional and administrative problems of enforcing Internal Revenue statutes: hearing before the Subcommittee on Administrative Practice and Procedure of the Committee on the Judiciary, United States Senate, Ninetieth Congress, second session pursuant to S.Res. 25. January 17, 1968 (Washington, US Govt. Print. Off., 1968) Page 13. Link: https://catalog.hathitrust.org/Record/008515190

40   United States. Congress. Senate. Committee on the Judiciary. Subcommittee on Administrative Practice and Procedure: Constitutional and administrative problems of enforcing Internal Revenue statutes: hearing before the Subcommittee on Administrative Practice and Procedure of the Committee on the Judiciary, United States Senate, Ninetieth Congress, second session pursuant to S.Res. 25. January 17, 1968 (Washington, US Govt. Print. Off., 1968) Page 7. Link: https://catalog.hathitrust.org/Record/008515190

41   Lydgate, Chris, Williamette Week. "FAMILY FEUD Who's gonna

wind up with Reuben Lenske's millions?" November 19, 2002. Link: https://www.
wweek.com/portland/article-1489-family-feud.html

42   "Peace Party Meets Told", Petaluma Argus-Courier, Petaluma,
California, 24 Feb 1968, Page 3

43   United States Congress, House Committee on Un-American Activities
"Report on the National Lawyers Guild, legal bulwark of the Communist
Party," September 21, 1950. Archive Link: https://archive.org/details/
reportonnational1950unit

44   Evanier, David, The Critic. "A spy all along," September 2020. Link:
https://thecritic.co.uk/issues/september-2020/a-spy-all-along/

45   Kaufman, Michael T. and Sam Roberts, "Morton Sobell, Last
Defendant in Rosenberg Spy Case, Is Dead at 101," Jan 30, 2019. Link: https://
www.nytimes.com/2019/01/30/obituaries/morton-sobell-dead.html

46   Official Government Biography (archived). "Meet Ron Wyden."
Archive Link: https://web.archive.org/web/20080130190834/http://wyden.
Senate.gov/ron/

47   Sanjek, Roger, University of Pennsylvania Press. "Gray Panthers," 2012.
Page 10.

48   Council for a Livable World Website, "Our Legacy in Congress:
Who We've Helped Elect". Archive Link: https://web.archive.org/
web/20220522030519/https://livableworld.org/meet-the-candidates/
our-legacy-in-congress-who-weve-helped-elect/

49   Wyden, Ron. Congressional Record. "Council for a
Livable World," June 7, 1995. Link: https://livableworld.org/
senator-wydens-statement-on-councils-50th-anniversary/

50   Loudon, Trevor, Breitbart News. "Blinded by the Left:
How Marxists Wrote Ron Paul's Defense Cuts Plan," January
8, 2012. Link: https://www.breitbart.com/politics/2012/01/08/
blinded-by-the-left-how-marxists-wrote-ron-pauls-defense-cuts-plan/

51   Arms Control Center, "Debt, Deficits, & Defense: A Way Forward"
Archive Link: https://web.archive.org/web/20100615145945/https://armscontrol-
center.org/media/Debt_Deficits_and_Defense.pdf

52   Council for a Livable Word, Twitter, June 11, 2010. Archive Link:
https://web.archive.org/web/20220623204522/https://twitter.com/Livableworld/
status/15949559834

53   Project on Defense Alternatives, "History" Archive Link: https://web.
archive.org/web/20220623190505/https://comw.org/pda/about-2/

54   Conetta, Carl, "RSB: justifiable reformers". Connecticut Daily
Campus. Wednesday, October 5, 1977, Page 2. Archive Link: https://web.
archive.org/web/20220623182221/https://archives.lib.uconn.edu/islandora/
object/20002%3A860231031/datastream/PDF/download

55   Conetta, Carl, C-Span. "Defense Spending Cuts", June
11, 2010 (Screenshot) Link: https://www.c-span.org/video/?294024-1/
defense-spending-cuts

56   Loudon, Trevor, Breitbart News. "Blinded by the Left:
How Marxists Wrote Ron Paul's Defense Cuts Plan," January
8, 2012. Link: https://www.breitbart.com/politics/2012/01/08/
blinded-by-the-left-how-marxists-wrote-ron-pauls-defense-cuts-plan/

57   Wyden, Ron, Official Government Website. "Congress Urges President's Deficit Reduction Commission To Look To Cuts In The Pentagon's Budget For Solutions," October 13, 2010. Archive Link: https://web.archive. org/web/20220623194645/https://www.wyden.Senate.gov/news/press-releases/ congress-urges-presidents-deficit-reduction-commission-to-look-to-cuts-in-the-pentagons-budget-for-solutions Letter Text: https://web.archive.org/ web/20211217100232/https://www.wyden.Senate.gov/imo/media/doc/Letter%20 from%2057%20Members%20to%20National%20Committee%20on%20Fiscal%20 Responsibility%20FINAL.pdf

58   Hudson, John and Paul Sonne, The Washington Post. "Trump administration discussed conducting first US nuclear test in decades," May 22, 2020. Link: https://www.washingtonpost.com/national-security/trump-administration-discussed-conducting-first-us-nuclear-test-in-decades/2020/05/22/a805c904-9c5b-11ea-b60c-3be060a4f8e1_story.html

59   Council for a Livable World, "Bill Foster for House (D-IL-11)". Link: https://livableworld.org/meet-the-candidates/house-candidates/ bill-foster-for-house-d-il-11/

60   Wyden, Ron, Official Press Release. "Wyden, Foster Lead Bicameral Warning Against Trump Administration Resuming Explosive Nuclear Testing," June 08, 2020. Archive Link: https://web.archive.org/web/20220623162720/ https://www.wyden.Senate.gov/news/press-releases/wyden-foster-lead-bicameral-warning-against-trump-administration-resuming-explosive-nuclear-testing Letter: https://web.archive.org/web/20220121095543/https://www.wyden.Senate.gov/ imo/media/doc/060820%20Wyden%20Foster%20Bicameral%20Nuclear%20 Testing%20Letter%20.pdf

61   Council for a Livable World, Twitter. Jun 9, 2020. Link: https://twitter. com/Livableworld/status/1270497168898523139

JEFF MERKLEY

1   Merkley, Jeff. Official Government Website: https://www.merkley. Senate.gov/download/official-biography-of-senator-jeff-merkley-

2   Merkley, Jeff. https://www.Senate.gov/general/committee_assignments/ assignments.htm Archive Link: https://web.archive.org/web/20220413210220/ https://www.Senate.gov/general/committee_assignments/assignments.htm

3   YouTube, "Jeff Merkley Pays Tribute to Senator Mark O. Hatfield." September 9, 2011, Link: https://www.youtube.com/watch?v=Fs-vfK0ntaw

4   Center for Arms Control and Non-Proliferation, "A Tribute to Senator Mark Hatfield." August 10, 2011. Link: https://armscontrolcenter. org/a-tribute-to-senator-mark-hatfield/

5   Judis, John, In These Times, "Democratic Socialism Will Prevail": An Interview with Ron Dellums in 1976," July 30, 2018. Link: https://inthesetimes. com/article/ron-dellums-death-democratic-socialist-dsa-antiwar-1976-interview

6   Communists in the Democratic Party ISBN: 0962742708 page 7

7   Szumilo, Dan, Black Swamp Gazette, "The Democratic Socialist Alternative DSA", January 17, 1983.

8   Concerned Voters, Inc., "Communists in the Democratic Party". ISBN: 0962742708, page 73.

9   Information Digest April 15, 1983 pages 77-79

10   Arnold, Laurence, "Mark Hatfield, Anti-War Republican Senator, Dies," August 8 2011. Link: http://www.bloomberg.com/news/2011-08-08/mark-hat-field-anti-war-republican-senator-dies.html

11   Kimball, Daryl G. Arms Control Association, "In Memoriam: Mark O. Hatfield (1922–2011)" Link: https://www.armscontrol.org/2011_09/In_Memoriam_Mark_Hatfield

12   Wittner, Lawrence S., Arms Control Association, "The Nuclear Freeze and Its Impact", December 2012. Link: https://www.armscontrol.org/act/2010_12/LookingBack

13   Markey, Edward J. Congressional Record "ON THE DEATH OF RANDALL FORSBERG" October 23, 2007. Link: https://www.govinfo.gov/content/pkg/CREC-2007-10-23/pdf/CREC-2007-10-23-pt1-PgE2210-4.pdf#page=1

14   Calkins, Jessie WAND Education Fund, March: "WAND@Work" March 5, 2014. Link: https://www.wand.org/2014/03/05/march-wandwork

15   Cortright, David, David Cortwright website "SANE is Back", March 7, 2012. Link: https://davidcortright.net/2012/03/07/sane-is-back/

16   Center for Arms Control and Non-Proliferation," A Tribute to Senator Mark Hatfield," August 10, 2011. Link: https://armscontrolcenter.org/a-tribute-to-senator-mark-hatfield/

17   Democratic Left "A BIG THANK YOU" • Winter 2016 • page 1

18   Council for a Livable World " Council for a Livable World 50th Anniversary Celebration" Link: https://armscontrolcenter.org/issues/recent/council_center_50th_anniversary/

19   Council for a Livable World "Summary of the Council's 50th Anniversary Senators Forum," June 21, 2012. Link: https://livableworld.org/summary-of-the-councils-50th-anniversary-senators-forum/

20   Council for a Livable World, "bio of Jeff Merkley", 2014. Archive Link: https://web.archive.org/web/20130811193242/http://livableworld.org/elections/2014/candidates/Senate/merkley/

21   Conley, Heather A., et al, Center for Strategic and International Studies. "The Future of US-Russian Arms Control: Principles of Engagement and New Approaches", March 12, 2021. Link: https://www.csis.org/analysis/future-us-russian-arms-control-principles-engagement-and-new-approaches

22   Council for a Livable World "Jeff Merkley for Senate (D-OR)" Link: https://livableworld.org/meet-the-candidates/Senate-candidates/jeff-merkley-for-Senate-d-or/

23   People's Daily World, "DSOC meet urges butter, not guns", June 11, 1981. Pages 5 and 18

24   Portland Democratic Socialists of America, "Report to National Democratic Socialists of America." July, 1982

25   Parks, Casey the Oregonian, "Steve Rudman led Home Forward with creativity, compassion and 'good hair,' bureaucrats and affordable housing activists say". Link: https://www.oregonlive.com/portland/2014/10/steve_rudman_led_home_forward.html

26   Merkley, Jeff, Official Government Website. "MERKLEY STATEMENT ON GRETCHEN KAFOURY", March 14,

2015. Link: https://www.merkley.Senate.gov/news/press-releases/
merkley-statement-on-gretchen-kafoury-

27   21st Century Democrats, "Jim Scheibel addresses 21st
Century Democrats 2008 Gala", Dec 19, 2010. Link: youtube.com/
watch?v=i68QXl6-ZVE

28   Fleishman, Harry, Democratic Left. "On the Left", July-August 1990.

29   Merley, Jeff, Jeff Merkley Campaign Website, "21st Century
Democrats Endorse Jeff Merkley" Link: https://2008.jeffmerkley.
com/2008/05/21st_century_de.html

30   NPR "Oregon's Jeff Merkley Becomes First Senator to Endorse Bernie
Sanders"
April 13, 2016. Link: https://www.npr.org/2016/04/13/474120856/
oregons-jeff-merkley-becomes-first-senator-to-endorse-bernie-sanders

31   Bachtell, John People's World, "Survey says, CPUSA members want to
be heard",
January 24, 2018, 2017. Link: https://www.cpusa.org/article/
survey-says-cpusa-members-want-to-be-heard/

32   Harami, Brandon, LinkedIn. "Brandon Harami Activities". Link:
https://www.linkedin.com/in/brandon-harami-4571453a/

33   Los Angeles Democratic Socialists of America, "Growing the
Movement with DSA Bernie Delegates". Link: https://dsa-la.org/event/
growing-the-movement-stream/

34   Our Revolution, "Our Revolution 2020 endorsements." Link: https://
s3.amazonaws.com/s3-ourrevolution/images/OR_Endorsemnts.pdf

35   International Coalition for Human Rights in the Philippines website.
Link: https://ichrp.net/

36   International Coalition for Human Rights in the Philippines website
"About" Link: https://ichrp.net/about/

37   State Library of New South Wales, MANUSCRIPTS, ORAL
HISTORY AND PICTURES CATALOGUE "Peter Murphy - papers, 1928-
1989." Link: https://archival.sl.nsw.gov.au/Details/archive/110311990

38   SEARCH Foundation website "SEARCH Foundation Committee
Elected at the 2002 AGM" Link: https://www.search.org.au/

39   SEARCH Foundation "About US" Link: https://www.search.org.au/
our_history

40   Murphy, Peter LinkedIn accessed July 25 2020, Link: https://www.
linkedin.com/in/peter-murphy-b516528/

41   International League of Peoples' Struggle "ILPS
International Coordinating Committee Elects Its Executive
Officers" November 20, 2015. Link: https://ilps.info/en/
ilps-international-coordinating-committee-elects-its-executive-officers/

42   East Wind, "Environmental Justice is Key to a Sustainable Planet,
Keynote Address to APALA Convention, Aug. 6, 2021. By Pam Tau Lee." Link:
https://eastwindezine.com/environmental-justice-is-key-to-a-sustainable-planet/

43   The Bancroft Library "Pamela Tau Lee COMMUNITY AND
UNION ORGANIZING, AND ENVIRONMENTAL JUSTICE IN THE
SAN FRANCISCO BAY AREA," 1967-200 pages 61, 65. Link: https://digital-
assets.lib.berkeley.edu/rohoia/ucb/text/communityunion00leeprich.pdf

44		YouTube. Pam Tau Lee: The Left Movement & Cadre Organizations--Integrating with the Masses" Feb 19, 2017. Link: https://www.youtube.com/watch?v=AI3K3Gg9Lv8

45		Out to Win, LeftRoots magazine. Volume 1, February 2019. "Preface, Who We Are" page 116 Link: https://journal.leftroots.net/downloads/out-to-win_eng_fin.pdf

46		PORTLAND COMMITTEE FOR HUMAN RIGHTS IN THE PHILIPPINES Duterte Extends Martial Law in Mindanao, US Senator Merkley Voices Support for National Campaign to Stop Killings in the Philippines December 14, 2017. Link: http://www.portlandchrp.com/national-statements/duterte-extends-martial-law-in-mindanao-us-senator-merkley-voices-support-for-national-campaign-to-stop-killings-in-the-philippines

47		Facebook, ICHRP US International Coalition for Human Rights in the Philippines, "Thank you Senator Jeff Merkley for your statement of support for ICHRP-US! #ICHRPUS #StoptheKillings," December 9, 2017. Link: https://www.facebook.com/ICHRPUnitedStates/posts/pfbid0yFrkYvBVX31dw-gaHJGeZ2hF6zWgcXAVbdHjpGmzTgxXxBZNBzvahvtHyQYa4HDZ8l

48		Ramirez, Rachel, Willamette Week. "Filipino Activists Demand a Stop to US Funding of the Duterte Regime
US Sen. Jeff Merkley stands with them." May 6, 2018. Link: https://www.wweek.com/news/2018/05/06/portland-filipino-activists-and-community-organizers-rally-demand-a-stop-to-u-s-funding-of-the-duterte-regime/

49		Ramirez, Rachel, Willamette Week "Filipino Activists Demand a Stop to US Funding of the Duterte Regime
US Sen. Jeff Merkley stands with them", May 06, 2018. Link: https://www.wweek.com/news/2018/05/06/portland-filipino-activists-and-community-organizers-rally-demand-a-stop-to-u-s-funding-of-the-duterte-regime/

50		Facebook, ICHRP US International Coalition for Human Rights in the Philippines, "Filipinos and Advocates in Oregon and Washington March Against Killings, Seek Support from US Senator Merkley and Legislators",
May 5, 2021. Link: https://www.facebook.com/notes/1158511241274294/

51		Philippine Human Rights Act One-Pager. Link: https://static1.squarespace.com/static/5ebd6cd50c128360664cb9bd/t/60a4688d3675cd0d7d6e4e61/1621387406475/One+Pager+on+ATA.pdf

52		Ramos, Christia, Maria, Enquirer.net. "11 US senators to Biden admin: Condemn 'pattern' of abuses under Duterte" August 02, 2021. Link: https://globalnation.inquirer.net/198204/fwd-us-senators-to-biden-admin-condemn-pattern-of-abuses-under-duterte

53		Jeff Merkley press release "MERKLEY, MARKEY, LEAHY, CARDIN, WYDEN, AND BOOKER, URGE SUPPORT FOR HUMAN RIGHTS AND DEMOCRACY FOLLOWING PHILIPPINES ELECTION" May 27, 2022 Link: https://www.merkley.Senate.gov/news/press-releases/merkley-markey-leahy-cardin-wyden-and-booker-urge-support-for-human-rights-and-democracy-following-philippines-election

54		Ibid.

55		Letter to Senator Merkley to support the PHRA February 10, 2022 Link: https://350pdx.org/wp-content/uploads/2022/02/Letter-to-Senator-Merkley-to-support-the-PHRA-1.pdf

56   Susan Wild, press release. "REP. WILD LEADS CALL FOR ACTION AGAINST PHILIPPINES HUMAN RIGHTS VIOLATIONS" May 27, 2022 Link: https://wild.house.gov/media/press-releases/rep-wild-leads-call-action-against-philippines-human-rights-violations#:~:text=In%20July%2C%20Rep.,accountability%20against%20the%20perpetrators%20commences.

PATRICK LEAHY

1   Leahy, Patrick. Official Government Website: https://www.leahy.Senate.gov/about

2   Leahy, Patrick. https://www.Senate.gov/general/committee_assignments/assignments.htm Archive Link: https://web.archive.org/web/20220413210220/https://www.Senate.gov/general/committee_assignments/assignments.htm

3   Patrick Leahy. https://www.appropriations.Senate.gov/about/chairman

4   Khouri, Jim, Renew America "Meet the new Chairman of the Judiciary Committee: Sen. Leaky Leahy", November 10, 2006, Link: https://web.archive.org/web/20140804044824/http://www.renewamerica.com/columns/kouri/061110

5   Carle, David Patrick Leahy press release "Statement at State and Foreign Operations Subcommittee Hearing On Assistance For Civilian Victims Of War" April 1, 2009 Link: https://www.leahy.Senate.gov/press/statement-at-state-and-foreign-operations-subcommittee-hearing-on-assistance-for-civilian-victims-of-war

6   Omang, Joanne, Washington Post "Leahy Says 'Contra' Aid Would Not Pass Senate" February 21, 1985. Link: https://www.washingtonpost.com/archive/politics/1985/02/21/leahy-says-contra-aid-would-not-pass-Senate/e954edfc-fdd1-4a02-a73b-5f7b62a602ca/

7   Discover the Networks "Patrick Leahy profile" Link: https://www.discoverthenetworks.org/individuals/patrick-leahy

8   Radu, Michael, Frontpage Magazine Colombia's "Revolutionaries" and Their Helpers", January 28, 2003. Link: http://archive.frontpagemag.com/readArticle.aspx?ARTID=20073

9   NAFSA website. "Cuba Placed Back on List of State Sponsors of Terrorism" January 22, 2021. Link: https://www.nafsa.org/regulatory-information/cuba-placed-back-list-state-sponsors-terrorism

10   Craven, Jasper, VT Digger. "The Leahy legacy: Fidel, fundraising and influential friends," October 26, 2016. Link: https://vtdigger.org/2016/10/26/leahy-legacy-fidel-fundraising-influential-friends/

11   Clymer, Adam, New York Times. "Republicans Take Raid Rage to TV, and Turn Up Volume," April 24, 2000. Link: https://archive.nytimes.com/www.nytimes.com/library/politics/camp/042400cuba-boy-pols.html

12   CNN Transcript of Press Conference, "Special Event: Senators Dodd, Leahy Hold News Conference Following Meeting with Attorney General Reno Regarding Elian Gonzalez Case," April 25, 2000. Link: http://us.cnn.com/TRANSCRIPTS/0004/25/se.03.html CSPAN Link: https://www.c-span.org/video/?156786-1/elian-gonzalez-custody-case

13   Weisman, Jonathon, New York Times. "Senators Urge Castro

to Release American" February 24, 2012, Link: https://www.nytimes.com/2012/02/25/us/politics/senators-meet-with-raul-castro-seeking-release-of-alan-gross.html

14   Associated Press, "Senator Patrick Leahy leads US group to Cuba to seek release of Alan Gross" February 18, 2013, Link: https://www.theguardian.com/world/2013/feb/18/patrick-leahy-cuba-alan-gross

15   Trotta, Daniel, Reuters. "US senators visit Cuba, hope Congress will ease restrictions" Sat Jun 27, 2015. Link: http://www.reuters.com/article/2015/06/27/us-cuba-usa-idUSKBN0P70UJ20150627

16   Leahy, Patrick, VT Digger. "Leahy reaction to Obama plan to open US embassy in Havana." Jul 2, 2015. Link: https://vtdigger.org/2015/07/02/leahy-reaction-to-obama-plan-to-open-u-s-embassy-in-havana/

17   Jim McGovern press release "McGovern Joins Secretary Kerry in Cuba for US Embassy Opening" HAVANA, CUBA, August 14, 2015

18   Heil, Emily. Washington Post "At re-opened Cuban embassy's first soiree, the crowd is eclectic, but the drink of choice is clear", July 20, 2015. Link: https://www.washingtonpost.com/news/reliable-source/wp/2015/07/20/at-cuban-embassys-first-soiree-the-crowd-is-eclectic-but-the-drink-of-choice-is-clear/

19   Democracy Now. "Secret Talks & Sperm Deals: Sen. Patrick Leahy Details Back Story to Renewed US-Cuban Ties", July 21, 2015. Link: https://www.democracynow.org/2015/7/21/secret_talks_sperm_deals_sen_patrick

20   Ibid.

21   French, Lauren Politico, "Pelosi, 15 House Democrats to join Obama trip to Cuba," March 14, 2016. Link: https://www.politico.com/story/2016/03/nancy-pelosi-cuba-trip-obama-220731

22   Fuerte, Cafe Havana Times "Trump Ally Joins Congressional Delegation to Cuba" February 20, 2017. Link: https://havanatimes.org/news/trump-ally-joins-congressional-delegation-to-cuba/

23   Jacomino. Pavel. Radio Havana. "Visiting US congressional delegation meets with Cuban Foreign Ministry officials, February 20, 2018. Link: https://www.radiohc.cu/en/noticias/nacionales/155673-visiting-us-congressional-delega-tion-meets-with-cuban-foreign-ministry-officials

24   The Hagstrom Report "Wyden introduces bill to repeal Cuba trade embargo with US ag exports down", | February 10, 2021. Link: https://www.thefencepost.com/news/wyden-introduces-bill-to-repeal-cuba-trade-embargo-with-us-ag-exports-down/

25   Vietnam Agent Orange Relief & Responsibility Campaign website "About". Link: http://www.vn-agentorange.org/about.html

26   NGO monitor "International Association of Democratic Lawyers (IADL)" February 10, 2022. Link: https://www.ngo-monitor.org/ngos/international-association-democratic-lawyers-iadl/

27   Vietnam Agent Orange Relief & Responsibility Campaign "VAORRC National Board" Link: https://vn-agentorange.org/vaorrc-national-board/

28   Institute for Policy Studies, "Phyllis Bennis" Link: https://ips-dc.org/ips-authors/phyllis-bennis/

29   International Association of Democratic Lawyers website "Marjorie Cohn" Link: https://iadllaw.org/officers-and-bureau-members-2/marjorie-cohn/

30   Liberation Road website "The Main Enemy of Our People" Link: https://roadtoliberation.org/the-main-enemy-of-our-people/

31   Tamiment Library website, "Descriptive Summary-Jeanne Mirer Papers" Link: http://dlib.nyu.edu/findingaids/html/tamwag/tam_383/

32   CofC website "Pay Fry's letter to the Metro DC CCDS" Link: http://www.dccofc.org/correspondence.htm

33   Liberation Road website, "The Young and the Leftless: An Open Letter on Organization" Link: https://roadtoliberation.org/the-young-and-the-leftless-an-open-letter-on-organization/

34   Portside, "LEFTROOTS & LEFT STRATEGIES HangOut on Strategy for Liberation," November 18, 2015. Link: https://portside.org/2015-11-18/hangout-strategy-liberation

35   CCDS MOBILIZER Vol 2 No 2 June 2006, "Nominations Open for National Leadership," Page 4. Link: https://www.cc-ds.org/IssueJune2006Version4.0.pdf

36   CUNY Academic Commons, "Merle Ratner (she/her/comrade)" Link: https://commons.gc.cuny.edu/members/minhkhai/

37   Jasper, Craven VT Digger "Leahy presses on with humanitarian efforts in Southeast Asia" Jul 9, 2019. Link: https://vtdigger.org/2019/07/09/leahy-presses-on-with-humanitarian-efforts-in-post-war-southeast-asia/

38   VAORRC blog "Senator Patrick Leahy to Retire" November 30, 2021. Link: https://vn-agentorange.org/senator-patrick-leahy-to-retire/

39   Ibid.

40   Aspen Institute: "Nine US Senators Visit Bien Hoa," June 4, 2019. Link: https://www.aspeninstitute.org/of-interest/nine-u-s-senators-visit-bien-hoa/
Ron Wyden

BERNIE SANDERS

1   Sanders, Bernie. Official Government website. Link: https://www.sanders.Senate.gov/

2   Sanders, Bernie. Link: https://www.Senate.gov/general/committee_assignments/assignments.htm Archive Link: https://web.archive.org/web/20220413210220/https://www.Senate.gov/general/committee_assignments/assignments.htm

3   Gutman, Huck Outsider in the House, By Bernie Sanders, page 14

4   Targ, Harry Diary of a Heartland Radical Link: https://heartlandradical.blogspot.com/2011/06/herb-march-and-vicky-starr-chicago.html HERB MARCH AND VICKY STARR: CHICAGO ORGANIZERS OF THE UNITED PACKINGHOUSE WORKERS OF AMERICA (UPWA-CIO) JUNE 9, 2011

5   Greenfield, Daniel Frontpage, BERNIE SANDERS SPENT MONTHS AT MARXIST-STALINIST KIBBUTZ February 4, 2016

6   Radosh, Ronald Hudson Institute: https://www.hudson.org/research/12194-bernie-s-adventures-on-a-stalinist-kibbutz Bernie's Adventures on a Stalinist Kibbutz Feb. 6, 2016.

7   Jewish Telegraphic Agency Link: https://www.jta.org/1980/10/01/archive/aharon-cohen-dead-at-70 Aharon Cohen Dead at 70 October 1, 1980

8   PITTSBURGH TRIBUNE-REVIEW By Dateline D.C. Sunday November 12, 2006

9   Howley, Patrick Daily Caller Link:https://dailycaller.com/2015/07/17/bernie-sanders-shunned-his-socialist-friends/ Bernie Sanders 'Shunned' His Socialist Friends 07/17/2015

10   Guma, Greg Tipping Point: Burlington's Progressive Revolution June 13, 2013. Link: http://muckraker-gg.blogspot.com/2013/06/tipping-point-burlingtons-progressive.html

11   The Militant May 1, 1981, page 13

12   The Daily Beast Link: Moynihan, Michael https://www.thedailybeast.com/when-bernie-sanders-thought-castro-and-the-sandinistas-could-teach-america-a-lesson April 12, 2017

13   Keywiki screenshot Link: https://keywiki.org/File:Mnnnnbvc.JPG

14   Sanders, Bernie Outsider in the House, p. 67

15   The Daily Beast Link: Moynihan, Michael https://www.thedailybeast.com/when-bernie-sanders-thought-castro-and-the-sandinistas-could-teach-america-a-lesson April 12, 2017

16   Walker, Hunter Yahoo News Link: https://www.yahoo.com/news/bernie-sanders-radical-past-how-the-vermont-230255076.html Bernie Sanders' radical past: How the Vermont firebrand started wearing a suit and gave up on taking over big companies Apr. 13, 2017

17   The Daily Beast Link: Moynihan, Michael https://www.thedailybeast.com/when-bernie-sanders-thought-castro-and-the-sandinistas-could-teach-america-a-lesson April 12, 2017

18   Radosh, Ron. Commies: A Journey Through the Old Left, the New Left and the Leftover Left, page 123

19   The Daily Beast Link: Moynihan, Michael https://www.thedailybeast.com/when-bernie-sanders-thought-castro-and-the-sandinistas-could-teach-america-a-lesson April 12, 2017

20   Ibid.

21   Moynihan, Michael. Daily Beast, "When Bernie Sanders Thought Castro and the Sandinistas Could Teach America a Lesson" April 13, 2017 Link: https://www.thedailybeast.com/when-bernie-sanders-thought-castro-and-the-sandinistas-could-teach-america-a-lesson

22   Seitz-Wald, Alex MSNBC Link: http://www.msnbc.com/msnbc/the-25-best-things-we-learned-bernie-sanders-book The 25 best things we learned from Bernie Sanders' book 05/28/15 01:38 PM—Updated 05/28/15

23   WSJ Sept. 24., 1990, page A16

24   Haynes, John Earl Commentary Link: https://www.commentarymagazine.com/articles/no-sense-denying-i-f-stone-was-a-soviet-agent/ No Sense Denying I.F. Stone Was a Soviet Agent, by John Earl Haynes June 2009

25   Keywiki screen shot Link: https://keywiki.org/File:Sanders-letter-page1.jpg

26   Pertman, Adam (November 11, 1990). "'The Times Caught Up' To Vermont Socialist". Boston Globe.

27   Keywiki screenshot DSA brochure screenshot Link: https://keywiki.org/File:Capture1995maybe.JPG

28   Democratic Left, Spring 2010

29   Montgomery County Press release Link:https://www2.montgom-erycountymd.gov/mcgportalapps/Press_Detail.aspx?Item_ID=2486 County Exec-Elect Ike Leggett Thanks Supporters, Lays Extensive Plans for November Transition November 8, 2006

30   Democratic Left, Jan./Feb. 1990, page 12

31   DSA News, January 1986, page 2

32   Green, David DSA Detroit newsletter March 2015 Link: https://d3n8a8pro7vhmx.cloudfront.net/detroitdsa/pages/70/attachments/orig-inal/1441479259/March_2015_DSA_Newsletter.pdf?1441479259 DSA Hosts Book Signing Event for Bonior Memoir

33   Baiman, Ron New Ground 56 Link: https://web.archive.org/web/20120322164027/https://chicagodsa.org/ngarchive/ng56.html Reorganized Illinois Citizen Action January - February 1998

34   JMU YDS website Link: https://web.archive.org/web/20151224042430/http://www.jmu.edu/orgs/youngdemsoc/aboutus.htm About the Young Democratic Socialists of JMU

35   Democratic Left, January/February 1987, page 17

36   Ibid.

37   DSA membership letter Oct 24, 1984

38   Ibid.

39   Democratic Left ♦ Issue #1 1997 * page 7-8

40   Democratic Left, Winter 1996, page 16:

41   Fishman, Joelle CPUSA website Link:http://www.cpusa.org/article/report-on-the-2002-elections/ Report on the 2002 Elections FEBRUARY 22, 2002

42   SolidNet Link:http://www.solidnet.org/article/7db8a9ef-e2cc-11e8-a7f8-42723ed76c54/ , Contribution of the Communist Party USA, 14th International Meeting of CWP, Presented by Erwin Marquit, member of International Department, CPUSA, 25 November 2012

43   Keywiki screenshot Link: https://www.keywiki.org/File:Bernireooo.PNG

44   Riley, Deidre Reading Times, 1/3/88, Socialist tells of need to expand awareness

45   Democratic Left, March/April 1995, page 22

46   Democratic Left, July/August 1996, page 21

47   Spring-Summer 2000 ♦ DemocraticLeft ♦ " Elections Statement 2000 -Electoral Politics As Tactic", page 3

48   Democratic Left, "Convention Resolution: DSA Priorities", Winter 2006, Page 4. Link: https://democraticleft.dsausa.org/files/sites/6/2018/12/DL_2006_V033_03.pdf

49   D'Angelo, Angelo - Wlody, Ed and Keating, Kevin CPUSA http://www.cpusa.org/party_voices/convention-discussion-to-build-our-party-rebuild-left-and-intermediate-forms/ Convention Discussion: To Build Our Party — Rebuild Left and Intermediate Forms MAY 19, 2010

50   The War Called Peace: Glossary, published 1982

51   Bell. David, Communist Party USA website Link: Convention Discussion: What Can We Learn From the Movement for Health Care Reform? February 2 2010 https://web.archive.org/web/20140422172447/http://www.

cpusa.org/convention-discussion-what-can-we-learn-from-the-movement-for-health-care-reform/

52   Turner, Melissa Black Past Link: https://www.blackpast.org/african-american-history/o-dell-jack-1924/ HUNTER PITTS "JACK" O'DELL (1924-2019) December 1, 2009

53   Kincaid, Cliff, AIM Link: https://www.aim.org/aim-column/should-the-nsa-be-watching-senator-sanders/ January 6, 2014

54   CORRESPONDER, August/September 1996 "US Progressives greet the Convention" page 10

55   Case, John Political Affairs Link: https://web.archive.org/web/20120606043150/http://politicalaffairs.net/sanders-for-president/?utm_source=feedburner&utm_medium=feed&utm_campaign=Feed%3A+Paeditorsblog+%28PA+Editors+Blog%29 Sanders for President? by: JOHN CASE Wednesday 29 December 2010

56   PWW, Chicago tribute hails work of Ishmael Flory October 12, 1991, page 8

57   CPUSA, Biography, Scott Marshall, accessed December 3, 2019. Link: https://www.cpusa.org/authors/scott-marshall/

58   Cambron, Rosanna and Wood, Roberta PW Link: https://peoples-world.org/article/chicago-elections-birthing-new-people-s-movement/ Chicago elections birthing new people's movement April 3, 2015

59   CPC link: https://cpc-grijalva.house.gov/caucus-members/ Caucus Members, accessed December 3, 2019

60   DSA website Link: https://www.dsausa.org/news/jan2019dispatch/ January DSA Dispatch
JANUARY 8, 2019

61   CBS News staff Link: https://www.cbsnews.com/news/couple-found-guilty-of-spying/
Couple Found Guilty Of Spying OCTOBER 23, 1998

62   Lenchner, Charles DL Link https://www.dsausa.org/democratic-left/political_revolution_101/ Political Revolution 101 NOVEMBER 3, 2015

63   Albert, Michael CounterPunch Link:https://www.counterpunch.org/2016/02/19/labor-the-left-sanders-an-interview-with-steve-early-and-rand-wilson/ Labor, The Left, & Sanders: An Interview with Steve Early and Rand Wilson FEBRUARY 19, 2016

64   Youtube "Anoa Changa on Young Women for Bernie Sanders" January 29, 2016, Link: https://www.youtube.com/watch?v=I5tUEO2pa3Q

65   Duhalde, David Organizing Upgrade Links" https://organizingup-grade.com/the-path-through-the-party-movements-and-the-democrats/ The Path Through the Party: Movements and the Democrats

66   Boone, Jeb Metro Atlanta DSA website Link: https://madsa.ga/blog/2018/04/19/statement_by_the_metro_atlanta_chapter_of_the_demo-cratic_socialists_of_america_on_the_hit_piece_against_member_anoa_changa/ Statement by the Metro Atlanta Chapter of the Democratic Socialists of America on the vulgar hit piece against member Anoa Changa April 19, 2018

67   Tilove, Jonathan MyStatesman.com Link: http://politics.blog.mys-tatesman.com/tag/bernie-sanders/ For Ted Cruz, Bernie debate previewed 'socialist' strategy against Beto, and one peril lying in wait September 25, 2018

68   Sanders Institute website Link: https://www.sandersinstitute.com/about/mission-statement Mission Statement

69   The Sanders Institute Fellows Link https://www.sandersinstitute.com/about/fellows accessed December 3 2019

70   Religious Socialism Link: https://www.religioussocialism.org/about Accessed December 3, 2019

71   Dem. Left July/August 1993, page 8

72   Jaffe, Sarah Truthout Link: https://truthout.org/articles/how-democratic-socialists-worked-with-sanders-s-our-revolution-and-other-grassroots-groups-to-sweep-november-s-elections/ How Democratic Socialists Worked With Sanders Supporters and Grassroots Groups to Sweep November's Elections November 16, 2017

73   NDP Link: https://nikiashton.ndp.ca/ Niki Ashton

74   Lewis, Jeffrey T.; Magalhaes, Luciana (11 September 2018). "Brazil's da Silva Steps Aside, Names Haddad as Replacement Candidate". Wall Street Journal – via www.wsj.com.

75   "An Open Call to All Progressive Forces". Progressive International. 30 November 2018. Retrieved 2 December 2018.

76   Day, Meagan (10 January 2019). "Trust the rich less, trust each other more". Jacobin. Retrieved 25 January 2019.

77   The Detroit Socialist Medium Link: https://medium.com/dsa-detroit-newspaper/electoral-victories-c82e1f7612fb 2018 Electoral victories

78   US News Link: https://www.usnews.com/news/politics/articles/2019-03-14/apnewsbreak-sanders-institute-closing-down-as-he-campaigns Institute Founded by Sanders' Wife, Son Is Shutting Down March 15, 2019

79   European Parliament website Link: https://web.archive.org/web/20190409211215/https://www.eu-events.eu/13284-building-transatlantic-bridges.html Building TransAtlantic Bridges 04 April 2019

80   PEL website Link: https://www.european-left.org/to-bernie-sanders-we-say-yes/ "TO BERNIE SANDERS, WE SAY YES! "Published on: 05.04.2019

81   PEL website Link: https://www.european-left.org/ruling-bodies/ Ruling Bodies, (accessed December 7 2019)

82   PEL website Link: https://web.archive.org/web/20190713014949/https://www.european-left.org/our-parties/ member paries (accessed December 7, 2019)

83   GUENGL website Link: https://www.guengl.eu/function/meps/ members (accessed December 7 2019

84   CSPAN https://www.c-span.org/video/?119897-1/pentagon-budget-increase-needed
"Is the Pentagon Budget Increase Needed?" FEBRUARY 3, 1999

85   Democratic Left, June 1982, page 14

86   Keywiki screenshot Link: https://keywiki.org/File:UntitledDL_Fall_2003.jpg John Conyers

87   Keywiki screenshot Link: https://keywiki.org/File:William-greider.jpg William Greider

88   Council for a Livable World Link: https://web.archive.org/web/20081023020002/https://livableworld.org/media/news/

council_celebrates_third_annual_drinan_peace_and_human_rights_award/
Council Celebrates Third Annual Drinan Peace and Human Rights Award

89   Council for a Livable World, Link: https://livableworld.org/elections/2012/candidates/Senate/bsanders/ Bernie Sanders endorsement Bernie Sanders endorsement

90   CLW website Link: https://livableworld.org/council-for-a-livable-world-celebrates-the-57th-presidential-inauguration/ Council for a Livable World celebrates the 57th Presidential Inauguration January 29, 2013

TIM KAINE

1   Kaine, Tim. Official Government Website: https://www.kaine.Senate.gov/download/official-biography-of-senator-tim-kaine

2   Kaine, Tim. https://www.Senate.gov/general/committee_assignments/assignments.htm Archive Link: https://web.archive.org/web/20220413210220/https://www.Senate.gov/general/committee_assignments/assignments.htm

3   Horowitz, Jason, New York Times "In Honduras, a Spiritual and Political Awakening for Tim Kaine" September 2, 2016, Link: https://www.nytimes.com/2016/09/03/us/politics/tim-kaine-honduras-jesuit.html

4   Ibid.

5   Catholic News Agency "The Honduras Tim Kaine knew" September 6, 2016, Link: https://www.catholicnewsagency.com/news/34512/the-honduras-tim-kaine-knew

6   Horowitz, Jason, New York Times "In Honduras, a Spiritual and Political Awakening for Tim Kaine" September 2, 2016, Link: https://www.nytimes.com/2016/09/03/us/politics/tim-kaine-honduras-jesuit.html

7   Ibid.

8   Ibid.

9   Ibid.

10   Catholic News Agency "The Honduras Tim Kaine knew" September 6, 2016, Link: https://www.catholicnewsagency.com/news/34512/the-honduras-tim-kaine-knew

11   Horowitz, Jason, New York Times "In Honduras, a Spiritual and Political Awakening for Tim Kaine" September 2, 2016, Link: https://www.nytimes.com/2016/09/03/us/politics/tim-kaine-honduras-jesuit.html

12   Ignatian Solidarity Network, "J. Guadalupe Carney, S.J. | 1983 | Honduras" Link: https://ignatiansolidarity.net/blog/portfolio-item/j-guadalupe-carney-s-j-1983-honduras/

13   Catholic News Agency "The Honduras Tim Kaine knew" September 6, 2016, Link: https://www.catholicnewsagency.com/news/34512/the-honduras-tim-kaine-knew

14   Ibid.

15   Horowitz, Jason, New York Times "In Honduras, a Spiritual and Political Awakening for Tim Kaine" September 2, 2016, Link: https://www.nytimes.com/2016/09/03/us/politics/tim-kaine-honduras-jesuit.html

16   Mazurczak, Filip, National Catholic Register "Archbishop Romero and Liberation Theology" May 7, 2015 Link: https://www.ncregister.com/news/archbishop-romero-and-liberation-theology-acs6n5kf

17   Gigg, Tom The Guardian "The killing of Archbishop Oscar Romero

was one of the most notorious crimes of the cold war. Was the CIA to blame?" 22 March 2000, Link: https://www.theguardian.com/theguardian/2000/mar/23/features11.g21

18   Ibid.

19   Senator Kaine press release "KAINE STATEMENT ON MARTYRDOM DECLARATION FOR SALVADORAN ARCHBISHOP OSCAR ROMERO" February 3, 2015, Link: https://web.archive.org/web/20150313023650/https://www.kaine.Senate.gov/press-releases/kaine-statement-on-martyrdom-declaration-for-salvadoran-archbishop-oscar-romero

20   Rossomando, John and Emerson, Steve, The Investigative Project on Terrorism, "Dems Tap Radical Islamists for Cash" November 1, 2012, Link: https://www.investigativeproject.org/3792/dems-tap-radical-islamists-for-cash

21   Ibid.

22   Ibid.

23   Rockwood Leadership Institute "From the Network: Alum News, Job Postings, & More" November 29, 2017, Link: https://medium.com/leading-from-the-inside-out/from-the-network-alum-news-job-postings-more-7e297552d8b

24   Democratic Socialists of America "Faith, Abolition, and Socialism: Panel and Discussion" July 16th, 2020, Link: https://www.dsausa.org/calendar/faith-abolition-and-socialism/

25   Washington Times, "Muslim group touts local political clout" October 1, 2007, Link: https://www.washingtontimes.com/news/2007/oct/1/muslim-group-touts-local-political-clout/

26   Liberation News "Brian Becker" Link: https://www.liberationnews.org/author/brian_becker/

27   MAS Con 2022, "ESAM OMEISH" Link: https://www.masconvention.org/esam-omeish.html

28   Islamist Watch "Islamist Money in Politics, Donor Name: Esam Omeish" Link: https://www.meforum.org/islamist-watch/money-politics/donor/667/

29   Mauro, Ryan "Clinton VP Pick Tim Kaine's Islamist Ties" July 23, 2016, Link: https://www.breitbart.com/politics/2016/07/23/clinton-vp-pick-tim-kaines-islamist-ties/

30   Ibid.

31   Swift, Matthew, The Hoya "MSA Founder Resigns After Israel Remarks" October 2, 2007, Link: https://thehoya.com/msa-founder-resigns-after-israel-remarks/

32   Ibid.

33   Ibid.

34   Osborne, James (June 8, 2009). "Clinton Invites Controversial Muslim Leader on Conference Call". Fox News. Archived from the original on August 24, 2009.

35   Mauro, Ryan "Clinton VP Pick Tim Kaine's Islamist Ties" July 23, 2016, Link: https://www.breitbart.com/politics/2016/07/23/clinton-vp-pick-tim-kaines-islamist-ties/

36   Swift, Matthew, The Hoya "MSA Founder Resigns

After Israel Remarks" October 2, 2007, Link: https://thehoya.com/
msa-founder-resigns-after-israel-remarks/

37   New Dominion PAC "Arab American Democratic Caucus of Virginia
hosts a dinner for Sen. Tim Kaine" Link: http://www.ndpac.com/home.html

38   NIAC Action "NIAC Action Statement on Tim Kaine Selection
as Clinton's VP" July 23, 2016 Link: https://www.niacouncil.org/news/
niac-action-statement-on-tim-kaine-selection-as-clintons-vp/?locale=en

39   Morello, Carol and DeYoung, Karen Costello, Washington Post, "US
sanctions Iran's foreign minister amid escalating tensions" July 31, 2019, Link:
https://www.washingtonpost.com/world/national-security/us-sanctions-irans-
foreign-minister-amid-escalating-tensions/2019/07/31/1d4f3780-7eaf-47cc-
8c55-569f6ede7615_story.html

40   Costello, Ryan, National Iranian American Council,
"Statement on House Passage of Kaine War Powers Resolution"
March 11, 2020, Link: https://www.niacouncil.org/news/
statement-on-house-passage-of-kaine-war-powers-resolution/

41   Iranian American Political Action Committee "Past Endorsements
- 2018 election cycle" Link: https://iranianamericanpac.org/candidates/
past-endorsements/

42   Council for a Livable World "Tim Kaine" Link: https://web.archive.
org/web/20120506172242/http://livableworld.org/elections/2012/candidates/
Senate/tkaine/

43   Council for a Livable World "Tim Kaine" Link: https://livableworld.
org/meet-the-candidates/Senate-candidates/tim-kaine-d-va-Senate/

44   Orrick, Dave et al, Twin Cities Pioneer Press. "3 cops, pepper spray
used in arrest of Sen. Tim Kaine's son near Trump rally at Capitol," March 7,
2017. Link: https://www.twincities.com/2017/03/07/son-of-sen-tim-kaine-one-of-
six-arrested-during-trump-rally-at-state-capitol-last-weekend/

45   2021 Minnesota Statutes, Office of the Revisor of Statutes. "Section
609.71 RIOT". Link: https://www.revisor.mn.gov/statutes/cite/609.71

46   Nelson, Tim, MPR News. "8 face criminal charges in dis-
rupted pro-Trump rally", May 26, 2017. Link: https://www.mprnews.org/
story/2017/05/26/8-face-criminal-charges-in-disrupted-pro-trump-rally

47   Ibid.

48   Associated Press, Twin Cities Pioneer Press. "Tim
Kaine's son placed on probation in Minnesota Trump protest",
December 28, 2017. Link: https://www.twincities.com/2017/12/28/
tim-kaine-son-linwood-woody-probation-minnesota-donald-trump-protest/

PATTY MURRAY

1   Patty Murray, "Biographical Directory," Congress.gov, http://bioguide.
congress.gov/scripts/biodisplay.pl?index=m001111, (accessed May 18, 2013)

2   Patty Murray, "Biography," Senate.gov, http://www.murray.Senate.gov/
public/index.cfm?p=Biography (accessed July 28, 2011)

3   Patty Murray official Senate website - Committee assignments Link:
https://www.murray.Senate.gov/public/index.cfm/committeeassignments

4   Committees of Correspondence National committee meeting, January
7-9, 1994, New York minutes

5   Soriano, Sally. Corresponder Volume 2, number 1 "Seattle activists' sendoff Friendshipment Caravan" January 1993, page 9

6   People's Weekly World November 8, 1997 page 3

7   Lumpkin, Bea Joy in the Struggle, My Life and Love, page 163

8   Seattle Times "Irene Hull, longtime labor-rights advocate, dies at 98" April 14, 2011 Link: https://www.seattletimes.com/seattle-news/irene-hull-longtime-labor-rights-advocate-dies-at-98/

9   Wheeler, Tim. Peoples World "Labor stalwart Lonnie Nelson dies at 83" February 14, 2014Link: https://peoplesworld.org/article/labor-stalwart-lonnie-nelson-dies-at-8/

10   People's Daily World "Awards banquet hears PDW editor, cites activists" May 25, 1989, page 5

11   People's Weekly World, "Labor women chart fightback," October 18, 2003 Link: http://www.peoplesworld.org/labor-women-chart-fightback/,

12   Washington State Labor Council blog, "Murray: More must be done for struggling working families," August 19, 2008, Link: http://www.wslc.org/reports/2008/august/19.htm

13   Senator Murray press release "Murray Joins Seniors to Protect Social Security and Fix the Medicare Prescription Drug Law Jun 30 2004" Link: https://www.murray.Senate.gov/public/index.cfm/lowbandwidth/newsroom?ID=BBE138BB-3B50-463E-AF75-ED1E91AC900C

14   Wheeler, Tim, Peoples World "Will Parry, labor and retiree advocate, 1920-2013" May 17, 2013 Link: https://peoplesworld.org/article/will-parry-labor-and-retiree-advocate-1920-201/

15   Social Security Works, "Celebrate Social Security's 75th Today with Murray, McDermott," Social Security Works, http://ssworkswa.org/2010/08/16/celebrate-social-securitys-75th-today-with-murray-mcdermott/, (August 16, 2010)

16   SS Works Washington, "Members of Social Security Works – Washington," SS Works Washington, http://ssworkswa.org/2010/08/01/members-of-social-security-works-washington/ (August 1, 2010)

17   Peoples Weekly World May Day Supplement May 6 1995

18   Ibid.

19   National Association of Disability Representatives press release. SENATOR CASEY INTRODUCES BILL TO EXPAND SOCIAL SECURITY BENEFITS September 19, 2018 Link: https://www.nadr.org/news/418973/Senator-Casey-Introduces-Bill-to-Expand-Social-Security-Benefits.htm

20   Swift, Mary Daily Record "Work on Roslyn's old City Hall begins next week" September 22, 2010 Link: https://www.dailyrecordnews.com/news/work-on-roslyn-s-old-city-hall-begins-next-week/article_2a1c758e-c5af-11df-9639-001cc4c03286.html (September 22, 2010)

21   Communist Party USA website "Marc Brodine biography" Link: https://cpusa.org/authors/marc-brodine/

22   People's Weekly World November 7, 1998 page 4

23   Tim Wheeler, People's World "The thumbs up win in Washington State,", http://peoplesworld.org/the-thumbs-up-win-in-washington-state/ (November 12, 2010).

24   Moore, Art. World Net Daily "Democrat senator praises bin Laden" December 20, 2002 Link: https://www.wnd.com/2002/12/16360/

25   CAIR WASHINGTON 2011 ANNUAL REPORT Link: https://cairwa.org/images/main/AnnualReport/CAIR-WA_Annual_Report_2011.pdf

26   CAIR Washington Facebook page "Training & meetings w/ Senator Patty Murray's Central WA Outreach Director Raquel Crowley, Benton County Democrats Chair Jay Clough, others" November 6 2015 Link: https://www.facebook.com/events/768167513295064

27   CAIR website, "What They Say About CAIR" 25 October 2017, Link: http://islamophobia.org/about-us/184-what-they-say-about-cair.html

28   VoteSmart "Patty Murray's Political Summary on Issue: Religion" Link:https://justfacts.votesmart.org/candidate/53358/patty-murray?categoryId=107&type=V,S,R,E,F,P

29   Council for a Livable World, "Meet the Candidates," Council for a Livable World, http://livableworld.org/support/meet_candidates/ (accessed December 31, 2010)

30   Council for a Livable World, "Senator Patty Murray," Council for a Livable World, http://livableworld.org/elections/2010/candidates/Senate/pmurray/ (accessed December 31, 2010)

31   Council for a Livable World website , "Senate Candidates" Link: https://livableworld.org/candidates/meet-the-candidates/Senate-candidates/

MARIA CANTWELL

1   Maria Cantwell, "Home/About Maria," Senate.gov, http://www.cantwell.Senate.gov/public/index.cfm/about-maria (accessed May 16, 2013)

2   Maria Cantwell, "Home/About Maria," Senate.gov, Committee Assignments https://www.cantwell.Senate.gov/about/biography/committee-assignmentsnt

3   Galvin, Kevin Seattle Times "A Will and A Way: Convinced that work can fix anything, Maria Cantwell takes on the Senate "December 2, 2001 Link: https://archive.seattletimes.com/archive/?date=20011202&slug=pmaria02

4   Congressional Record April 24, 2001 - Issue: Vol. 147, No. 52 — Daily Edition 107th Congress (2001 - 2002) - 1st Session TRIBUTE TO SENATOR ALAN CRANSTON (Senate - April 24, 2001) Link: https://www.congress.gov/congressional-record/2001/4/24/Senate-section/article/s3834-2?q=%7B%22searc h%22%3A%5B%22%5C%22Adoption+and+foster+care%5C%22%22%5D%7D

5   Inc. Concerned Voters, Communists in the Democratic Party January 1, 1990 page 37

6   The Stanford Daily, Volume 87a, Issue 9, 23 July 193

7   Inc. Concerned Voters, Communists in the Democratic Party January 1, 1990 page 37

8   Ibid.

9   Congressional Record April 24, 2001 - Issue: Vol. 147, No. 52 — Daily Edition 107th Congress (2001 - 2002) - 1st Session
TRIBUTE TO SENATOR ALAN CRANSTON (Senate - April 24, 2001)
Link: https://www.congress.gov/congressional-record/2001/4/24/Senate-section/article/s3834-2?q=%7B%22search%22%3A%5B%22%5C%22Adoption+and+foste r+care%5C%22%22%5D%7D

10   Post-Intelligencer, How to meet an 8:15 deadline on election night, November 8, 2006

11   Wheeler, Tim, People's World "Labor stalwart Irene Hull dies at 98" March 24, 2011 Link: https://www.peoplesworld.org/article/labor-stalwart-irene-hull-dies-at-9/

12   Common Dreams, Morning After Bush's Speech, Progressive Activists to Unite February 28 for Conference on 'Working Family' Agenda, WASHINGTON - February 26 - News Advisory Link: http://www.common-dreams.org/news2001/0226-05.htm

13   Democratic Socialists of America website. 1997 Directory of Locals, Organizing Committees, and Youth Section Chapters of the DEMOCRATIC SOCIALISTS OF AMERICA Link: http://web.archive.org/web/19970706172357/www.dsausa.org/Locals.html

14   Shue, Chad. examiner.com. "Cantwell to be guest speaker at upcoming awards banquet", June 3, 2010

15   Dring, Jason Dring; Shellenberger, Michael ; Hendricks, Bracken. Apollo Alliance press release, January 14, 2004 "New Study Finds Strategic Investments in Clean Energy, Efficiency Would Create 3.3 Million High-Wage Jobs and Pay for Itself" Link: https://web.archive.org/web/20040117024201/https://www.commondreams.org/news2004/0114-11.htm

16   Democratic Underground "The Apollo Alliance for Good Jobs and Clean Energy" Link: https://www.democraticunderground.com/discuss/duboard.php?az=view_all&address=115x37653

17   Democratic Socialists of America website: "In Memory of Julian Bond (1940-2015)" August 18, 2015 Link: https://www.dsausa.org/democratic-left/julian_bond_dl/

18   New Ground 112 Chicago Democratic Socialists of America "49th Annual Debs - Thomas - Harrington Dinner program" Link: https://web.archive.org/web/20080516071713/https://www.chicagodsa.org/d2007/index.html

19   Matt Labash, Matt The Weekly Standard "JOHN SWEENEY AND THE STATE OF HIS UNION" October 21, 1996 Link: http://www.ipsn.org/characters/coia/magazines/john_sweeney_and_the_state_of.htm

20   Garver, Paul. Talking Union "SEIU VP Explains Strategy: Build a Progressive Movement with Labor at Its Core" January 22, 2009Link: https://talkingunion.wordpress.com/2009/01/22/building-a-new-progressive-movement-with-labor-at-its-core

21   Council for a Livable World website: Our Legacy in Congress: Who We've Helped Elect Link: https://livableworld.org/meet-the-candidates/our-legacy-in-congress-who-weve-helped-elect/

22   Board Members, Council for a Livable World, accessed October 19, 2022. Link: https://livableworld.org/about/board/#MSixkiller

23   Sixkiller, Mariah, LinkedIn Account, accessed October 19, 2019. Link: https://www.linkedin.com/in/mariah-sixkiller-39529b86/details/experience/

24   Socialist International Website, "Full list of member parties and organisations", accessed October 19, 2022. Link: https://www.socialistinternational.org/about-us/members/

25   Senate, Daily Digest, July 18, 2022. Link: https://www.congress.gov/117/crec/2022/07/18/168/118/CREC-2022-07-18-dailydigest.pdf

26   Gould, Joe, Defense News. "White House aims to release overdue security strategies within weeks," dated August 1, 2022. Link: https://www.defensenews.com/pentagon/2022/08/01/white-house-aims-to-release-overdue-security-strategies-within-weeks/

27   White House, Washington. "Biden-Harris National Security Strategy," October 2022. Link: https://www.whitehouse.gov/wp-content/uploads/2022/10/Biden-Harris-Administrations-National-Security-Strategy-10.2022.pdf

28   Bernton, Hal, Seattle Times. "EPA proposes Bristol Bay protections in potential blow to Pebble Mine development," May 25, 2022. Link: https://www.seattletimes.com/seattle-news/epa-proposes-bristol-bay-protections-in-potentially-fatal-blow-to-pebble-mine-development/

29   Maria Cantwell press release. "Cantwell: Cuba to Purchase $4.5 million of Washington State Peas and Apples
Announcement comes on heels of Senator's agricultural mission to Cuba" March 7 2002 Link: https://www.cantwell.Senate.gov/news/press-releases/cantwell-cuba-to-purchase-45-million-of-washington-state-peas-and-apples

30   Alamar Associates photo gallery "2000s" Link: http://www.alamarcuba.com/photogallery5.html

31   New Orleans CityBusiness (New Orleans, LA) "La. Sen. Landrieu seeks to grow US small business' opportunities with Cuba" May 11, 2009

TAMMY BALDWIN

1   Baldwin, Tammy. Official Government Website: https://www.baldwin.Senate.gov/about

2   Baldwin, Tammy. https://www.Senate.gov/general/committee_assignments/assignments.htm Archive Link: https://web.archive.org/web/20220413210220/https://www.Senate.gov/general/committee_assignments/assignments.htm

3   Kwo, Tre and Vergara, Jimena, Left Voice, "DSA in the Democratic Party Labyrinth," June 19, 2017. Link: https://www.leftvoice.org/The-DSA-in-the-Democratic-Party-Labyrinth/

4   Tammy Baldwin Wisconsin State Journal (Madison, Wisconsin), 19 Oct 1992, Mon, Page 1

5   Wypijewski, JoAnn. The Nation, The Rainbow's Gravity Twenty years after Jesse Jackson's historic run for President, what does it all mean? JULY 15, 2004, Link: https://www.thenation.com/article/rainbows-gravity/

6   Fleischman, Harry. Democratic Left "On the Left" page 14, January 1983

7   Fleischman, Harry. Democratic Left "On the Left" page 15, Nov./Dec. 1983

8   Fleischman, Harry. Democratic Left "On the Left" page 15, Nov./Dec. 1983

9   Tipler, Gary Our Lives, "Making History" Apr 19, 2018. Link: https://ourliveswisconsin.com/article/making-history/

10   DSA Members support Tammy Baldwin, The Capital Times (Madison, Wisconsin), 31 Oct 1992, Sat, Page 11. Link: https://www.newspapers.com/clip/106064920/dsa-members-support-tammy-baldwin-the-c/

11   Ibid.

12   Collins, Mary Jean. Veteran Feminists of America "Women's Liberation Will Not Be Achieved Until All People Are Free." Interview with Christine Riddiough, October 2018. Link: https://veteranfeministsofamerica.org/vfa-pioneer-history-project-chris-riddiough/interview-chris-riddiough/

13   Riddiough, Christine Democratic Left, "DSA Co-Founders: Organizers Need Better Political Education" May 29, 2022 Link: https://www.dsausa.org/democratic-left/dsa-co-founders-organizers-need-better-political-education/

14   Fleischman, Harry. Democratic Left "On the Left" page 14, January 1983

15   Tipler, Gary Our Lives, "Making History" Apr 19, 2018. Link: https://ourliveswisconsin.com/article/making-history/

16   Letter to Editor, The Capital Times (Madison, Wisconsin), 31 Oct 1992, Sat, Page 11. Link: https://www.newspapers.com/clip/106064920/dsa-members-support-tammy-baldwin-the-c/

17   Fleischman, Harry. Democratic Left "On the Left" page 14, January 1983

18   Tipler, Gary Our Lives, "Making History" Apr 19, 2018. Link: https://ourliveswisconsin.com/article/making-history/

19   Roddy, David and De La Rosa, Alyssa, Sacramento DSA "A People of Color's History of DSA, Part 2: DSA Enters the 80s" September 11, 2019 Link: https://www.sacdsa.org/blog/2019/09/11/a-people-of-color-s-history-of-dsa-part-2-dsa-enters-the-80s/

20   Democratic Left, March/April 1986, page 12

21   Gorosh, Kathy, New Ground 33. "Ron Sable: A Life of Health and Justice" March - April, 1994. Link: https://chicagodsa.org/ngarchive/ng33.html

22   Llewellyn, Frank, Democratic Left, "DSAPAC Swings into Action" Summer 2006 Page 3

23   Roman, Bob New Ground 61 "Other News", November - December, 1998 Link: https://chicagodsa.org/ngarchive/ng61.html

24   Alt, Theresa and Hirsh, Michael Democratic Left "Beyond Kerry: DSAers Back Local Candidates," Spring 2004 page 6.

25   Schwartz, Joseph Democratic Left, "Morning Afterthoughts: Myriad Musings on the 1996 Elections & Beyond", November / December 1996 page 12

26   Carey, Nick and O'Brien, Brendan, Reuters, "Wisconsin's progressivism faces a recall" May 25, 2012. Link: https://www.reuters.com/article/usa-politics-wisconsin/wisconsins-progressivism-faces-a-recall-idUSL2E8FO5XD20120525

27   Resnick, Gideon The Daily Beast, "The Democratic Socialists of America Have Actual Political Power. What Will They Do With It?" Updated Aug. 09, 2017, Link: https://www.thedailybeast.com/the-democratic-socialists-of-america-have-actual-political-power-what-will-they-do-with-it

28   Nichols, John, The Capital Times (Madison, Wisconsin). "Monument to the Good Fight", Monday, July 19, 1999, Page 9A Link: https://www.newspapers.com/clip/106066114/old-commie-friend-of-tammy-baldwin/

29   Congressional Record Volume 14, Number 149 Pages E2209m Extensions of Remarks, Thu, Oct. 28, 1999

30   Riddiough, Chris, Democratic Left, "Present Progressive" Winter 1999 page 2

31   Progressive Majority website, Progressive Majority's Advisory Committee Link: http://progressivemajority.org/leadership/index.asp

32   Szumilo, Dan, Black Swamp Gazette, January 17, 1983 page 6

33   Democratic Left, January 1983 issue, page 14

34   Democratic Left, Jan./Feb. 1990, page 7

35   DSA News, January 1986, page 2.

36   Progressive Majority website, "About Progressive Majority" Link: https://web.archive.org/web/20051223034655/http://www.progressivemajority.org/about/

37   Progressive Majority website, Board of Directors Link: http://www.progressivemajority.org/board/

38   Truehart, Charles, Washington Post, "The rainbow's Political Gold" Link: https://www.washingtonpost.com/archive/lifestyle/1992/06/13/the-rainbows-political-gold/1f121927-1f44-48dc-b1d9-5faa7bf7f76d/

39   Progressive Majority website, Board of Directors Link: http://www.progressivemajority.org/board/

40   Kincaid, Cliff Accuracy in Media, "Castro's Puppet Works for "Progressive Congress" June 26, 2012 Link: https://www.aim.org/aim-column/castros-puppet-works-for-progressive-congress/

41   Phillips, Steve, PowerPAC+, "The Progressive Case for Cory Booker", December 20, 2012 Link: http://www.powerpacplus.org/the_progressive_case_for_cory_booker

42   PowerPAC+, Board of Directors Link: http://d3n8a8pro7vhmx.cloudfront.net/pacplus/pages/244/attachments/original/1396464159/mini-state-w-board-final.pdf?1396464159

43   Ibid.

44   Troller, Susan The Capital Times, "Chalkboard: MTI to accept national award for helping organize protests" May 22, 2012 Link: https://madison.com/news/local/education/blog/article_f5cae6fc-e886-11e0-b1a0-001cc4c03286.html

45   Progressive Democrats of America, PDA Blog, Jim Hightower, John Nichols, Michael Lighty and Tim Carpenter in Janesville Nov. 1, 2012 Link: https://www.prlog.org/12014034-jim-hightower-john-nichols-michael-lighty-and-tim-carpenter-in-janesville.html

46   Democratic Left, "Remembering Tim Carpenter" May 2, 2014 https://www.dsausa.org/democratic-left/remembering_tim_carpenter/

47   Lighty, Michael, Democratic Left, "Everybody In, Nobody Out" August 25, 2020, Link: https://www.dsausa.org/democratic-left/everybody-in-nobody-out/

48   LA Progressive, "Judith LeBlanc bio" Link: https://www.laprogressive.com/author/judith-leblanc

49   Metro Detroit Democratic Socialists of America JIM HIGHTOWER'S KEYNOTE ADDRESS AT THE DSA'S ANNUAL DOUGLASS-DEBS DINNER Link: https://www.metrodetroitdsa.com/jim_hightower

50   PDA, Jim Hightower, John Nichols, Michael Lighty and Tim

Carpenter in Janesville, Nov. 1, 2012 Link: https://www.prlog.org/12014034-jim-hightower-john-nichols-michael-lighty-and-tim-carpenter-in-janesville.html

51   Progressive Democrats of America, PDA Blog, Jim Hightower, John Nichols, Michael Lighty and Tim Carpenter in Janesville Nov. 1, 2012 Link: https://www.prlog.org/12014034-jim-hightower-john-nichols-michael-lighty-and-tim-carpenter-in-janesville.html

52   Council for a Livable World, Senator Tammy Baldwin Link:http://livableworld.org/elections/2012/candidates/Senate/tbaldwin/

53   Council for a Livable World, "Council for a Livable World celebrates the 57th Presidential Inauguration" January 29, 2013 Link: https://livableworld.org/council-for-a-livable-world-celebrates-the-57th-presidential-inauguration/

54   Council for a Livable World, "Tammy Baldwin " Link: https://livableworld.org/meet-the-candidates/Senate-candidates/tammy-baldwin-d-wi-Senate/

55   Colombia Support Network "About Us" Link: https://colombiasupport.net/about-us/

56   Blinken, Anthony, US State Department "Revocation of the Terrorist Designations of the Revolutionary Armed Forces of Colombia (FARC) and Additional Terrorist Designations" November 30, 2021 Link: https://www.state.gov/revocation-of-the-terrorist-designations-of-the-revolutionary-armed-forces-of-colombia-farc-and-additional-terrorist-designations/

57   Colombia Support Network, Facebook. Post dated November 7, 2012. Link: https://www.facebook.com/ColombiaSupportNetwork/posts/pfbid02exGnhkj1xhW8hUcHsg1d2TBLJULE68c118EYwJJk48jxBS48j1xjVut6C5g-BK3Uvl

58   Whitney, W.T. Marxism-Leniniesm Today "
COLOMBIA'S PATRIOTIC UNION TRAGEDY: LESSONS LEARNED" November 12, 2010. Link: https://mltoday.com/colombias-patriotic-union-tragedy-lessons-learned/

59   Colombia Support Network, "Senator Feingold: Oh how we miss you!" February 23, 2011. Link: https://colombiasupport.net/2011/02/senator-feingold-oh-how-we-miss-you/

60   Colombia Support Network, Action on Colombia, "Open Letter to Presidents Clinton and Samper", Summer 1994

61   Committees of Correspondence for Democracy and Socialism "Leadership - Advisory Board members" Link: https://web.archive.org/web/20070204061846/https://www.cc-ds.org/advisory_bd.html

62   Colombia Support Network, "DEAR COLLEAGUE LETTER", May 15, 2002. Link: https://colombiasupport.net/archive/dearcolleague.html

63   Vanovac, Ned Colombia Reports, "US Congress concerned by Colombia bases agreement" September 8, 2009. Link: https://colombiareports.com/us-congress-concerned-by-colombia-bases-agreement/

64   Madison.com, Capital Times editorial. "Tammy Baldwin's people-powered politics" October 19, 2011. Link: https://madison.com/news/opinion/editorial/tammy-baldwin-s-people-powered-politics/article_e4707a01-0aec-5a88-ace5-6cd5c12e87ee.html

65   Zoominfo. Tammy Baldwin Employee Directory Link: https://www.zoominfo.com/pic/tammy-baldwin/37503361

66   Olig, Haley Colombia Support Network "Colombia Should Not Enter

Trans-Pacific Partnership" Posted on October 21, 2015. Link: https://colombia-support.net/2015/10/colombia-should-not-enter-trans-pacific-partnership/

67   Colombia Support Network National Conference June 2017 Link: https://colombiasupport.net/wp-content/uploads/2017/05/CSN-Annual-Meeting-Program-2017.pdf